**Emotional First Aid
For You and Your Loved Ones**

MANAGING ANGER

A Handbook of Proven Techniques

Mitchell H. Messer, M.A., L.P.C.

Credits

Editors:	Richard Greb and Kally Fraser
Book Design and Illustration:	James Maivald, Desktop Design, Skokie, IL
Manuscript Preparation:	A-OK Business Service, Skokie, IL

Inquiries should be addressed to:

The Anger Institute™
111 N. Wabash
Suite 1702
Chicago, IL 60602,
Phone: (312) 263-0035, (800) 334-ANGR or
E-mail: mmesser@angerclinic.com
Websites: angerclinic.com and angerinstitute.org

Illustrations © 2001 James Maivald, All rights reserved.

ISBN 0-9636776-08

Second Edition. Third Printing June 2002

02 03 04 05 10 9 8 7 6 5 4 3

DEDICATION

This book is dedicated
to the memory of

Dr. Rudolf Dreikurs.

He was our teacher.

He is still our teacher.

ACKNOWLEDGMENTS

We wish to acknowledge the patience and skill of all the unsung people behind the scenes, without whose efforts this book would have remained a glimmer in its author's eyes. Our thanks go to Rebecca Cady Patton, the staff at A-OK Business Service and a special thanks to Jim Maivald of Desktop Design, Skokie, IL, Linda Dillon and Richard Greb. Thanks also to Joyce Messer who lent moral support and emotional first aid to our endeavors when we needed them, which was most of the time.

ABOUT THE AUTHOR

Mitchell H. Messer, M.A.

The founder and executive director of the Anger Clinic and the Anger Institute, Mitch Messer received his Master's Degree in Clinical Psychology from Roosevelt University. He took advanced work in marriage and family counseling at the Alfred Adler Institute of Chicago. He has served with the Suicide Prevention Service of the State of Illinois Department of Mental Health and is a counselor in private practice. Mr. Messer has been a consultant to the American Telephone and Telegraph Company, and Ameritech, the Chicago Board of Education, and the Cook County Educational Service Region. He is a frequent lecturer on anger topics and has appeared as a guest on television and radio programs, both locally and nationally.

He is a member of the Chicago Psychological Association and the International Society of Marriage and Family Counselors.

Table of Contents

INTRODUCTION

You may have read books on dysfunctional families, co-dependency, communication, shame, violence, abuse, guilt, addiction and grief. There are plenty of books on these topics, but very few on the subject of anger. They are important, but anger is the specific emotion that can destroy your marriage, your relationship with your loved ones or your job. It is the necessary precursor of violence. In fact, it is the emotion that can blow up this planet. So why are we so strangely reluctant to take this powerful emotion as seriously as it needs to be taken? Anger is like a crazy relative in the attic who everyone knows is there but no one talks about. That is the problem.

Anger is an emotion that causes terrible damage every day, but no one wants to talk about it because it isn't nice. If we do talk about it, it's in terms of hitting a pillow with a bat, walking around the block or thinking happy thoughts. Even professional counselors are shy about confronting this scary – but perfectly normal – emotion. Understandably, most counselors feel inadequately prepared to cope with anger problems because there is no course in Angerology 101 in our counselor preparation institutions.

You may have been told you are "aggressive," "bitchy" or "hostile." You may have been told to "control yourself," or "Take anger out of your vocabulary." You almost certainly have not been told how to stop controlling negatively or how to take anger out of your heart. There is no cure for "bitchy," but there are many ways to relieve your legitimate, valid anger.

Do you wonder why you are walking around talking to yourself, feeling confused, dissatisfied, discouraged or "out of it," as they say these days? It is because life gives us an anger problem every twelve minutes, and we are inadequately prepared to solve it.

Despite what you have been hearing all your life, you are not a bad person if you get angry. Nice people like you get angry all the time, but they have learned to manage it between the extremes of too much (erupting like a volcano) and too little (smiling through their tears).

Some cope with these unwelcome episodes by denying them out of existence. When you deny this aspect of your personhood, you deny the whole thing. It's a package deal. You have arranged to be out of control of your own reality. This is not living, it is merely existing. Life is too short to play these games with our legitimate human emotions. Sometimes our emotional problems escalate until we can't stand it. These problems are painful to us. Our pain is compounded by our anger at ourselves for not being able to solve them. It is not our fault that we never learned anger management techniques before this. This book is your resource for filling this void in your education and relieving your pain the right way.

In this book, you will learn how you can manage your anger. You will learn that you can stop feeling frustrated, depressed or anxious very quickly. You will learn that you have choices you didn't know you had. When you exercise your power of choice, joy-killing hang-overs from the past will finally begin to go away. You will be able to stop just existing and start living.

Why Manage Anger?

In our twenty years of experience at the Anger Clinic in Chicago, we have seen the terrible things that mismanaged anger can do to a marriage, a career and a life. We have also seen how quickly this damage can be repaired, even reversed, when people are given tools they did not even know existed. Marriages on the brink of disaster have been turned around when destructive anger practices were replaced by interventions that made things better instead of worse. Employees facing the choice of quitting or being fired have learned how to cope successfully with their boss's childish temper tantrums to the benefit of themselves, the boss and everyone in the division.

Even insoluble anger problems from forty years ago can be relieved. By putting them in a new perspective, we find they do not have to be solved at all; they can be drained out of our system in the right way so we can get on with our lives with more energy and joy than we had before.

One of our anger management tools is the power of choice. People keep making the same mistakes because no one ever told them what their other options are. They come in to the Anger Clinic feeling discouraged and unable to cope because they know only one way to handle anger and it is not working. They don't know what else to do, and not knowing makes them feel out of control and fearful.

After people meet with us about managing their anger, they leave with many new choices and specific new tools. They can't wait to try them out on their jobs or at home with their spouses, their parents or their kids. They come back with reports of their successes and they want to know more, so we tell them. The more successes they have, the better their relationships become, and the better they feel about themselves.

That is the point of this book. We teach people how to use an anger situation to strengthen our most important and most overlooked relationship: *our relationship with ourselves*. We learn to stop being afraid of our anger and to start seeing negative situations as opportunities to do something productive and constructive for both ourselves and our loved ones. We feel empowered, competent, in control, independent, mature, encouraged and confident. These are all facets of self-respect, which is our reward for an anger job well done.

In *Managing Anger*, we will introduce you to some of the specific anger management techniques we use in the Chicago Anger Clinic.

At first reading, you may say to yourself, "Oh, this is too easy. This is too simplistic." If these techniques were as easy to use as they appear to be, you would have been using them for years. They only seem to be easy on the printed page.

The first problem in adapting these anger management techniques is the universal inertia that kicks in whenever we try anything new for the first time. It is so much cozier to perform the same old routines even when they have not worked for years.

A second difficulty is that we may have impediments in our personal makeup that are inconsistent with these new approaches. We will try to identify some of these impediments for you as we go along. We will also provide you with the tools to help you grow, both personally and socially.

Don't Fight the Feeling

When an old attitude, such as "It is my role in life to please others at my own expense," runs into a new technique, such as "Tell the Truth," the conflict becomes painfully apparent. You want to tell the truth, but you fear that the truth will be very displeasing and that you will not be able to find a rational compromise between the two warring attitudes in your heart.

We are letting you know in advance that we do not advocate open warfare between your contradictory attitudes. Do not fight the feeling. Instead, work carefully over time to replace one attitude with another, so that you can make conscious choices on an informed basis. We need not go head to head with ourselves. We can gradually outgrow that which needs to be outgrown. Replacing, choosing and outgrowing, rather than fighting ourselves to a standstill, are the preferred operations for implementing these techniques that we failed to acquire on our way into adulthood.

Roles In The Family

Anger management techniques fall into two major categories – good and bad. Good techniques make things better, while bad ones make them worse. Bad techniques include punching, swearing, sulking, cursing, hitting and screaming. Our use of these techniques does not mean we are bad people. It may mean we are just loyal, obedient students of the parental models who gave us these examples to follow.

Your choice of techniques often has something to do with your role in the family constellation. For example, if your older sister was a screamer, you were sure you couldn't catch up to her in that arena, so you may have chosen to use *sarcasm* as your way of expressing your anger. If your baby brother had flaming temper tantrums that were worse than yours, you may have surrendered that technique to him and opted for *the silent treatment* as your way of heightening the contrast between your developing personhood and his.

Your Parental Models

Perhaps your parents were evenly matched sparring partners and seemed to value solving problems by squaring off in the bedroom. You may have assumed this was the technique of choice and you therefore carried this parental example over into your own adult relationships.

We learn anger management in the same way we learn to wash dishes and make beds. There is not a whole lot of intellectual debate or rational discourse prior to the adoption of a mannerism that will last a lifetime. In other words, in the area of anger management, there hasn't been a brain cell working for four generations.

It is no wonder we find ourselves in an ocean of seemingly insoluble social problems, including child abuse, spouse battering, and granny bashing; runaway kids; drive-by, shootings; racial tension and labor strife. All of these problems arise out of the mismanagement of anger problems that may have been minor disruptions at one time, but have become major social problems now.

You would think that our social engineers, political experts and corporate tycoons would have long ago established institutes and academies for the study and improvement of anger management practices in this country. One reason they have not is that, for nice people, getting angry in the first place is a "No, no." It isn't pleasant; it's scary. We all like pleasant things and do not like scary things, except on the big screen where we know they will all be over soon. Therefore, why should we study an emotion we aren't supposed to have? Why should we learn how to solve a problem that isn't supposed to exist?

We cannot argue with that logic. It is not the logic of the grown-ups we are now. It is the logic of the four year-olds we used to be. We never outgrew it. As long as we are the prisoners of this infantile logic, our anger problems (which — remember — we aren't supposed to have but we do) will get only worse. Anger problems will continue to push husbands and wives to the brink or over the edge, disrupt business partnerships, and inflame working relationships. They will impel young people into the whirlwind of self- destructive behavior. Our mangled anger patterns will stress our bodies with hypertension, ulcers and strokes. They will plunge us into depression, anxiety and suicidal impulses.

After our anger attack blows over, we will not understand why we did the things we did. We will say, "Something came over me," "It was a crime of passion," or "I killed her because I loved her." For a population that prides itself on its technological and medical accomplishments, these throwbacks to the Stone Age are an enduring disgrace.

The Anger Management Techniques

In the following pages, we look at both good and bad anger management techniques. These include several that were not apparent when we prepared the first edition of this book but emerged in our practice over the past decade. You can learn from examples of both kinds of techniques. If you recognize yourself in the bad kinds, you can identify what you have been doing wrong all these years. Then, if you are so disposed, you can choose to replace your current counter- productive techniques with one or two that might make things better for you, your loved ones and the generations to come.

"The unexamined life
is not worth living."

Socrates

ANGER TERMS

Here are our definitions of some of the major concepts we use throughout this book:

Anger is not a weakness or a crime. It is merely unpleasant. We define anger *as an emotional response to a grievance.* The immediate grievance can be real or imaginary, but the anger itself is valid. Between the extremes of too much and too little in managing our anger, we try to find the middle ground. Socrates called it "the Golden Mean."

When someone is angry at us, our approach is to *validate* the person's anger first and save our defensiveness for later. Conducting an inquisition into the truth or falsity of the grievance when someone is in pain is a negative technique that we call, "the Perry Mason Syndrome." We can choose not to do it. It never helps.

The **gamut.** Many people believe that anger refers only to blowing one's stack. Anger runs the whole gamut from mild irritation to homicidal rage, even to World War III. It is all anger, whether we express it openly or not, and whether the grievance is accidental or on purpose. The emotional response takes place and it must be managed. If we don't manage it, it will manage us.

Frustration is a compound emotion. It consists of feeling *angry* plus *powerless* and *out of control.*

Mischief often makes us angry. We define mischief as *"that which does not need to be done."* When we learn how to recognize mischief and put it in its proper perspective, we free ourselves to deal with it appropriately. We will not get so angry so often.

Good intentions are a type of *mischief*. When people feel inadequately prepared to solve a problem, they make up a solution that sounds good at the time and proceed to inflict it upon us. We aren't supposed to protest because they "mean well." It is very frustrating. Like all mischief, good intentions are *self-indulgent, counterproductive* and ultimately *self-destructive*. They make us angry but our anger has no place to go.

We can learn to replace our own inappropriate good intentions with **real intentions**, which means doing what reality requires us to do, no more and no less. We must be able to perceive what is required of us. We can use our adult judgment to determine what to do about it, and we must have the courage to do what needs to be done.

Courage is the *willingness to take a risk*. It is our adult judgment that tells us which risks are worth taking and which are not.

Super-anger means *feeling angrier than the situation requires us to feel*. We understand the excess anger as arising from a similarity perceived below conscious awareness between the current situation and an unresolved anger problem from the past.

An **attitude** is a *predisposition to behave in a certain way*. We don't even have to think about it. We have attitudes about our anger that get us in trouble that could have been avoided. We can learn to identify these attitudes and replace them with more appropriate ones.

Absurd attitudes. Some attitudes from childhood are absurd, but we do not have words for them in our language. For instance, it is absurd for an intelligent person to feel stupid if he forgets his mother-in-law's birthday or his boss's wife's name. An appropriately absurd name for this predisposition to call ourselves and each other stupid is "stupiditude." We cannot bring ourselves to respect stupidity in ourselves or others, but "stupiditude," while absurd, is a forgivable human imperfection.

Another word we use is **rationalitosis**, which is the absurd delusion that the person we are talking to is in his right mind — and vice versa. It includes the notion that we can solve every problem rationally to the third decimal place. Emotional problems need to be solved subjectively by replacing one set of feelings and attitudes with another. This cannot be done with a computer or by the pep talk method.

The **anger roles** we play in the present originated in childhood. We have carried them into adulthood with us. We can use an anger situation to actively replace our role as Victim, Avenger, Pleaser, Rebel, Scapegoat and so on with a mature identity of our own.

Homework is the name that we have given to the act of replacing our old attitudes and roles with new ones. When life gives us an opportunity to change our way of responding, we actively choose to shift our gears, and to behave in the new way we have learned. For example, we use one of the anger management techniques. We take an appropriate action on our own legitimate terms in our own behalf. We are not making mischief. We are doing what needs to be done. That is a Homework.

Catch yourself is one technique for remembering to do our Homework. We can see an anger situation as an opportunity to do something that we have never done before. We are about to react in the old way and we choose not to. We have *caught ourself in the act*. We have shifted our gears. And what is it that we are free of? Our old attitudes. We are in the process of replacing inappropriate attitudes with more effective ones in the present. We are free to make new choices from now on. It may be scary at first. It takes courage, but the reward is worth it.

Self-respect. In our anger therapy, we use an anger situation as an opportunity to grow. Specifically, we change the way we express our anger or respond to the anger of a loved one. In that moment, *we* are changed. Our self-doubt, even self-contempt has been replaced by something better: Self-respect. We have earned it. After accomplishing a few such Homeworks, our periods of self-respect start to run together. We are no longer our parents' inadequate, inferior child.

10

We are *a worthwhile human being in spite of our faults and imperfections.* We can feel it in our bones.

Angerphobia. We suppress and repress our anger because we have learned to be afraid of it. We are afraid that if we express our anger openly, we will be victimized, abandoned, even annihilated. We spend our lives and energies trying to prevent these things from happening.

Suppression means stifling our anger because we are afraid to express it openly. Our suppressed anger does not fade away with time. We can tap into it years later with a few well-chosen focusing questions. It needs to be identified for what it is and removed once and for all so it won't erupt later when something reminds us of our old grief.

Repression refers to anger that has been pushed below the level of conscious awareness because it is too dangerous to deal with, or even remember. Repressed anger, too, can be recovered and relieved in the right way. We will feel liberated from our depression and anxieties. We have gotten our life back.

Control. To prevent these negative consequences, we instituted a system of control when we were still a young child. We taught ourselves to express our anger in ways that were safe, but which did not give us any real relief from the emotional pressure. We defined control as if it meant *preventing bad, scary things from happening to us.* This immature definition set us up to control in crazy ways that can only work in reverse. We will feel out of control most of the time, we call it *negative control.* A better definition of control is *taking life as it comes and doing the best we can with it.* That is called *positive control.* That is what self-respecting people feel adequately prepared to do.

Anxiety is the feeling that a bad thing is going to happen any minute and we can't prevent it. When our anger is out of control, we are out of control. We experience this out-of-controlness as anxiety.

If we negatively control in the same ways we did as children, we are going to be out of control most of the time:

- When we live on other people's terms instead of our own,
- When we live in the future not the present,

11

- When we have a problem we cannot solve, such as trying to prevent disaster perfectly.
- When our anger is out of control.

The antidote to anxiety is to live in the present on our own appropriate terms and take life as it comes. We can do this more easily if we have learned to manage our anger successfully.

Panic is the feeling that the bad thing is happening to us right now and we are going to die! We feel totally out of control and doomed to destruction. These panics subside, too, when we learn how to replace our negative attitudes toward control with new, appropriate ones.

Early recollections. The early recollections we use in this book are not dramatic or sensational. They did not *cause* the individual's problems in later life. We are interested in these events people remember for thirty or more years because they reveal attitudes about the self, others and life that the individual acquired in childhood. For example, "I am a victim;" "People are out to get me;" "Life is scary and dangerous." These built-in attitudes predispose us to be scared and angry even when there is no basis for these feelings in the real world. They are often mistaken, and they interfere with our coping in the present. They are often negative and preclude a happy, successful passage through life. If these mistaken attitudes can be held up to the individual for what they are, a child's misperceptions and misconstrusions, there is the possibility they can be discarded and replaced with attitudes that conform to the realities in which we find ourselves. If we can make that replacement, the probabilities of our achieving happiness and success will be increased.

Taking it personally. Life presents us with problems every time we turn around. As children, we did not know how to solve problems. We remember our humiliating failures and the painful consequences of our ineptitude. We took these failures personally, *as if they were a reflection on our worth as a person.* We acquired feelings and attitudes about problems that were exaggerated and scary. We bring these carryovers from the past to our problems in the present, where they interfere with our functioning. One such attitude is, *"Life is pleasant for me when I can solve problems; it is very unpleasant for me when*

12

I cannot." Another is, "*I feel like a worthwhile human being when I can solve a problem. I feel worthless when I can not.*" The problem itself is not the issue now. The problem is the way we feel about the problem and about ourselves as a person in the world. We can learn how to put ourselves on a basis of self-respect which will make us much less vulnerable to taking the ups and downs of life as personally as we used to when we were five years old. We will be free to solve more problems than ever before.

Pain creates problems for us that we do not know how to solve. We want to relieve our psychological pain, but we never learned how to give ourselves *emotional first aid*. We have good intentions for ourselves which only make things worse. Anger is painful, anxiety is painful, the loss of our self-respect is painful. Not knowing how to solve these painful problems compounds the pain of our everyday existence.

Making the situation more complicated is that we do not know what our pain is. **Self-contempt**, which is the opposite of self-respect, is a pain that we all feel to a greater or lesser degree. We try to relieve it by overcompensating and making either fools or tyrants of ourselves. Or we give up and stop trying. We sink to the bottom.

Or we try to numb the pain of our self-contempt by escaping into drugs, alcohol, sex, gambling and other *negative excitements*. In any event, we lose, and so do our loved ones.

Anger is painful, too. We may try to relieve this pain by *displacing* our anger onto an innocent party, or rationalizing it away, ("He didn't really mean it") or other inappropriate techniques that we picked up in grade school.

Since these pain-relieving techniques do not really work, the pain does not go away. We may have pushed it below the level of conscious awareness, but it is still there. We now have a pain we cannot feel: It is a pain that ruins our happiness without our even knowing it is down there. That is a problem that very few of us know how to solve all by ourselves.

Overcompensation is the process of trying to prove that we are not worthless and inferior. This is our solution to the problem of feeling **not good enough**. It is a *good intention* we have for ourselves without even

13

knowing it. It is a **negative ambition**. Since it works in reverse, we wind up confirming our self-contempt in the end. We feel compelled to keep trying forever. Mischief often comes from this attempt to prove something that cannot be proved. We try too hard. We make up these *good intentions* that make no sense in the real world. The real antidote to our painful feelings of worthlessness is to replace them with feelings of self-respect by doing Homework that needs to be done.

Enough. Unself-respecting people cannot feel good enough. They cannot feel smart enough, pretty enough, thin enough, successful enough or strong enough. Their overcompensatory striving to achieve "enoughness" can only make things worse. When we do our Homework, we feel competent enough, responsible enough, smart enough and worthwhile enough. We have earned the right to feel that *as good as we are right now, that is good enough. If we are better still next week, that is all right, too. We are worthwhile human beings in the meantime.*

This is not a prescription for stagnation or smug self-satisfaction. Self-respect gives us the freedom to do what is in us to do. Self-respecting people have no intention of vegetating. That would be inconsistent with their self-respect.

Emotional First Aid™. We can learn how to identify our emotional torments and call them by their rightful names. One such pain is self-anger, another is self-contempt. Having these handles is a first step toward relieving our emotional pain in the right way. We can learn how to catch ourselves about to overreact out of these griefs and choose not to. We can validate our loved one's pain and find that we have relieved our own at the same time. We can choose to express our anger like a mature adult for a change, and experience feelings of relief, control, security, identity and all the other facets of self-respect. We can learn how to disengage from the pain-inducing mischief of others. We can even learn to identify *our own mischief* and disengage from that, too. Emotional first aid brings down the unnecessary pain of everyday life.

Our power to **disengage from mischief** is perhaps the most potent remedy in our emotional first aid kit. As soon as we have identified someone's negative, provocative behavior as mischief, we enable ourselves to do something about it. We are empowered to do the unexpected. Instead of defending, protesting, explaining or cajoling, which are all good intentions, we can choose to have a real intention for ourselves. We can use our adult judgment to tell us what the situation really requires us to do, and then we do it. Sometimes the situation requires us to do nothing. This is a conscious choice, too. We are choosing to let it go.

Vignette: Let it Go

Sarah was upstairs in the shower. She heard three-year-old Bradley crying and thirty-three-year-old Larry trying to talk him out of it. Larry was saying, "If you can't tell me why you are crying, then you shouldn't be crying." In the old days, before the Anger Clinic, Sarah would have been out of that shower, into her robe and down those stairs in 6.5 seconds flat. This time was different. She had the course and she applied what she had learned to the real world. She decided not to run down there and give Larry another useless lecture on the absurdity of his logic, or to scoop up the child and rescue him from his inadequately prepared father. She decided to let go of her self-assigned responsibility to solve every family problem perfectly and instantly. She realized that the old way never changed anything. It hadn't helped anyone.

For the first time in her life, Sarah consciously and deliberately chose to do nothing. She let it go. She went on with her shower. The crying and yelling stopped much sooner than it had in the past.

Sarah had disengaged from the mischief in the kitchen. These two people, without knowing it, were used to putting on a show for mom. They expected her to come down and react to it. It didn't need to be done. Sarah chose not to be a part of their mutual mischief. She arranged to live on her own appropriate terms for a little while. It felt good. She didn't feel guilty of the crime of negligence or irresponsibility. She didn't feel out of control; she felt in control of herself. She had spared her husband and child the pain of an out-of-control, super-angry, super-counterproductive Mother from Hell. She had made it happen. No one had to know about it but her. She felt she had assumed appropriate responsibility and allowed both Larry to learn from his own mistakes and Bradley to solve his own interpersonal relationship problems. He was going to need the practice.

Sarah had given herself *"Emotional First Aid."* She had replaced her *good intention* to rescue her child with a *real intention*: To let them work it out for themselves. This was not selfish, it was appropriate behavior. It deprived these mischief makers of their negative payoff. She experienced all the facets of self-respect (See "THE COMPONENTS OF OUR CHARACTER" on page 265.). She had used an anger situation to move from a felt minus (self-doubt) to a felt plus (self-respect). She had set an example of appropriate responsibility and admirable restraint for her loved ones to see and follow. She had solved the problem in the right way. She was healing herself.

I'm abandoned forever and it's all my fault!

1. ABANDONMENT

We rarely experience anger in its purest state. Our anger in the present is often contaminated by remembrances of angers past that were never dealt with properly. As children, we did not know how to manage them properly, so we mismanaged them. We did not get relief from them at the time, so they are still circulating down there below the level of our conscious awareness. When something in the present reminds us of an anger from the past, we often become angrier than we need to be. We call this, *"super-anger."* For example, when our wife, Doris, does not come home at the time she said she would, it makes us angry. If it reminds us of an abandonment we experienced in our early childhood, our anger in the present is reinforced. We experience the overwhelming feeling that we are being abandoned all over again, which of course we are not. When Doris finally does come home, we aren't relieved to see her safe and sound. We are angry at her for causing us this unnecessary pain and grief. We learn nothing from this mistake. Nothing has changed. We will repeat it again the next time.

Our anger management technique is to identify the contaminant from the past so we can put it into a more realistic perspective in the present. When we become angry, we should remember that we do not want to go through that agony again. We have a choice now that we did not have before. We can remind ourselves to ask a focusing question such as, *"Wait a minute. I am not 'upset,' I am angry. What angers me the most? Is it that Doris is 47 minutes late?"* Very often the answer from the past will pop into our consciousness. "I feel alone and abandoned, just like I felt when I was a kid." We may have a recollection of a terrified child pressing his nose to the cold window pane waiting for the headlights of a car pulling into the driveway, a car that never came. We can say to ourselves, *"That was then and this is now. I am an independent grown-up now. I have a personhood of my own that I did not have as a child. I have adult resources. I have choices and I have me. I cannot be abandoned anymore. I can be angry at Doris for being late, but that is manageable. I will tell her I am angry at her for not calling me, but I am glad to see her. We might even have a pleasant dinner for a change."*

18

2. ABUSE

One of the most prevalent anger mismanagement techniques in America today is abuse. We have an epidemic of abuse, including: wife abuse, husband abuse, child abuse, sibling abuse, teacher abuse, student abuse, employee abuse and elder abuse. If there is one thing that we abuse more than substances, it is each other. How do we understand abuse as a social phenomenon?

Is it a reflection of the proliferation of media violence? We had abuse before television and movies were invented.

Is it a reflection of hard economic times? We have abuse in good times, too.

Is it a matter of low self-esteem? People who profess to have high self-esteem abuse each other, too.

Is abuse an urban phenomenon? No, for we have abuse surrounding us everywhere.

Under what circumstances are abusers provoked to inflict pain on their fellow human beings?

- When they have a problem they cannot solve;
- When they are not getting what they want;
- When they have a hard day;
- When they are not appreciated;
- When they are inconvenienced;
- When they are feeling victimized;
- When they feel out of control;
- When they have suffered a loss;
- When they do not receive "proper" respect.

All of these circumstances are actually grievances. We all have grievances, but a major characteristic of abusers is that they do not manage their grievances very well. When we peel their *anger artichoke* down, we find these grievances are not the real issue. They are only the occasion for the real issues, which are hidden farther down. For

19

example, these people feel inadequate to cope with the ups and downs of everyday life. When life or a loved one presents them with a problem that they cannot solve instantly and perfectly, as they require themselves to do, their preexisting feelings of inadequacy to cope are ignited and they explode.

The Issue Is Not the Issue

When abusers try to justify their hurtful behavior by screaming, "I just want to teach you a lesson" or "It's's for your own good," these excuses are not to be taken at face value. It is ironic that they are abusing their victims with the best of intentions. When they yell, "You made me do this" or "You make me so mad" the purpose is not to convey the truth about their motivation. These are self-serving, self-deceiving cover stories. The abusers are trying to put the guilt and blame on the person being abused, and very often they succeed. They arrange to have it both ways: They can indulge themselves and it is never their fault. These are not valid statements to be taken at face value, but a smokescreen behind which the abuser can operate in safety.

Abusers will say, by way of explanation, "That's just the way I am." What they are really saying is, "I have no interest in changing for you or anyone else. Take it or leave it. Don't say I didn't warn you."

They may seek to justify their abuse by claiming, "I'm under too much pressure." We are all under pressure. Self-respecting people take the trouble to learn how to manage the pressures of everyday life.

What the abusers are really saying is, "I am inadequate to cope with life as other people do and I have no intention of doing anything about my inadequacies. I expect you to do something about them and when you fail to achieve the perfection I require, that causes me a grievance. I have the right to complain about the service, even to punish you for disappointing me."

Many therapists focus on the abuser's overt behavior. They say, "You've got a temper. You've got to control that temper," as if abusers were interested in giving up an anger technique that has been successful all these years. Practitioners often consign abusers to self-help groups where they can exchange war stories with their fellow abusers, feeling sorry for their misunderstood selves all the while.

There are many more such surface issues. Many of us stop looking right there and take these phony issues at face value as if they made sense. We debate with the abuser as if we could make him understand the error of his ways.

But there are deeper issues that underlie all of these surface considerations. Most of us experience these negative situations, but we do not abuse each other when we do. We do not use these disappointments and grievances as an excuse to inflict pain on a safe target. Abusers never pick an unsafe target. They are mean, but they aren't stupid. What do we non-abusers have that abusers do not have and do not even wish to attain if they could? What are the real issues?

The answer to this is twofold:

1. The first factor *is anger*. Negative situations make us angry. Some of us have learned how to manage our anger during our childhood or in therapy as adults. Abusers, on the other hand, do not know how to manage their anger in appropriate, civilized ways and many of them are not interested in learning how. So they mismanage it. They express their anger in destructive ways that can only make the situation worse. They do not learn from their repetitive experiences. Often, there is no logical consequence (See "LOGICAL CONSEQUENCES" on page 126.) from which they can draw a constructive conclusion. Even when there is a consequence, it may not scratch where they itch. They miss the point of it and repeat their offensive behavior anyway.

2. The second factor is *self-contempt*. Since abusers hold themselves in contempt, it follows that they can only have contempt for those who love them. Their abusive behavior is a derivative of their contempt for themselves. Their self-destructive behavior is consistent with their feelings that they are worthless and undeserving of happiness and success. We cannot reason them out of their negative attitudes towards themselves and others.

21

The newspapers often say a particular case of abuse was sense-less. We know that sense has nothing to do with it. (See "RATIO-NALITOSIS" on page 160.)

These factors — mismanaged, out-of-control anger in a context of self-contempt — are the real issues. They predispose abusers to behave in ways they do not understand or even want to understand. Their anger and self-contempt are painful, and abusing others is how they relieve their pain. This is how they solve problems they feel inadequately prepared to solve otherwise. Unfortunately for them and for us, they are relieving nothing and solving nothing. That's the catch. The pain will be back tomorrow and the problems will be worse than they were before.

Some of us try to make these people understand the error of their ways. Our mistake is to think they are just like us, just regular folks who need a little helping hand to make them see the light. They are not like us. We need to stop trying to help these people out until we discover the source of their real issues.

At the Anger Clinic, one of the first steps in our therapeutic approach is to help abusers learn the underlying *purposes* of their abusive behavior. For instance, their purpose may be:

- To get attention, even if it is negative. To them, it is better than no attention at all. Attention validates that they exist. They cannot validate their own existence.

- To gain power and control over others. Not so they can use this power in positive, constructive ways, which they do not know how to do, but so that they can reduce the pain of their power-lessness. Their pain makes them totally self-preoccupied. They do not care about others. What is worse, they *cannot* care about others.

- To get revenge on people who have caused them a grievance, even if the grievance is imaginary, fictitious or a misperception. The pain of the grievance is real and they must relieve it by hurt-ing others in the name of *equity* and *fair play* as they define it.

- To drive people away from them so they can withdraw from life into a cocoon of discouragement. That is how they hope to keep from failing even more in the future.

Their loved ones may mean well, for they do want to help. However, they do not understand the abuser's underlying anger and self-contempt. They do not know how to identify or relieve the negative purposes of the abusive behavior. Their good intentions can only make things worse. The abuser will beat them until they give up and stop trying to help. When they do, they will lose and the abuser will win. Our goal is to replace these negative purposes with positive ones. We do this by giving both parties appropriate Homework to do.

Another step in the healing process is to find out how the abuser got this way. We do this by asking a focusing question such as, *"What is the first thing you remember from your childhood?"*

Vignette: Victim or Victimizer?

Ron was an abuser. His wife divorced him because of his cruelty to her and the children. He has not learned a thing from the experience. He is now abusing his new girl friend, Sylvia. He is in danger of losing her, too. He came in for counseling because she insisted. He doesn't think he needs it.

Ron's first early recollection was of his father forcing him into a corner of his room and beating him with a rolled up newspaper. Investigation does not end with the finding that Ron was an abused child. We wish to identify the specific conclusions, attitudes and expectations Ron derived from this experience.

Using the limited insight of a five-year-old child, these are some of the lessons that Ron learned on that day that his father beat him. He has never unlearned them:

- "I must have done something wrong. Wrongness is to be punished violently."
- "Control is used for inflicting punishment on persons weaker than oneself."
- "I am a victim; I am weak."

- "My father is a victimizer, he is strong. He can do as he pleases. I would much rather be a victimizer than a victim."
- "I was wrong. My wrongness made my father angry. It is my own fault for being wrong."
- "The only time my father pays attention to me is when he beats me. At least it proves I am alive."
- "I cannot cope. I cannot solve my problems. When I can't solve problems in the present, it reminds me how weak and inadequate I really am. I do not want people to find out my secret inadequacy. I must control them to prevent that. I must be stronger than they are."
- "My father solved his problems by beating people. If it's good enough for him, it's good enough for me."
- "Strong people are entitled to get revenge on loved ones: It's for their own good. It will make them a better person."

One intervention that worked with Ron focused on his tendency to go into his victim role whenever he had a grievance. For instance, when Sylvia tried to defend herself against him, Ron perceived her behavior as an attack on him: a victimization. He hates to be victimized, especially by someone who is physically weaker than he is. He cannot permit that to happen. His only method of relieving the pain of his victimization was to become the counter-victimizer. He was able to stop her "attack" by doing to her what his father did to him.

We agreed that Ron felt victimized by Sylvia's behavior. No one had ever agreed with him before. He had always been told that he had to understand the other person's distress. No one ever tried to understand his, which just compounded his feeling that he was a misunderstood, guiltless victim.

After validating Ron's perception of himself as the "innocent" victim of Sylvia's wrath, we said, *"Could it be, Ron, that you are perceiving victimization where no victimization is intended?"* We are not invalidating him, we are merely asking a question. Even if Ron says "no," which is not necessarily the truth, we have at least introduced to him the concept that perceptions can be mistaken and that it is all right to make mistakes. He will not be beaten for his wrongness. We have created an atmosphere in which it is possible for Ron to accept his imperfection, which no one ever created for him before. He can begin to consider the possibility that he is not life's perpetual victim at all, but that he is a worthwhile human being in spite of his faults and imperfections.

Ron's Homework is to see Sylvia not as a victimizer like his father, but as an imperfect human being. She is not wrong and he is not right. They are both imperfect human beings who make each other angry from time to time. Anger is not to be feared anymore. Ron is not seven years old. He can learn to say, *"It makes me angry when you do that, Sylvia."* He has a choice now that his father did not have. He can also learn to validate Sylvia's anger by saying, *"I'm sorry you are so angry."* That is what self-respecting people do.

Ron did his Homework the next day. Sylvia did not understand something he said. She asked him to repeat it. In the old days, Ron would have felt *controlled* by her, like an inferior person about to be victimized. He would have taken her request *personally,* as if it were a reflection on his worth as a person, as if she were blaming him for not speaking clearly. He would have become angry and abusive in self-defense. But he *chose* not to. He just repeated what he had said. He had chosen to cooperate with her as an independent and equal member of the human race. He had never seen an example of cooperation between his father and mother. He became his own model. He made it happen. It was his choice. He felt in control of himself, and he had used mature judgment. He had an identity of his own to replace his old role as his father's terrified, inadequate victim. His Homework had earned him the right to respect himself as an independent human being in his own right.

That same night, Sylvia talked on the telephone for an hour. Ron wanted her attention and he wasn't getting it. This grievance made him angry, too. He was feeling victimized again. Ron gave himself the choice of expressing his anger the "new way" or the "old way." He chose the new way. He said, *"Sylvia, it makes me angry when you tie up the phone so long."* She said, *"You're right. I'm sorry."* There was no explosion of anger, no defensiveness, no name calling. Ron didn't miss the negative excitement of the bad old days. He felt relieved, liberated, calm and at peace with himself. These are all facets of self-respect.

The more Homework Ron does, the more he replaces his self-contempt, with its negative attitudes and roles, with self-respect. The more adequate Ron feels to cope with life, the less he needs to express his anger with his fists.

Some abusers are not ready to make these difficult transitions. They only do what is easy. That way, they cannot fail. Perhaps they have not suffered enough and cannot see why they should change at all. They think their way of living is working. They are not paying any price for their misdeeds, but their loved ones are. They cannot see why they should quit when they are winning.

Do's and Don'ts:

- Do not attack or defend on the abuser's terms. You can choose to behave on your own valid terms.
- The issue is not what the abuser is complaining about; the issue is his anger in the context of his self-contempt.
- Use a focusing question to help the abuser identify the real source of his pain. *"What happened to make you so angry?"*
- Validate the abuser's anger. *"I'm sorry you are so angry. I'd be angry too, if that happened to me."*
- Identify the "victim" component of the abuser's distress. *"You must have felt like a victim when that happened."*
- You can even say, *"I didn't mean to make you feel like a victim. I am not your enemy. I am on your side."*

3. ACTIVE REMORSE

Active remorse does not mean feeling guilty for what we did and buying an expensive gift to cover our tracks. It does not mean brooding forever over our sins of omission and commission.

Active remorse means using our adult judgment to determine an appropriate course of remedial action. Sometimes it means saying, *"I'm sorry"* (page 118). We may never have said "I'm sorry" in our life. We didn't want to give anyone the satisfaction. Maybe it is time we did. We will find it costs us nothing. In fact, it might pay big dividends.

On other occasions, active remorse may mean actually spending money to buy a replacement. Some of us are willing to go as high as two bucks. Grown-ups are prepared to go as high as the reality of the situation requires them to go. If we do not know what the injured party wants us to do, we can ask something like, *"What remedy do you seek?"* This is not abject submission, this is cooperation between two imperfect human beings.

4. ADMIRABLE RESTRAINT

Some people express too much anger, while others express too little. Very few people express their anger right down the middle between the two extremes and get the relief they need to get.

Sometimes, it is not possible or practical to express our anger openly. On such occasions, managing our anger means *riding it out*, keeping our feelings to ourself and resisting the often powerful temptation to "let 'er rip," which takes no brains at all.

When we exercise Admirable Restraint, we are not suppressing our anger below the level of conscious awareness or rationalizing it away ("Oh, he doesn't really mean what he is saying," or "He can't help himself.") We are fully aware of the fire in our belly. We are making wide-awake choices in the real world and using our adult judgment to determine our behavior at every point.

We are not doing it for the other person; we are doing it for *us*. We know what the consequences will be if we let fly and we are consciously choosing to spare ourself this unnecessary fallout. We are not taking the other person's mischief personally or literally. We are managing our anger and our life competently as a self-respecting human being should under combat conditions. We are not fighting harder; we are fighting smarter.

5. AFFIRM LIFE

When our anger gets the better of us and ferments into vindictiveness, depression, discouragement and despair, the oil in our lamp burns very low. Our energy is bound up in negative emotions and there is not much left for us. That is when we are tempted to chuck it all, crawl in our hole and hibernate until spring.

Many of us give in to this temptation, until, after a while, our hibernations seem to run together and life has passed us by. It was the only one we had.

Self-respecting people use a technique called "Affirming Life." They have a choice that their vegetating neighbors do not have. They can choose to manage their anger properly and keep it from turning into such emotional symptoms as depression, anxiety and paranoia. They can get back in the flow. It is hard to do, but they know that the other way is even harder.

Here is an example of how we can make appropriate anger choices in the moment that we are angry:

Vignette: Shifting Gears

Julie and Jim were engaged. Jim wanted to buy a brand new stereo set that they would both enjoy. He read all the catalogues and magazines until he found one that really filled the bill. He took Julie downtown to see it in the store. He couldn't wait to see her reaction.

"Is that the one?" she said. "It's so bulky. I thought it would be smaller. Don't they have it in blonde mahogany? This is so dark. Don't they have anything else?"

Jim could feel the old pulling in his gut. He had learned to recognize that pulling as his organism's anger response to a grievance. He wasn't

28

exactly sure what the grievance was. It angered him that his beloved did not share his taste in acoustical hardware, but more than that, he felt that his hours of research in this field were insignificant and unappreciated. He felt *good for nothing* which means "worthless." That hurts.

They had planned to go to dinner afterward at their special restaurant on the waterfront. Jim felt sick to his stomach and had no appetite for dinner now. He felt like going back to his apartment and dozing off. That was when he remembered his choices: He could choose to withdraw from life as he had all through college when the going got rough, or he could allow himself to be angry at Julie for her lack of consideration for his feelings and her failure to appreciate his expertise. He chose not to take Julie's preferences in den furniture personally and not to get angry at himself for *allowing* the disappointment to happen. He was still angry, but he was managing it like a grown-up. He shifted his emotional gears, explained his preferences to Julie in language she could almost understand and made his purchase.

He was still angry as he left the store, walked to the car and steered toward the restaurant. Julie began talking about other things, never realizing how close she came to having canned tuna for dinner that night, while Jim found himself involved once again in the human race. His anger dissipated, as it had before when he had remembered to manage it correctly. It seemed to him that it was dissipating sooner each time.

He had voted against withdrawing into his hurt feelings, which he knew was a prescription for a solitary, joyless existence. Instead, he had affirmed life on his own valid terms.

6. AGREE WITH IT

This technique is a specific example of, Do The Unexpected (page 57). When your provokers are venting their anger, taunting you with nonsense that they will probably regret in the morning, you can defuse their unreasonable, non-objective emotionality by finding something in their tirade to agree with. Here are some game-enders:

Provocation	Disagreeing, (Defending/Explaining)	Agreeing
"I've never seen a mess like this."	"You're always complaining."	"It's awful, isn't it?"
"Can't you do anything right?"	"I do plenty of things right, but you never notice."	"I don't blame you for being angry."
"Your mother is driving me crazy."	"You never liked my mother, admit it."	"She sure has her ups and downs, doesn't she?"

We are not agreeing that they are right, only that they *feel the way they feel*. We are letting them know we have no intention of trying to talk them out of it or of defending our integrity or anyone else's. Neither do we have any intention of making useless countermischief on their terms. They cannot take away our self-respect. Such a response costs us nothing. It takes the wind out of their sails. They cannot fight with agreement.

The Wimp Factor

Some people are resistant to using the "Agree With It" technique. They have never agreed with anyone and they are not about to start now. It would be *wimpy* and they couldn't live with themselves. *Real* grown-ups stand up for their rights; only *wimps* are agreeable.

Their definition of "wimp" is one they acquired in the early stages of their personal development. To a four-year-old, people are either weak or strong, right or wrong. There is no middle ground between the two extremes. To this day, they cannot compromise with their immature, self-indulgent definitions of themselves as people in the world. These are some of their impediments to agreeing with their fellow human beings:

- They take what other individuals say personally. They then feel compelled to defend their threatened personhood at the other person's expense.
- They take what is said *literally*, as if it made sense. Most of the time, it is only nonsense intended to provoke a negative reaction, which it does. They are going to fall for it every time.
- They confuse agreement with submission and inferiority. They cannot allow themselves to be inferior to anyone.
- They stand in judgment on other people's nonsense and find them guilty of a *wrongness*. They cannot agree with wrongness; they can only agree with rightness. Since they are the only ones who are ever right, they can only agree with themselves.
- They feel it is their responsibility to teach people the error of their ways. They cannot do that by agreeing with error.
- They feel it is up to them to make wrongdoers understand their version of the truth. They would feel guilty of irresponsible behavior if they let them persist in their error.
- They have played the role of the Oppositional Child all their lives. They define themselves by contrasting themselves with everyone else. They are not really *for* themselves; they are just *against* others.

The irony is that people who can retain their composure under these anger attacks are not wimps at all. They are showing resolute competence under fire. They are not reacting to these negative stimuli like laboratory rats; they are using their adult judgment to make appropriate choices under difficult circumstances. They are showing their independence, individuality and their strength of character by doing the unexpected on their own valid terms.

Some people admire aggressiveness under all circumstances. To the aggressive person who feels like a hammer, every problem is a nail. But some problems are not nails. They require a degree of flexibility and

31

accommodation. That is not wimpiness, but self-respect. It is a sad reflection on our contemporary way of life that we value the mindless, spunky counterattack over a thoughtful, stress-relieving intervention.

Agreeing with what the other person says is not to be confused with appeasement, placating or kowtowing, which are all forms of wimping out. The self-respecting person is merely agreeing that these other people feel the way they feel at the time. They may feel differently tomorrow. We can agree with them tomorrow, too. Here are some more examples:

"People are no damn good."

It seems that way, doesn't it?

"Nobody likes me."

It's very lonesome, isn't it?

"I can beat up anyone in the joint."

You certainly can.

It costs us nothing to let these other people know that we heard what they said. We are also letting them know we have no intention of letting them manipulate us into defending the opposite point of view. We have no such responsibility to correct another human being's world view or to debate nonsense as if it made sense. As self-respecting grown-ups, we have the power of choice. We can choose to let it go and say something appropriate that is conciliatory. We do not make things worse. Our goal is to make things better. It is written, "A soft answer turneth away wrath." Some of us are still having a hard time believing it.

7. THE ANGER LETTER

One way to solve an insoluble anger problem is to write our anger down on a piece of paper. This seems too easy to be of any use, yet this technique is very successful if we do it in the right way. We are not writing a hate letter or a laundry list of complaints and criticisms. We are directing our specific angers toward another entity outside of ourself.

- Writing our abstract feelings and attitudes down on a piece of paper makes them tangible and concrete before our very eyes. We cannot manage abstract thoughts about our life or about ourselves. However, we can begin to evaluate and sort them out when we see them in black and white in front of us.

- Writing our thoughts and feelings down can begin a process of association that brings up ideas from the past that are not accessible otherwise. Seeing these ideas before us in the present through adult eyes gives us a chance to evaluate them as we might not have otherwise. If we see that they are no more than childhood misperceptions, we can choose to replace them with more appropriate ideas and attitudes.

- Writing is an action in the real world. When we take this overt action, it gives rise to psychological, biochemical and physiological responses that brooding or intending cannot evoke.

- Writing is a choice we have made. The power of choice is in itself a welcome antidote to the miserable feeling that there is nothing we can *do* about the pain our anger is causing us. We have given ourselves the feeling that there is something we can do about our anger and we are doing it. The power of choice liberates us from our frustration: The feelings of anger, powerlessness and loss of control.

These letters do not have to be mailed. That is optional. We are not writing the letter to enlighten the other person. We are doing it to give ourselves some timely relief from our own distress. If we are angry at a deceased loved one, at God, at life, at the system or even at ourselves, we can write our anger down. Afterwards, we can file our letter, tear it up or burn it. That is our choice, too.

This technique even works with children. They, too, should be encouraged to express their anger appropriately, even if it is at us. They are not saying, "I hate you," only that we caused them a grievance whether it is real or imaginary, and it made them angry. If they are too young to write a letter, they can draw a picture (See "DRAW A PICTURE" on page 66.).

8. BLAMING
(The Perry Mason Syndrome)

When we are angry, we are in pain. One of our first priorities is to relieve our pain as fast as we can. We want fast, fast, fast relief. We imagine that we can solve our problem by:

- Identifying the culprit who caused our pain.
- Transferring our pain to the offender in a way that will give us gratification. The pleasure of this gratification, we hope, will assuage the pain of our anger.
- Distracting others from our own contribution to our present distress.

We imagine we are proceeding in a rational, logical manner when we point fingers of guilt, shame, fault and blame, but we are not. This entire operation is born of emotion, and our intellectual faculties are just going along for the ride.

An emotion is a feeling that impels us to move. When we feel angry sitting on the sofa, we are not doing anything about it. It is not yet an emotion, but just a feeling. However, when our anger energizes us to track down the miscreant who left the skateboard on the basement stairs, that is an emotion. We are seeking relief from the pressure, tension and stress that this emotion is causing us. We are behaving according to attitudes we learned when we were four years old, if not earlier: "Find the one who did it and do it back worse." Our reasoning is equally immature: "If you cause me pain, I have the right to cause you pain in return. That's fair." This is not the logic of a mature adult. These attitudes are out of our conscious control.

When we blame someone, we are inflicting the pain of guilt, which we hope is commensurate with the degree of pain he or she caused us. When we dump guilt, we are at the same time tearing down the alleged offender's self-respect. Even young children know that guilty people are worthless, and that is how they come to feel. The issue is no longer guilt or innocence. It is the fact of the accusation itself that turns their self-respect to self-contempt. If the accusation is correct, the children do not learn from their mistakes. They take the accusation personally, as a reflection on their worth as a person. The child is *wrong*. There is no appeal to a higher court. There is no cure for being *wrong*. Even when the child is exonerated, the scar of that accusation remains behind. The damage has been done.

A better technique than blaming, guilting, ridiculing, fault-finding and criticizing would be to tell the truth. That is the last thing we think of doing. We think the truth lies in unmasking the perpetrator, even if it is a hapless child or a well-intentioned spouse, but that is not the truth. The truth is that there was a grievance and the grievance made us angry. Our pain is real and we need to relieve it in ways that work. We can choose to say, *"It makes me very angry when you leave things on the stairs that cause me to slide all the way down into the basement."* That is a powerful, impressive statement. Children can understand that our anger is a logical consequence of their not picking things up. Our anger is not a wipeout of their personhood. We are only saying that what happened made us angry. We are making a distinction between the deed and the doer. They are worthwhile in spite of what happened, and so are we. Blaming is not a logical consequence of anything. It is an illogical, destructive consequence.

Do's and Don'ts:

- Do not take your blamer's mischief personally as a reflection on your worth as a person.
- Do not defend, debate or rebut the substance of the blame. It is not a crime, it is only mischief or an unfortunate happenstance in an imperfect world.
- Do not try to make sense out of nonsense.
- Instead, we can choose to do the unexpected:

"All my life I've wanted to
be somebody, but I see now
I should have been more specific."

Lily Tomlin & Jane Wagner
The Search For Intelligent Life In The Universe
1986, Harper Collins, NY, NY

"Thank you for calling this to my attention."

"I know you are doing this for my own good and I appreciate it, but I will be fine."

"How does that help?"

9. CATCH YOURSELF IN THE ACT

Most of our present anger management techniques are no more than bad habits we picked up along the way and never outgrew. Now we can. We can use an anger situation to begin the process of replacing these old habits with some less offensive new ones. The first step is to be aware that we have these inappropriate carryovers from our childhoods. Whether we are using sarcasm, revenge, sulking, the silent treatment, hitting, wall-banging or other negative means, our Homework is to catch ourselves in the act of doing it and then choose not to. We can choose to stop it at any time. With practice, we will catch ourselves sooner each time and, therefore, stop sooner. We can choose to replace our inappropriate, relationship-killing habits with one or more of the new techniques in this book.

Someday, we will be able to catch ourselves before we start! That's *bingo*! That is our self-respect kicking in.

10. COMMUNICATING IN A NEW KEY

You do not realize it, but you are communicating in different keys all day long. You use one key for your spouse, another for your two-year-old daughter, yet another for your boss and still another for your racquetball buddies. Often, you change from one key to another instantly — for instance, when you pick up the telephone in the middle of a fight. You do it without being consciously aware of it. It would be useful if you could learn to do it in the middle of an anger attack.

Some keys are scary, unpleasant and anger provoking: *"Do this! Do that! Jump when I tell you!"* This is the imperative voice. We are not even aware we are using it half of the time. This key is not taken kindly by our hearers. They become testy and rebel against us or they become intimidated by us and resentfully submit to our tyranny. Neither response is conducive to happy relationships. People tend to resent being torn down to bolster our shaky egos. They are not favorably impressed by our imperiousness. They are negatively impressed, which to some of us is better than not being impressed at all.

We can choose to modulate our tone into one that encourages cooperation between equals. We may have to practice, just like when we were learning to play the saxophone. If we do not know how it is done, we can look around and listen. There are people around us who are securing cooperation all the time. Listen to the tone they use. Listen to their *music.* Watch what they do. Instead of saying, "Why can't I ever get any help around here?" which is merely your mismanaged anger talking, some of them choose to say, *"I would like your help over here."* That has the advantage of offering the other person the choice of helping or not. If we do it in the right key, the other person often makes the right choice. We will often find that the music we choose is more important than the words!

Another key we do not need is the accusatory voice, such as, "Why did you do that? Why are you so stupid?" This is not a request for factual information, but an angry accusation of guilt. People resent being found guilty without a trial, and they resent our standing in judgment on them without ever having been elevated to the bench.

A better technique would be to stop talking about the other person, which is called a "You message," as in, "You make me sick," and choose to use an "I message" instead, such as, *"I am angry at you"* or *"It makes me angry when you pour gravy in my shoes."* This is an affirmative voice. Now the ball is in the other party's court. Let's see what he or she does with it. In the meantime, we are generating less anger in other people and affording ourselves some relief from our excessive anger that we were not getting the old way.

People who don't respect themselves are liable to use these inappropriate voices from their childhood. People who have worked through their childhood carryovers are more likely to use a voice that is appropriate to the situation in the present. They can sound firm or gentle, angry or kind. The music changes, but their self-respect stays the same.

11. CONFRONTATION

To most people, the thought of an angry confrontation is scary. They feel inadequately prepared to cope with anger problems. To prevent this humiliating exposure of their inadequacy, they withdraw from the problem into silence and submission. Their suppressed anger ferments into clinical symptoms such as depression, anxiety and suicidal impulses, or into physical symptoms such as stress, burnout, ulcers, colitis and hypertension. Mismanaged confrontations escalate into domestic violence, drive-by shootings, police brutality, mob demonstrations and even war.

We need not fear that a confrontation will turn into a shootout at the OK Corral. A shouting match need not bring up fears of losing control or being victimized. A confrontation, if it is managed properly, very often clears the air and enables us to get on with the business of living our lives and solving our problems.

We are liable to mismanage confrontations because of our vulnerability to taking the other person's anger at us personally, as a wipeout of our self-respect. Under these circumstances, the risks are too high. It isn't worth the risk of losing our self-worth. We submit too soon or we go into an overcompensatory counter-offensive. We lose either way.

It takes courage to solve these problems and that is what we do not have. We do not even know what courage is nor how to attain it. Courage is the *willingness to take a risk*. If there were no risk, there

39

would be no need for courage. Without courage, we cannot grow out of our childhood fears and inadequacies. We cannot solve problems without courage. We cannot change. We can only stagnate and fall behind those who are willing to take life as it comes and do the best they can with it. Self-respecting people have courage. They are scared too, but they are willing to take the risk. They are free to change.

The prerequisite for a successful anger exchange is self-respect. This in turn, is the prerequisite for mutual respect. Self-respecting people have the courage to tell the truth, even when that truth is displeasing. They can speak their unpleasant truths in a mature, responsible manner, such as:

"It's makes me angry when you do that."

"I'm glad you can tell me that, because if you don't tell me, I won't know. I'm not a mind reader."

"Are you going to change it?"

"No. It's too late to change it now. It has to be done this way. I don't blame you for being angry, but I'm glad you could tell me. That took courage."

"Can we do it the other way next time?"

"If we prepare for it in the right way, we can give it a try."

The issue is not so much the topic under discussion. It is the positive context of mutual respect in which this conversation takes place. When one person has self-respect, the other person often follows that example. A context of mutual respect has been created. If the context is a negative one based on mutual contempt, there can be no constructive outcome. That is when the drive-by shooting starts.

12. CONSIDER THE SOURCE

When we are under an anger attack, we are so busy reacting to the provocation that we forget to realistically consider the person who is provoking us. It may be our boss, and we see him as ten feet tall, or it may be our sassy three-year-old whose newly minted cuss word is a threat to our standing in civilized society. It may be the girl of our dreams, or a beefy truck driver on the freeway who has just come within two inches of our rear bumper. We tend to invest these people with various fictitious qualities and attributes, which makes it very difficult for us to relieve our anger problem in a constructive, nonfatal way.

We can choose to catch ourselves inflating or deflating these parties of the second part and then choose not to. We can choose, instead, to consider the source of the provocation. The source is, despite these intimidating auras, halos, horns and tusks, an imperfect human being behaving imperfectly as humans are wont to do from time to time. Put in that perspective, their provocation loses some of the power to blow us through the roof. We are now free to say to ourselves, *"It's only Marvin being Marvin."* We are less likely to take his mischief personally. It has nothing to do with our worth as a person. It never did.

13. CRYING

Crying is a healthy, natural way of releasing strong emotion. The Greeks called it a catharsis. Unfortunately, we have developed attitudes towards crying that interfere with this sanity-saving process. Some of us see crying as a sign of weakness to be rejected and despised. We create a conflict between our natural impulse to cry out our anger, and our exaggerated fear of *what the neighbors will think.* Some of us will never resolve this conflict. It tears us apart from the inside.

Crying is behavior, and like any behavior, it can have negative as well as positive purposes. When we use our tears for negative purposes, we are making mischief:

- We use crying to get attention and pity for our suffering. "If I ever stop crying, how can I get the attention that I need to prove I still exist?"

"Some people can resist anything
but temptation."

Rudolf Dreikurs

- We use crying to obtain power over others and to make them feel guilty and ashamed so they will do what we want, such as to stop hurting us or take us to the movies. There are more mature techniques for securing cooperation. This misuse of our tears is called *water power.*

- We use our tears to get revenge and to hurt people as they have hurt us. We are reproaching them and punishing them for what they have done. Unfortunately, the issues involved in the negative transaction have not been dealt with constructively and the whole scenario will be repeated shortly.

- We use tears as an excuse to withdraw from the situation or from our relationships. We lack the courage to find out what is really going on so the underlying problems can be solved.

When we are depressed *(anger at ourselves in a context of self-contempt)* we cry at the slightest provocation. The issue is not tears; the issue is the unresolved anger that has never been worked through and relieved. After we have sorted out our anger, identified the objects of our anger, peeled our anger artichoke using focusing questions and written our anger letters, the depression often lifts and the crying stops.

Sometimes we weep tears of impotent rage, while other times we weep tears of despair. These tears are legitimate and valid. We need to cry them out on our own terms and not suppress them because of our image. What kind of people cry sometimes? Imperfect human beings cry from time to time and we are worthwhile in spite of it.

14. DEBRIEFING OUR ANGER HOMEWORK

The Anger Clinic isn't just about Anger. It's about using an anger situation as an opportunity to move from carryover childhood self-doubt to adult self-respect. That is our larger therapy goal: To relieve the pain and unhappiness of doubting our worth as a person and replacing it with the feeling that we are *a worthwhile human being in spite of our faults and imperfections*, not because we won the baton twirling championship in seventh grade. That's not self-respect. It's merely self-esteem, which is only an estimation, an opinion we have of ourselves. Such opinions can be taken away very quickly and replaced by a negative, discouraging self-concept.

Here's how this process works.

We reveal to people that they have two choice the next time they get angry at their child, their spouse, or their co-worker:

- The old way, which is to either suppress their anger or blow up, or,
- Plan B, which is to manage their anger like a grown-up. They can choose to tell the truth as in, "It makes me angry when you do that." Or, they can write their anger out of their system onto a piece of paper and tear it up.

That's the action stage of the process.

The second stage is the follow-up: the process of replacing the facets of self-contempt with the facets of self-respect, which we call, "The Debriefing."

We ask, *"How did you feel after you did your Homework?"* They will say, "I felt good" or "I felt great!" These words are generic and non-specific. We want to zero in on this good feeling and squeeze the juice out of it, so they can use it to grow on.

We know that this good feeling has many components. They are like the facets of a diamond. We ask, "What is that good feeling called?" The sad fact is that most people don't know the name of their own good feelings. They don't have a handle on it and cannot summon it up whenever they want to. We ask this question, not to expose their ignorance, or to embarrass them, but to show them they have spent all these years on earth not knowing what *self-respect* is, how it feels, or how to recapture it when it gets away from them.

We debrief their Homework by enumerating the many emotional/attitudinal components of self-respect they experienced on that occasion. They were not able to appreciate what they accomplished in

44

their own behalf at the time. They had, for a moment at least, replaced their self-doubt with self-respect. Our goal is to stretch these periods of self-respect from a few minutes, to a few hours, days and months until they have crowded out the self-doubt of a lifetime. Not perfectly, just well enough.

We validate the *accomplishment*. For many, it is an All-Time First. We reveal that they haven't done it before, or if they have, they let it slip away from them like water in the sand. We want to capture it and savor it so we can do it again next time and the time after that. These successes are the building blocks of our new personhood. With repetition, these good feelings run together. The clients have become full-time self-respecting human beings. They are not the person they were before.

The Debriefing Questions might include:

- How did you feel after you did your Homework? *Relief* from the pressure, tension and stress.

- Were you out of control? You made it happen. That's positive *control*.

- Were you frustrated? Or did you have the *power of choice*? How good was your choice? It was good enough.

- Did you use your own judgment? How good was your *judgment*? Was it perfect? Or, was it good enough? Can you trust it next time?

- Did you feel a sense of *accomplishment*? You were building up, not tearing down.

- Did you feel *success*? It was positive — not negative mischief.

- Can you do it again? What's that feeling called? It's called *confidence*. Who gave you that confidence? You did.

- Were you playing a role? Were you a victim, a rebel, a pleaser? Or did you have an *identity* of your own, a self, not a role from childhood.

- Did you feel *mature*? This is not kid stuff, this is a grown-up.

- Did you tell the truth? How did you feel? *Liberated*. From whom? From the old you. Your truth has set you free.

"I don't want to!"
"Do we only do what we want?
Some of us do what life
requires us to do.
I didn't say you had to like it."

Rudolf Dreikurs

- Were you dependent? Co-dependent? Or did you feel *independent*?
- Did you feel inferior? Superior? Or did you feel *equal*? In what way are you equal? You are no more and no less human than anyone else. You are equal.
- Were you being super-responsible? Were you irresponsible? How responsible were you? Perfectly? You were assuming *appropriate responsibility* for yourself.
- Were you living in the past? Were you trying to prevent the future from happening? No. You were *living in the present*, right now, on your own valid terms.
- What happened to your insecurity? It went away. What took its place? *Security.*
- How smart were you? What happened to your stupiditude? You were *smart* enough. You don't have to be any smarter than that.
- What happened to your feeling that you didn't belong? You do *belong.* To whom? To yourself. There is a self now to belong to. And you belong to the human race.
- What happened to your feelings of inadequacy? Did you feel competent? How competent were you? You were *competent enough.*What happened to your anxiety? You had *peace of mind*, serenity.
- Was it scary? Did you do it anyway? What is that feeling called? *Courage.*

These qualities are components of self-respect. We are holding the mirror up to their faces and they can see themselves in it. They have gone through the fire. They did what reality required them to do. They have earned the right to outgrow their childhood self-doubts and replace them with appropriate self-respect.

15. DENIAL

A very common method that people have of coping with anger is to deny that they have it: "I am not angry. Shut up!" This denial is their way of solving a problem that nice, strong or superior people are not supposed to have.

We should not make the mistake of trying to penetrate the denial by saying, "Yes, you are angry. Don't lie to me." This makes us sound like an accuser, an attacker or a victimizer, which is exactly what our anger-denying loved ones do not need right then.

They need a friend — someone who will validate them as worthwhile human beings in spite of the present unpleasantness. We can validate them by validating their anger, which they have just denied having. When they say, "I'm not angry, I'm just hurt," we know that their anger is the emotional response to the hurt. It is down there, but we are not supposed to know it because anger is not nice. We can say something supportive, such as, *"I'd be angry if that happened to me"* or *"The same thing happened to me in fifth grade and I was so angry."* We are giving them permission to follow our example of anger management if they choose to do so. It is all right if they choose not to. It is their preference right now. Their preference may change in ten minutes. We can wait.

We can even ask a focusing question: *"How do you feel towards people who hurt you?"* The answer that comes out is often, "Angry."

We do not demand that they confess their anger to us instantly. That is a *good intention*, and it will backfire. A good intention is *our attempt to solve a problem when we really don't know what to do.* To conceal our feelings of inadequacy to cope, we make up something that sounds good at the time. Our behavior is not reality oriented. It is self-serving and counter-productive. In fact, it is mischief.

We need to have real intentions (See "THE COMPONENTS OF OUR CHARACTER" on page 265.) and to do what reality requires us to do, not what we hope will help but never has in the past. We can say, *"I'm sorry you're so upset. If you would like to talk to me about it later, I'll be glad to listen. If not, that is all right, too."* That is empowering. It gives them the power of choice when they need it most. They are feeling angry and powerless to do anything about it. They feel *frustrated.* Now they have the power to choose when and if they want to talk to us about their feelings. By giving them a choice, we avoid a power struggle over who can force whom to express what. When we validate the legitimacy of their anger there is nothing for them to deny or rebel against.

If they choose not to talk about it, that is their legitimate preference. We are not going to deny them that preference. It may be their way of testing us to see if we really mean it when we say we will respect their right to be left alone. Do not flunk the test. They are worthwhile human beings whether they confess their anger or not, and so are we. Sometimes it is appropriate to just let it go and let them heal themselves as best they can. You have already set an example of acceptance and it will help, whether they admit it or not. This is one way to begin creating an atmosphere of positive trust in which such problems can be resolved in the future.

16. DEFENSIVENESS

When people are angry at us, we hear their anger as if it were an attack on our personhood and an assault on our personal worth. This mistake is called *taking it personally.* We take their anger personally because we do not know we were not supposed to. Moreover, we do not know how else to take it.

We may rise to the defense of our integrity, innocence and high moral character. We cannot see what is wrong with this response. It seems logical to us to meet an attack with a counterattack, but this technique never solves the problem.

Our mindless reaction is not logical. It is an attitude kicking in. An attitude is *a predisposition to behave in a certain way.* An attitude has no brains. It doesn't care. It *can't* care. We have brains. We can choose to care in appropriate, responsible ways. The issue is not our character or our worth as a person; the issue is their *anger* and we need to deal with it effectively and constructively. We cannot do that by saying, "I didn't do it. You lie. I was out of town the whole time."

After we learn that the issue is not one of guilt or innocence, we can let go of our defensive propensities and, instead, we can choose to intervene appropriately. Once we have done so, we are free to say, *"I'm sorry you are so angry,"* or *"It makes you angry when that happens, doesn't it?"* When they hear us empathizing with their pain, they just may calm down so we can discuss their grievance with us like equal members of the human race.

17. DISCRETION

For many years, "total honesty" was a buzzword in the counseling industry. Every self-help book took pride in espousing the high ideal of perfect honesty at all times. Today, practitioners are reporting that relationships have broken down because of too much honesty! What are we to do?

The first thing we can do is to stop treating honesty as if it were an isolated attribute that exists apart from our personal context. If our personal context is negative, we are going to have honesty problems. We will have too much or too little. Self-respecting people have fewer honesty problems because they can be *appropriately* honest.

Appropriate honesty does not mean spilling the beans at every opportunity, nor does it mean telling people the awful truth "for their own good." That is a self-serving good intention. It is an overcompensation for feelings of inferiority by being super-truthful. Our attitude is, "Look how honest I am, everybody. I'm not inferior at all. I'm really superior. I have the power to inflict the awful truth upon you and you can't stop me."

Discretion does not mean clamming up, either. We cannot prevent disaster in the future by suppressing unpleasant communication in the present. It takes courage to tell the truth in a discreet manner, as in *"Pardon me, but your spouse has fallen asleep in the punchbowl again."* It takes no courage to look the other way and pretend it isn't happening.

Self-respecting people do not play destructive games with the truth. They have attributes that immature people do not have: They have mature judgment and the power of choice. They know how much honesty is appropriate for each given situation. This knowledge enables them to be discreet, which means they have *the ability to decide how much or how little they wish to reveal about themselves.* They are not compelled to flaunt their knowledge for overcompensatory purposes. Neither do they suppress information for fear of what others might think. They have the courage to live on their own valid terms.

Sometimes it is appropriate to express our anger openly. Other times it is not. Self-respecting people know the difference. When restraint is appropriate, they do not suppress their anger behind a smiling facade and deny they are angry. They are consciously choosing not to reveal their anger at the present time for legitimate reasons of their own. They may choose to express their anger later, after all the company has gone home, or they may choose to Give It a Pass (page 96), Consider the Source (page 40) or Write an Anger Letter (page 32). They can choose to mail the letter or to tear it up. That is discretion, too.

Do's and Don'ts

- Do not let other people control your power of choice. If they insist that you be open and honest "for your own good," identify their request as mischief. It does not need to be done. Rather, it is a self-serving good intention on their part. You can choose to say, *"I know you want the best for me and I appreciate it, but I'll be just fine this way,"* or *"Thanks for asking, but I would rather not."* As a worthwhile human being, you have the right to your own preferences.

- When someone tries to penetrate or overcome your discretion, do not get into a power struggle over who can make whom tell what. You can choose to deflect the attention away from yourself. You can use focusing questions to expose the underlying purposes of this mischief:

"I wonder why you want to know that."

"In the past, you have used these things as ammunition against me. Are you planning to do that again?"

"Could it be that you are trying to control me? I am not trying to control you. I am only trying to secure your cooperation."

- Do not try to make people understand you. Your life goes on whether they understand your motivation or not. You can be discreet about your purposes. They are no one's business but your own.

You can choose to be discreet about your opinions. When someone says, "Your uncle is a lazy bum," you can catch yourself about to play into this mischief. You can choose not to defend or explain. Instead, you can choose to agree that the other person feels that way. You can say, *"You may be right."* They can't fight that. You are setting appropriate limits on the mischief. You are aware that the issue is not your uncle, but power and control. The other person is seeking the power to provoke you into a counter-reaction. As a self-respecting person, you are free to make other arrangements.

18. DISENGAGE FROM YOUR OWN GOOD INTENTIONS

Why do we fight with someone we love? It makes no sense on a rational level. Our child has never said to us after a fight, "You know, I never thought of it that way, Mother dear. I see the light now. I will change my ways forthwith." But we keep hoping. We keep wanting the best for our loved ones without ever knowing how to bring that about. We never find out how to do that without insulting their intelligence.

On a deeper level, we fight because we have an agenda of our own that has nothing to do with wearing galoshes or eating more roughage. We may, in our hearts, want to "improve" our loved ones so they will be as happy, prosperous and as successful as the law allows. But basically, we are trying to prove to them how good we are to them. This is how we overcompensate for our feelings that we are really *not good enough*. Conversely, we may be fighting off the intrusive manipulations of our parents, elder sibling or maiden aunt to protect and defend our right to be miserable in our own way. This is a good intention we have for ourselves. Both parties are engaged in an absurd, mutually destructive struggle over who can make whom happy whose way.

After forty years of trying to change someone in ways that are obviously not working very well, we can choose to stop. We can let go of our ambition to improve people according to our own nebulous specifications. We can let go of our futile efforts to stop them from inflicting their mischief on us by making them understand how wrong they are, which is another self-serving good intention on our part. We can disengage ourselves from their mischief without disengaging from them. Or, we can minimize our contacts with them and see if the pattern changes. If it does, we can resume our relationship on a new, more mature basis. However, if the other party is too far gone, we can make the sad decision that the relationship is too painful and destructive for both of us and that it has become necessary to make other arrangements altogether. We can choose not to send good years after bad.

19. DISENGAGE FROM THE MISCHIEF

People make mischief at our expense. They tease, insult, criticize and patronize us. It all makes us angry. The angrier we get, the more they do it. They can't stop and neither can we.

If we want to break this cycle of provocation and anger, we have to figure out what is going on.

Our first step is to identify their provocative behavior as mischief. *Mischief is that which does not need to be done.* Teasing and criticizing do not need to be done, but people do it anyway. They do it because they can. We don't know how to stop them, so why should they stop when they are winning? We are so easy.

Our second step is to take away from them the power to provoke us with their nonsense. Identifying it as nonsense in the first place helps take some of the impact away from it. We are not impressed with nonsense.

There are two mistakes we often make when people make mischief. These mistakes make us vulnerable to overreacting to their childish behavior, which always makes things worse.

1. We take their mischief *seriously* as if it made sense. When they say, *"Can't you do anything right,"* they know very well that we do many things right. That is not the issue. We do not argue with them or defend our track record. Our track record is not the issue. The issue is that the other person is angry and we need to deal effectively with the anger. We cannot do that if we have made the mistake of taking this exaggerated accusation literally as if it meant what it seems to mean. It just means "I'm angry at what happened just now," and that is what we attend to.

2. We take mischief statements *personally*, as if they were a reflection on our worth as a person. Our antidote to taking the other person's anger personally is our *self-respect*. We can choose to remember that we are worthwhile human beings in spite of our faults and imperfections, one of which seems to have caused them a grievance. We regret that they are angry, but we are not guilty of a crime, nor are we worthless. We are worthwhile in spite of it. Only perfect people can go through life without making their fellow human beings angry, and we are not one of them. We don't have to be.

The third step in the process of disengaging is to respond to the other person's provocation in a way that is appropriate to the situation. For instance, you can say, *"You're right, I'm sorry it happened. I'll take care of it."* If their grievance is not a legitimate one, but only an excuse to get a rise out of us, it is appropriate to return their absurdity with another absurdity. We are now free to say anything we want to say, as long as it is on our terms and not theirs. We can say, *"Isn't it awful? It's been like that all day."* In so saying, we are letting the other person know that they have lost the power to provoke us to madness with their nonsense. They won't stop until we do.

20. DISPLACEMENT

This is the most common anger mismanagement technique of all. When daddy is angry at his boss, for instance, he cannot very well express his anger directly. He lives in fear of the consequences of his anger: of displeasing, of being victimized, of losing control and of ultimate abandonment. He suppresses his anger until he gets home where there is a whole houseful of safe targets. He takes his anger out on his loved ones. They have to take it. He is not powerless anymore.

He has power and control over their pain, and the victim has become the victimizer. His problem has been solved at the expense of his loved ones. He cannot see what is wrong with that. He does not see what they have to complain about.

Many of the cases of spouse battering and child abuse that we read about today can be understood as the effects of displaced anger. The original anger may be a few hours old or it may be decades old. A father may be displacing his anger at his parents onto his child. A mother may be displacing her anger at her pretty sister onto her pretty daughter. These behaviors are inappropriate, destructive and out of conscious control. They have less to do with current reality than they do with the carryover anger that the individual brings to reality from the past.

Displacers are trying to accomplish three underlying purposes:

1. Relief from the pain of their suppressed rage.

2. Relief from the pain of playing the role of the out-of-control victim.

3. Revenge upon those who hurt them by hurting others who cannot hurt back.

When these people feel victimized, a dynamic tension is set up and:

- They feel inferior to their victimizer.
- This state of inequality is painful and they feel impelled to relieve the pain of their inferiority and worthlessness.
- They seek this relief by displacing their anger onto others.
- They build themselves up by tearing others down.

Their equilibrium is restored, while others have just begun to suffer. When these victims are able, they will, in turn, seek relief from their torment by following their tormentor's pattern of displacing anger onto safe targets who do not deserve it.

The displacer's cover story is that it is fair to hurt others as they have been hurt. It comes out even. This is not fairness at all, but mischief — it does not need to be done.

Displacers can feel victimized by another person, by the system, by life. They may even feel victimized by themselves and think, "Why was I so stupid? The grievance that caused the anger may be real or imaginary, rational or nonrational, but it is a grievance just the same. The pain of it must be assuaged one way or another.

One reason the father displaces his anger onto his child is that he does not know what else to do. He is following his father's example of problem solving, or perhaps he developed this bullying technique himself on the schoolyard in the third grade. Our antidote is to reveal to him that he has a choice now. He can choose to express his anger verbally like a grown-up or he can tell his loved ones what the boss said to him at lunch. That would give them the opportunity to validate his anger and give him some relief. But the displacing father cannot do that yet, because showing his feelings would be a sign of *weakness*. To over-compensate for this threat of exposure as a weak, feeling person, he demonstrates his awesome power over terrified women and children. This is not strength, but phony, overcompensatory *strongness*. It is an absurd attitude. He does not respect himself on an appropriate basis and he will not stop beating up his loved ones until he does.

We can encourage him to make this new choice on his own behalf by asking, *"Did something happen to make you angry?"* This question shows that we respect him in spite of his emotional imperfection. No one ever showed him respect under these circumstances before. In time, he may come to respect himself. It will be easier for him to express his real feelings. That will take courage. That will take strength.

21. DO THE UNEXPECTED

When we are angry, we are very vulnerable to being manipulated to our own detriment. Our usually acute thought processes have been swamped by a tide of nonrational reactions and counter reactions. We are, in this state, very likely to do exactly what our sparring partners expect us to do. They do not expect us to do anything reasonable or constructive. They expect us to be as immature and vindictive as they are. "That's fair." We accommodate them when we sink to their nonsensical level of discourse: "You stink." *"I do not stink."* "Yes you do." *"You take that back."*

We will get nowhere that way. One of us has to make a break for it. If they do not know how, then we must. We know, after the two hundredth time, exactly what they expect us to do when they provoke us. We can choose, when we are ready, not to do it. We can choose to do something else instead. In fact, we can do anything we want as long as it is on our own terms and not a mindless reaction to their provocation. If we are tired of this useless third-grade game, we can learn some new responses to old jabs:

Game-Enders

When they say:	They do not expect us to say:
"You stink."	"There's a lot of that going around."
"You're stupid, too."	"I don't know how you stand it."
This report isn't as good as Miss Rumplemeyer used to turn out, bless her soul."	"Yes, she was a saint, wasn't she. Too bad she died so young."
"Come back here and fight like a man."	"Second graders fight. Grown-ups do not. I am leaving now. I hope you feel better in the morning."
"I hate you."	"I am sorry you are so angry."
"I am not angry. That's stupid."	"You could have fooled me."

The content of our reply does not have to make sense. We are using our response to reveal to our partner that the game is over and that we have ended it. We have done what reality has required us to do when confronted with mischief.

They can no longer control us into reacting destructively on their terms. We have a choice now, an alternative mode of responding. This alternative gives us a 100-percent improvement over the old days when we had only one choice, a knee-jerk reaction to defend ourselves, which was not much of a selection.

22. DO WHAT PLEASES YOU

One of the main impediments to managing our anger appropriately is our fear of displeasing others. We pull our punch. We stuff our anger. We make ourselves emotionally and physically sick. We are living on other people's terms instead of our own. We are controlling negatively instead of positively which means we are effectively out of control. We have good intentions for the other person instead of appropriate intentions for our own best interests.

This impulse to stuff our anger is not a well-thought out measure that we have arrived at consciously and deliberately. We may have learned early in life that living on our own terms is selfish and inconsiderate. That is not acceptable in polite society. As a consequence of this early learning, we give away our terms and live on someone else's. Their terms may not be any more valid than ours. We do it without thinking. We don't have to make a conscious choice. Our *attitudes* make these choices for us.

The antidote to operating out of attitudes is to use our adult judgment to make an appropriate choice in our own behalf. That is *thinking*. That is assuming appropriate responsibility for our own well-being. We can use an anger situation as an opportunity to break out of this unhappy mold after all these years. We can catch ourselves reacting out of immature attitudes towards ourselves ("If I'm displeasing I will be abandoned.") and towards others ("Others have the power to hurt me terribly. I'd better not do anything to offend them."). Since these are negative attitudes, the outcome cannot be positive for us or the other people in our lives. They will never know where they stand until our anger erupts like a volcano under pressure. Then we find ourselves going to the other extreme. Yelling, hitting, slapping, swearing . . . What happened to the Pleaser Role we've been playing all our life? It's been overridden by the self-contempt that lies below these superficial facades. Our role will come back after the dust settles. Nothing has been learned. Nothing has changed.

To relieve the built-up pressure, we can choose to express our anger appropriately in the middle ground. We can choose to tell the truth: *"It makes me angry when you do that on my shoes."* We have had the courage to overcome our old attitudes and do what is appropriate in our imperfect world. We have risked abandonment, loss of love, even annihilation of our lifelong role as The Pleaser. In so doing, we have liberated ourselves from a lifetime of reacting on other people's terms. We have affirmed ourselves as equal members of the human race. These feelings of relief, accomplishment, success in our own behalf, and confidence we can do it again are all components of *self-respect*. They are our reward for having made a break with our old attitudes which were impeding our effectiveness and our happiness as adults. This is not self-indulgence at all. This is appropriate responsibility for ourselves and for our half of our adult relationship. We are independent now. We are free to become *inter*dependent as equal members of the human race. We have chosen to do what pleases us. We are confident we can do it again. It gets easier each time.

We wouldn't think that a homely anger situation in our kitchen would serve as a stepping stone to replacing years of self-doubt with healthy self-respect. We wouldn't think that expressing an unpleasant emotion would come under the heading of *Doing What Pleases You*. We wouldn't have thought this because we *couldn't* have. Our old attitudes were in the way, controlling our thoughts and behaviors for us. But this is how we can use a potentially unpleasant disagreement as an opportunity to outgrow years of early mis-learning. When we do, it's a breakthrough for us and for the relationship.

Telling the truth about our anger is not pleasant for the other person, but it's a lot less unpleasant than not knowing where they stand with us, or what we would like them to do to make things better. The irony is that our old attempts to avoid displeasing were no more than good intentions. They turned out to be consistently *dis*pleasing.

If it pleases us to say, "It makes me angry when you do that," or "I'm sorry you're so angry" or "I don't blame you for being angry" or to use some other new, more appropriate way of coping with anger, we will find that we have pleased the other person more than we ever did in the bad old days like last Tuesday.

Many of us *think* we are pleasing ourselves when we *let it all hang out*, when we rant and rave out of control. That is not *expressing ourselves*. That is letting our anger manage *us!* We are not in control at all. Our anger attitudes are in the saddle as usual. They are predisposing us to say hurtful things to our friends and loved ones that we will all regret in the morning. For some of us, our lives are one regret after another.

This *Shooting From The Hip* is not *liberation*, it is immature self-indulgence and there is a price to pay every time we do it. We may think that we have gotten away with our abusive outburst, but it will take its toll over time in terms of our personal relationships. The other people in our life may not tell us what they think of us. They're too polite or too intimidated. They just leave our life, often without telling us why. But the worst damage that our suppressed anger does is to ourselves. We are doing damage to our circulatory system, our digestive system, our nervous system and our endocrine system. This is called *internal stress*, and it will show up on an X-ray some day. We will wind up very displeased with ourselves, indeed.

When our attitudes override our adult judgment time after time, we are not making appropriate, constructive choices on the basis of adult judgment; we are having a tantrum. We may say to ourselves, "It feels good to get it out of my system." There are better, more effective ways of getting it out of our system so it doesn't keep coming back every time an old attitude is triggered. One better way is to consciously choose to do an anger Homework in our own behalf, to vent our anger positively instead of negatively (See "VENTING – POSITIVE AND NEGATIVE" on page 217.).

23. DO YOUR HOMEWORK

In our vignettes, we show people doing their Homework. This is an important concept in our system of anger management. A Homework is an action we take on our own behalf. It is not *against* the other person; it is *for* us. We are not reacting to a provocation, but are taking an independent, appropriate action that the reality of the situation requires us to take. We have used our adult judgment to sort out what reality does and does not require and we have made a decision based on that judgment. We must now have the courage to do what we have decided to do. When we take this step, we have done our Homework.

The payoff for doing our Homework is the ensuing feeling of accomplishment, success and confidence that we can do it again. We will also feel identity, maturity, trust in our judgment, security within ourselves, liberation from our childhood fears and doubts, feelings of equality, belonging, appropriate responsibility and competence. We will also experience relief from our tension, pressure and stress. We will feel peace of mind. These are our rewards for our courage under fire.

These feelings are all components of self-respect. Each time we do our Homework, especially an anger Homework, we take another step towards outgrowing our childhood roles and replacing them with a mature identity in the present. We are using these negative situations as opportunities to grow. We are replacing our self-contempt with self-respect.

Until we do our Homework, all of this is theoretical and hypothetical. After we have done our Homework, it is not theoretical anymore and we can feel it. We have been there and we made it happen. We feel in control, not of the other person or the relationship, but of ourselves. We have earned the right to respect ourselves as worthwhile human beings in spite of our faults and imperfections.

24. DON'T GET MAD, GET EVEN

This is a new name for an old mischief called revenge. It is as old as Cain and Abel. It has made all of the wars in history longer and bloodier than they would have been otherwise. It is the energy that erupts in shootouts on our freeways, saloons, sidewalks and bedrooms. There is nothing cute about it.

"Example isn't the best way
to teach self-respect;
it's the only way."

Albert Schweitzer

First of all, it is too late for them to say, "Don't get mad." We are already angry or we wouldn't be thinking about getting even. If we try to deny our anger out of existence, we will pay a price for such foolishness.

Secondly, getting even with our provoker does not constitute *problem solving*, even though some folks thought it did. At least they thought so when they were alive.

Thirdly, getting even with them entitles them, under the *"fair trade laws"* to get even with us! There are places in the world this very day where the residents have been getting revenge and counter revenge on each other for hundreds of years. It is not a pretty sight.

Civilized human beings do not seek revenge. It is mischief that does not need to be done. They do not go for counter revenge, either. They resolve their anger problems in ways that integrate their head and their heart, which takes a little more forethought. It is not nearly as exciting, but they do not mind.

25. DON'T LET THEM MAKE YOU ANGRY

This negative technique is a product of modern American psychology, which holds that, "The issue is the issue, and if you don't like it, get rid of it." American psychology advocates such techniques as "will power," "pulling yourself up by your bootstraps," "controlling yourself," and "self-motivation." It also recommends "putting the past behind you. It's dead, forget about it." The goal is to have a nation of perfectly nice people acting perfectly nicely to each other at all times. "Play nice and don't fight," seems to be one of its catch phrases.

Its line on anger management seems to be, "No one can make you angry unless you let them, so don't let them." The implication is that if we become angry, it is our own fault for being weak and not strong. It is never our counselor's fault that his techniques did not work in the clinches. That is our fault, too.

We are seeing in these pages that the real issue is what we bring to the present grievance from our childhood. We have unresolved issues from the past that are ignited by analogous situations in the present. It is not a weakness in our character when this happens; it is human nature. It is one of our many faults and imperfections. We are worthwhile in spite of it. Blaming individuals for having human imperfections is not an encouraging technique.

With the right kind of help, we can attain insight into our private agenda of childhood carryovers that predispose us to overreact in the present. The past is not dead and gone. It is alive in us right now and, to some extent, it is interfering with our current relationships.

The issue is not "letting" them make us angry, as if we failed to prevent this incoming provocation from affecting us. We are not made of stone, and we are not required to be.

When our residual anger from the past is drained out in the right way, we will be less vulnerable to the provocative mischief of the people around us. There will not be as much anger to manage as there is now, and we will be able to manage it much better than we have ever managed it before. We will never be able to manage it perfectly, but we are not required to do that, either. Another example of this mentality is "No one can make you angry but yourself." (page 138)

26. DON'T TAKE IT PERSONALLY

Our biggest vulnerability to an anger attack is our susceptibility to taking things personally. When something makes us angry, for instance, if our ten year old is called out at first by the Little League umpire, we become angry at the wrongness and the unfairness of it all. We are angry at our powerlessness to do anything about it. These are all facets of our anger attack, and they are painful. But the biggest pain comes when we take our child's *grievance* personally, as if it were *a reflection on our worth as a person*. Then our anger turns to super-anger. We lose control, overreact and do something irrational we will be sorry for.

Anger management means identifying these predispositions that we acquired in childhood and learning how to replace them with more appropriate predispositions in the present. In this case, we can catch ourselves taking these ups and downs of everyday life personally and choose not to. Instead, we can replace our feelings of self-doubt with feelings of self-respect. *"I am a worthwhile human being whether my kid is tagged out at first or not. My kid is a worthwhile human being, too."* We can also say, *"I am a worthwhile human being whether my boss shakes my hand or not. My worth is not dependent upon these external considerations. I am a worthwhile human being in spite of my faults and imperfections. That is my antidote to taking things more personally than I need to take them."*

Our anger at the grievance is legitimate. It is not legitimate to take the next step and wipe out our own self-respect. We can choose not to take it. We are not powerless and out of control in the face of an anger attack. We have this power of choice now.

27. DRAW A PICTURE

Children have much to be angry about, but they have trouble expressing their anger. Some of them have never learned the proper names for their feelings, while others have learned not to express feelings for fear of being beaten. They also have attitudes toward their feelings, such as "feelings are bad," which makes their problems too complicated to articulate clearly. So they keep their feelings in to be on the safe side. Children cannot control much, but they have learned to control their feelings if they know what is good for them.

We want to encourage them to let their feelings out in the right way so they can get the relief they need right now, not twenty years from now in a therapist's office.

If they cannot use a verbal medium, we can try another. We can give them paper and coloring materials and suggest that they draw their anger. We do not structure it too much for them, for it has to be their expression.

Afterwards we do not say, "That's a beautiful picture." We say, *"That's very interesting. Tell me about it."* We focus on their anger. *"What angered you the most when that happened? Who are you angry at? Who else are you angry at?"* Very often they are angry at themselves for failing to prevent the grievance. This is the anger that tears down their self-respect.

We can also say, *"If this person could talk, what would they say?"* and *"What would this other person say?"* If they want to stab the paper or tear it up, we must let them. That is part of the process. The child is more important than the piece of paper. If the child needs to draw another picture tomorrow, that is all right, too.

When we see that the child has had some relief from the pent-up emotion, we can ask, *"How did you feel after you drew your picture?"* We can run down the facets of self-respect that we think are appropriate for the child's age. *"Did you feel relief? Did you feel that you were making this picture happen? That is control. Did you feel a sense of accomplishment and success? Can you do it again? That is confidence. Did you feel like you belonged? Well, you do. You belong to yourself and to the whole human race."*

Do's and Don'ts

- Do not have good intentions for these children; let them have real intentions for themselves.
- Do not invalidate their unpleasant but valid anger. When you invalidate the anger, you invalidate the child. After a while, there's nothing left.
- Do not worry about the mess. Messes can be cleaned up. Neatness does not count.
- Do not defend the people they are angry at. They are not the issue. The issue is the child's anger.

- Do not try to make a child understand. That is intellectualizing and it defeats the purpose. Some things are not intellectual. Emotions are valid, too. Even the unpleasant ones.

When you validate children's anger, you validate them as worthwhile human beings in spite of this unpleasantness. You also validate yourself. That is emotional first aid.

28. EMOTIONAL FIRST AID

The first thing our medical first aid manual tells us to do is to stop the bleeding. Wouldn't it be nice if there were a way of putting a tourniquet on a loved one or a co-worker who was raging out of control or silently bleeding inside from a grievous hurt?

Well, there is.

First, we have to find the bleeding or the anger, which is not as easy as it sounds. Our teenagers may use words like "upset," "hate" or "I don't like it" to describe the situation that tore them apart. These are euphemisms for anger. They may even deny they are angry at all and attack us for suggesting they are. "I am not angry. Shut up!"

It is like a drowning victim beating off the lifeguard who is trying to save him. The professional lifeguard does not say, "Ok, fella, if that's the way you're going to be, go ahead and drown. See if I care." He perseveres. Similarly, we are not put off by inappropriate behaviors that arise under emotional stress. We disengage emotionally from their mischief. We even disengage from our own mischief. We do not say, "That's the thanks I get for trying to be helpful. Well, I won't make that mistake again." That is taking their mischief personally. This is not about you. It is about their pain. After we have disengaged, we are free to address the real issues behind the smokescreen they have thrown up. The issue is not hate, either. It is anger.

After we have identified their emotion properly as anger, we can proceed to call their anger by its rightful name. We say something like, *"I'm sorry you are so angry"* or *"What happened to make you so angry?"* If they are cooperating with us, we can go on to ask, *"What angered you the most?"* or *"What was the worst thing about it?"*

Calling their anger to their attention in this way gives them a handle on what is going on inside of them. It gives them a gearshift they can use to manage their out-of-control feelings. It is up to them to use this tool constructively, but they cannot use it if someone does not put it into their hands. Very often, this alone will stop the bleeding. We have validated their *anger* as a legitimate, though unpleasant, emotion, and we have validated *them* as worthwhile in spite of it. If we do it right, we will even find we have validated *ourselves*.

29. EUPHEMIZING

This unhelpful technique involves treating anger problems by calling them something else: "I'm not angry. I'm just miffed, tiffed and spiffed." By so saying, these angry people are able to deny to themselves and others that they have a "not nice" emotion in their bosom. The purpose of their denial is to prevent the negative consequences they are sure would follow if they were to utter the "A" word, such as abandonment, rejection, victimization, loss of control, loss of love, loss of prestige, disapproval, and being sent to their rooms forever.

These deniers are also preventing the painful feelings of guilt that nice people feel when they fail to be perfectly pleasing. To them, these griefs are not worth the trouble of calling their anger by its legal name, so they trivialize their own emotion. By extension, they are also trivializing themselves. Moreover, they are keeping themselves from getting the relief they might get if they were to acknowledge the legitimacy and validity of this unsettling but unavoidable aspect of their earthly existence.

These cutesy names for anger, which include "ballistic," "bummed out," "bent out of shape" and so on, can be called "downscale" euphemisms.

There are also "upscale" terminologies such as "hostility," "outrage," "violence," "acting out," "passion," "aggressiveness," etc. These words are often used to enhance the impressiveness and potency of our homely, garden variety anger. These euphemisms, too, make the anger problem worse instead of better. We are putting on airs to distance ourselves from the earthy emotion that we feel in our hearts. This is another example of overcompensation for feelings of inferiority.

Sometimes we use euphemisms because we think daddy really is "grumpy," "grouchy," "mean," "in a bad mood," "crabby," "hateful," "cranky," "down" and a hundred other stand-ins for the offensive sounding, but more definitive, word: "Angry." There is no cure in the world for crabby.

30. FAMILY-FREE DIET

If chocolate makes us break out in a rash, we make the sad decision to put ourselves on a chocolate-free diet for our own good. By the same token, if we see that our family reunions do nothing but upset us for weeks afterwards, we may have to make other arrangements next year.

Our families have come to see us in a certain role since we were five years old. Our loved ones will not let us outgrow our childhood role as "The Victim," "The Stupid Child" or "The Scapegoat." No matter how competent we are in the outside world, they treat us the same way they did when we were clumsy kindergartners. The more we yell at them to start treating us like a grown-up, the more we confirm that they are correct in their assessment of our mental state. We are obeying their implicit expectation that we will regress to a more primitive stage of development. It is maddening.

One way to manage our anger at these obtuse folks is to stay away from them. It may be sad and lonely, but they may come to respect us at last. It will be the smartest thing we have done in twenty years. They may have been wondering how long it would take us to catch on.

71

"Power is an issue
only when it is contested
We have the power of choice.
We can choose not to
contest for power.
We can drop our end of the rope."

Rudolf Dreikurs

After we have been on our family-free diet for a while, we can test the waters. We can call or go over there to see if anything has changed. They may have missed us during the interim, maybe even learned to appreciate our good qualities. Maybe nothing has changed. In any event, we do not have much to lose by staying away, except hours and hours of abuse and grief that they do not need any more than we do.

31. FIGHTING

Some of us mismanage our anger by fighting. We see physical aggression as an outlet for our pent-up energies. It is an outlet all right, but at what price? When two people have been raised by parents who were evenly matched fighters, they are compatible with this so-called problem-solving technique. However, when one of the parties has been raised in a fight-free environment, it is a different matter. We call this a "mixed marriage." The husband may feel comfortable having a good, clean fight like his parents. In his view, this is how loving couples solve problems. There are no hard feelings afterward. They kiss and make up. Sometimes they cannot kiss *unless* there has been a fight. His nonfighting wife, however, sees confrontation as barbaric and scary. It is foreign to her upbringing. She refuses to participate. The husband feels *"betrayed"* by her refusal to *"cooperate"* with him. His expectation of emotional release is thwarted. They begin to fight over not fighting.

When does a disagreement turn into a fight? When one of the parties *takes an issue personally.* As soon as that happens, the original issue is no longer the issue. The issue has become the individual's shaky self-respect. The other party is often not aware that this subtle shift has taken place. These two are now arguing on two different wavelengths and there cannot be a rational resolution of their differences.

One of our hopes in writing this book is that you will be enabled to fight smarter, not harder. We hope, for instance, that you will respect yourself on a new basis so that a difference of opinion will

not cost you your self-respect. We also hope you will be able to identify the mischief component in the dispute. *"This does not need to be
done. I can choose to disengage from it and resume the conversation at a more
appropriate time and place."* You can identify the anger component in
the argument and when it is reaching dangerous levels, you can use
your new-found power of choice to make other arrangements in your
own behalf. You can disengage with your feet right out of the room.

We hope you are learning a new and better definition of control.
Control does not mean preventing bad things from happening.
People resent being controlled for their own good because it implies
they are stupid and inadequate. A fight often starts over who can
inflict whose good intentions upon whom.

Most fights are over such absurdities. The precipitating factor is
often trivial, such as burnt toast. If one partner sees burnt toast as a
reminder of irresponsibility from the past or a victimization by a
loved one, then all bets are off and the fight is on.

We can no longer afford this horrendous loss of time, energy and
love. We cannot afford to keep destroying our potential for happiness in these mindless squabbles over absurdities. Life is too short to
spend it wrangling over Aunt Blanche's thoughtless remark. We can
"Consider the Source (page 40)" "Give It A Pass (page 96)" or any
other of the many positive anger management techniques in this
book. We will be giving emotional first aid to ourselves, to our partner and to our relationship. When we learn to fight smarter, we may
find we do not have to fight at all.

32. Five Steps to Fighting Smarter

1. **Identify the problem.** What is the real issue behind the surface
   issue? Ask a focusing question:
   - What happened to make you so angry?
   - What angered you the most when that happened?
   For example, the other person might say:

"I was trying to help and you wouldn't let me."

Could it be that you had good intentions for me?

"That's right, I meant well and you didn't appreciate it."

Could it be that you feel your 'goodness' was all for nothing?

"I sure do."

I'm sorry you are so angry at me for not appreciating you, but who else are you angry at besides me?

"I'm angry at myself for trying so hard to be helpful. Maybe I should stop trying so hard."

I'm sure you meant well, but maybe I would appreciate you more if you asked me how I wanted to be helped.

2. **Neither fight nor give in**. Fighting is negative cooperation and it takes two. If one of you stops, the fight becomes irrelevant. As soon as you fight, you lose. You can choose to disengage from the fight, which is only mischief, at any time. If you give in, you are submitting, out of control, discouraged. You cannot secure positive cooperation when you give away your power and your self-respect.

3. **Secure positive cooperation**. You can choose to replace your negative cooperation with positive cooperation. You can ask something like, "What remedy do you seek?"

4. **Establish an atmosphere of mutual respect**. These are the Four Components of Mutual Respect:

   - You must respect yourself.

   - You must respect the other person.

   - The other person must respect you.

   - The other person must respect himself or herself.

This atmosphere of mutual respect is hard to establish, but fighting is even harder.

"Mischief is that which
does not need to be done."

Rudolf Dreikurs

5. **Do what *you* can do.** You can catch yourself depending on the other person to solve the problem. You have left yourself out of the equation. You have the power of choice and adult competencies. There are many things you cannot do, but you *can* use your adult judgment to tell you what you can do instead. It is then your responsibility to do it on your own valid terms. When you do, you will be replacing your dependency with independence.

33. FIND THE PURPOSE

We understand negative human behavior not in terms of *causes* such as peer pressure, television violence, socioeconomic deprivation, breakdown of the family or low self-esteem, but in terms of its *purposes*. When we misbehave, we may not be consciously aware of our purposes, but we have them just the same. We acquired our attitudes and purposes early in life and we have not examined them since that day. We are not mindless rats in a maze, but members of the human race. Laboratory rats do not have purposes; they have drives. Human beings have purposes.

For example, our tardiness makes people angry and their anger makes us angry! We do not need this warfare, but we keep coming late anyway. We might ask ourselves a focusing question — not, "Why am I doing this?" It is not that easy. Our psyche will defend itself against exposing our infantile, potentially humiliating attitudes even to ourselves. It will come up with something useless such as, "I try so hard to be on time. I guess I'm just built that way. I can't help it." As adults now, we can go about getting the answer in a more productive way. We can ask ourselves another focusing question, *"How would my life be different if I stopped coming late?"* Here are some of the answers we may get:

- "I'd be happy." The purpose of our tardiness may be to keep us from getting any happiness that we believe we do not deserve.
- "I wouldn't be rebelling against my father anymore." Perhaps we are trying to prove our independence from our father by

disobeying his order to come on time. He isn't even around anymore. This is not adult independence; it is only rebellious mischief.

- "They might not notice me if I came at the same time as everyone else. If people don't notice me, how can I be sure I exist?"

- "If I get there early, other people will have the power to keep *me* waiting. I will feel powerless and out of control. I'd rather keep them waiting for me. That way I am in control."

- "I am angry at these people, but I dare not express my anger openly. I can punish them by keeping them waiting. Why should I stop? It's working."

- "I'd be seen as a responsible person, but I was never the responsible person in my family growing up. My sister Suzie was the responsible one. I'm just the baby of the family, always bringing up the rear. At least I'm consistent. I'm still me and I hate it."

These are just some of the *negative purposes* that underlie our mischief. Self-respecting people can identify these attitudes in themselves and replace them with more positive purposes in their lives. The more self-respecting we are, the more positive and constructive our purposes will be and the more likely we will be to come on time.

Negative Purposes

Our underlying purpose usually turns out to be to prevent something bad from happening, like losing control, failing, feeling guilty, being exposed and humiliated, or ceasing to exist. Our goal sounds positive, but upon further examination, its negativity becomes apparent. "Preventing" is a negative approach to solving problems, and predicting a negative outcome that has to be prevented is an exercise in pessimistic fortune-telling. We are setting ourselves up to fail because we cannot do it. We are not fortune-tellers. When we hear ourselves saying, "What's the use, I am going to fail anyway," this is not extra-sensory perception, but our discouragement and self-doubt talking to us. Self-doubt cannot be optimistic and happy. It can only be negative and counter-productive.

The Antidote to Negative Purposes

Old Tapes	New Tapes
"My negative purpose, now that I have identified it, is in the service of my feelings of inadequacy and worthlessness."	"When I remind myself I am a worthwhile human being in spite of my faults and imperfections, my negative purposes will become irrelevant."
"My purpose is to prevent happiness, which to you is a positive quality, but to me is a negative quality. I'm afraid I'll be caught enjoying happiness that I do not deserve to enjoy. I'll feel guilty. It isn't worth it. I have to keep it from happening."	"Worthless people don't deserve to enjoy happiness, but self-respecting people do. As a worthwhile human being, I can catch myself sabotaging my happiness and stop it."
"My purpose is to prevent success because I know that I won't be able to keep it up. My inadequacies will catch up to me and my success will end in failure, so why bother succeeding in the first place?"	"I am not inadequate or incompetent. I only feel that way sometimes. I deserve to succeed and I am competent enough to take life as it comes and do the best I can with it. If I have ups and downs, it will prove merely that I am imperfect. I am worthwhile in spite of it. I am not required to succeed perfectly and forever."

Old Tapes	New Tapes
"My purpose is to maintain and perpetuate my unhappy childhood perception of myself. I cling to this role because I do not know what will take its place. Maybe nothing. That is too scary."	"As a self-respecting adult, I know that my childhood roles will be replaced by a mature identity, and it's about time. I can stop living in the past and stop trying to prevent the future. I can choose to start living in the present.
"My purpose is to prevent losing control. I never knew what control was; I only thought I did. I have been out of control all my life. I must hang on for dear life to keep from going over the cliff."	"Control means taking life as it comes, not preventing disaster. I couldn't take life as it came when I was a child. I can now. I can choose to stop hanging on to thin air. I can let go of these mistaken attitudes from the past."

34. FOCUSING QUESTIONS

When we are angry, we are up in arms, carried away with our emotions. We are not using our heads. Civilized people have learned to use their heads in the right way, not to suppress their anger or rationalize it away, but to sort out what is real from what is not real.

We can do that by asking ourselves, *"What is angering me the most right now? Is it the fact that I didn't make the sale? No. That is merely the occasion for my anger. What angers me the most is that I am feeling victimized by this customer. I am feeling unappreciated and good for nothing."*

The next focusing questions might be, *"Who am I angry at? The customer, of course. Who else am I angry at? I am angry at me for being so 'stupid' and for not doing it the right way. I am taking this whole thing personally and feeling worthless."*

These questions have helped us get at the issues beneath the surface issues. Now we can work through them in a more appropriate, mature perspective:

- "I am not a victim. I am an imperfect human being."
- "It is not a matter of fairness. It is just business, that's all. I win a few; I lose a few. I am worthwhile in spite of it."
- "I am not dependent on my customers or this sale for my personal worth. They cannot make me feel good for nothing like my dad used to do. I am worthwhile in spite of them."
- "I am not stupid or worthless. I need not be angry at myself. I did the best I could at the time. I'll try them again next month. I am a self- respecting human being in the meantime." (See "PEELING THE ANGER ARTICHOKE" on page 147.)

35. FORGIVING OTHERS

The first step towards managing our anger appropriately is the identification of the mistaken attitudes and convictions that predispose us to being excessively angry in the first place. Once these mistakes have been corrected, we will be less likely to fly off the handle than we were in the past.

The second step is the identification of those factors from our childhood that prevent us from expressing our anger as appropriately as we otherwise might. These factors include fear, denial, parental examples, family constellation, etc. These impediments can be removed so our suppressed anger will not compound itself inside of us, as it has been doing for years.

The third step is to relieve our residual anger by writing anger letters to those who have caused us grievances in the past.

The fourth step in the process is learning appropriate modes of expressing our legitimate anger so we can begin to cope effectively with anger-provoking situations as they come up.

But the management of our anger does not end in the instant that we articulate our emotion in these new, appropriate ways. There remains one last stage in the process that must be completed to bind up the wounds left by this devastating emotion. If we do not complete this mopping-up stage, we will carry the festering residue of our rage in our hearts forever. It will make us sick.

To Forgive or Not To Forgive

The antidote to this residual anger is *forgiveness*. Many of us cannot bring ourselves to forgive those who have "trespassed against us." Below the level of conscious awareness, there are attitudes and predispositions that prevent us from relieving our residual anger in this way, and we carry grudges in our hearts for years. These impediments to forgiveness are carryovers from our childhood, when we learned all kinds of things about ourselves and about life that were not true. They are still not true, but we behave as if they were. We do not even know they are there.

One carryover from our childhood is our total ignorance of what forgiveness means. In the absence of an appropriate definition, we make up inappropriate, mistaken definitions.

Then, we proceed to withhold forgiveness according to our misdefinition.

We imagine forgiveness is arrived at through a logical, rational sorting-out process of assessing degrees of guilt and innocence or the relative evil of the perpetrator's intent, as if we were a Supreme Court of one. This mistaken *scientific* approach to relieving our pent-up is an example of *rationalitosis*, which is the attitude that nonrational problems can be solved rationally.

Some of us forgive too soon, saying things like, "Oh, they didn't mean to do what they did. They didn't know any better." We would say that reality required these people to find out what they didn't know, but they failed to assume that responsibility. We suffered as a direct consequence of their negligence.

Some of us try to wish away our anger by saying, "They were doing the best they could." We would say they were not doing their best at all. They were behaving out of their ignorance, discouragement and self-contempt. They caused us a legitimate grievance and it made us angry. We have a right to our anger and we must not sugarcoat it by forgiving our victimizers on these superficial bases. We will never get rid of our anger if we do. This type of forgiveness is no more than a good intention that we have for our perpetrators. We need to replace these good intentions with real intentions for our own mental health.

Forgiveness is not arrived at or achieved intellectually. Our anger is a subjective, nonrational problem and it must be solved subjectively. That means replacing one subjective feeling or emotion with another subjective feeling or emotion. When we are angry, we are, in a sense, at war. We must replace these warlike feelings in our bloodstream with the feeling that we are at peace.

Before we can show how that is done, let us identify some of the most common impediments to replacing our angry feelings with feelings of peace, serenity within ourselves and blessed relief from the pressure, stress and tension of our lifelong internal warfare.

The Impediments to Forgiveness

These are some of the unconscious attitudes that prevent us from forgiving others:

- "Why should I forgive them? They never forgive me. It's not fair."

How are you helping the cause of justice and fairness by harboring this anger inside of you forever? It doesn't work that way.

- "When I am angry, there is nothing I can do about it. I feel so powerless and depressed."

*There **is** something you can do. There is one power you have and that is the power to forgive and give yourself some relief.*

- "No one ever told me I had the power to forgive. I've been so busy asking people to forgive me I never realized that I had the power to forgive them."

You are not a child any more. Adults have the power to forgive anyone they want to.

- "Who am I to forgive anyone? I'm nobody."

You are not a nobody. You are a worthwhile human being in spite of your faults and imperfections. You have as much right to forgive as anyone else, no more and no less.

- "Why should I bother to forgive them? They don't care whether or not I forgive them, so what's the use?"

You are not doing it for them. You are doing it for yourself. This is a choice you can make on your own terms to relieve your own pent-up emotions.

- "Why should I forgive them? What they did was wrong."

Do we only forgive people who do right? Such people don't need our forgiveness.

- "I cannot forgive them. It is my moral responsibility to condemn these wretches forever for what they did!"

Your eternal righteous indignation makes you feel morally superior to these wretches. Big deal! Morally superior to a wretch! Your superiority is a fiction. You can choose to set a limit on your responsibility for judging the imperfections of your fellow human beings. You are not more human than they are, nor are they less human than you. They are only imperfect human beings, and their imperfections made you angry.

- "It's the principle of the thing. I must not compromise my abstract ideals even though they have nothing to do with the real world."

You must catch yourself trying to relieve your painful feeling of inferiority by identifying yourself with high sounding and irrational abstractions such as:

- 'If my kids make me unhappy, I am entitled to make them unhappy. That's fair!'

84

- 'I am their parent and I am entitled to their respect whether I know what I am talking about or not. I don't care if I have to beat them into respecting me.'
- 'I am trying to make this a better world by stamping out rudeness, offensiveness, inconsideration and other forms of not acting appropriately. If I start forgiving these incorrect people, what will the world come to?'

These are not high principles or ideals at all. They are self-serving, overcompensatory attitudes carried over from childhood. Super-angry idealists can relieve themselves of these destructive determinants of their behavior by reminding themselves that they are worthwhile human beings on their own terms, not because they are upholding some absurd good intention from first grade.

- "I have been carrying this anger for so long that it's like a harpoon in my side. It is a part of me. I am afraid that if I pull it out, I will bleed to death. I don't know who or what I would be without it. I will be annihilated. It's scary."

It is true that your old role as the angry, impotent victim will begin to fall away from you after you have chosen to forgive, but you will not be left in a void. In place of this unhappy role you will find an identity of your own as a worthwhile human being in spite of your faults and imperfections. You will feel better about yourself and about your life than you ever did.

- "If I forgive them, I might become like them and I don't want that to happen."

Your defense against losing your identity is not your suppressed rage. That is not what sets you apart from the people who hurt you. You are more than a bundle of anger. You are a worthwhile human being in spite of your faults and imperfections.

Once you have experienced yourself in these new terms, you will not be like anybody else. You will have an independent identity of your own.

- "If I forgive them, it will be as if I were condoning what they did."

Do not confuse forgiveness with condoning. Condone means to let pass without punishment. You are not being asked to condone their behavior nor to punish them for it, but to forgive them for perpetrating it. It is written: 'Hate the sin, not the sinner.' Hating these sinners poisons our lives and does not have much of an effect on them in the end, anyway.

- "Why should I give them the satisfaction of forgiving them?"

Are you living your life in terms of depriving others of satisfaction? That is a negative ambition and it cannot be a very gratifying lifestyle for you. Moreover, it does not deprive them of anything they can't live without. It's a game you are playing with yourself. You can choose to live your life on more realistic terms.

Plus, they need never know you have forgiven them. There's no law you have to tell them.

- "If I forgive them, they will keep doing it. I have forgiven them three times already and they haven't stopped yet."

The purpose of forgiveness is not to control or prevent behavior. It is to give you some relief from your pain. It may be that you have been forgiving them in the wrong way and they are still taking advantage of your vulnerability. Forgiving them in the right way and for the right purposes will make you less vulnerable, whether they stop doing it or not. Your good intention is to change them for the better so they will stop hurting you. You need to replace this useless good intention with a real intention to change yourself. You need to do some Homework in your own behalf. You can choose to set limits on their behavior by changing your actions or by imposing some logical consequence. You will feel stronger in your self-respect after you have done so. They will respect you more, too. That is when they will stop.

- "I am afraid that if I forgive them it will make me vulnerable to being hurt again in the future."

Where is it written that if you don't forgive, it will make you tough or immune? You cannot prevent hurtful things from happening to you in the future by refusing to forgive. There is no connection between unforgiveness and security. As a worthwhile human being, you can cope with hurtful things in the future as they come, just like anyone else. You don't need to prevent them

86

from happening. In the meantime, you can choose to live in the present and do the best you can with it. That is a positive ambition.

- "If I forgive them, my suffering might stop. I'm not sure I am worthy to get relief from my suffering. All I have ever deserved is to suffer. Not suffering might make me happy. I'm not sure I deserve that. Besides, if I ever stop suffering, what will I have to talk about?"

You have suffered long enough. As a worthwhile human being, you deserve to be as happy as anyone else, no more and no less.

- "If I forgive them, I will forfeit my entitlement to get revenge on them someday."

You are afraid that if you forgive them, the judge will throw your case out of court. This is another fiction. Does this dream of vindication in the unspecified future make you happy? Or does it merely prevent you from living your life in the meantime? Life is too short for this mean, petty spitefulness. You pay a high price for reserving the right to be as cruel to them as they were to you. Besides, such revenge promises a lot more than it delivers.

- "If I forgive them, I might have to start living my life in the present and assuming appropriate responsibility for my own situation. If I did that, I might fail. It's much safer to hide behind my old grudges and resentments."

You are using your ancient grievances as an excuse to withdraw from your appropriate tasks and responsibilities in the present. You are seeking to exempt yourself from having to cope with life because you are afraid you'll fail if you try. But hiding behind your anger is a fictitious solution to a pseudo-problem. You need not live in fear of failure to assume your responsibilities perfectly or to exempt yourself from tasks that other people seem to be accomplishing without too much difficulty. If you can learn to respect yourself as a worthwhile human being, you will be able to find the courage it takes to do the best you can with what you've got. If you slip up, it will only prove you are an imperfect human being. You are worthwhile in spite of it.

- "If I forgive, I'll forfeit my right to get angry again."

Forgiveness now does not preclude becoming angry again. You can always forgive again if you do.

- "My parents never forgave anybody. If I start now, I will betray their ideal of eternal grudge bearing."

Is there no better way to honor our mothers and fathers than to uphold their mistaken coping techniques? You can honor them by freeing yourself to be all you can be, and that means throwing this dead weight overboard and respecting their best, not their worst.

- "If I forgive them, it means I have to go over there and kiss them on the cheek. I'd rather die!"

There is no such "have to." Cheek kissing is entirely optional. Do not confuse forgiveness with reconciliation.

What Forgiveness Is

We have just seen some of the things that forgiveness is not. It is not condoning, permitting, or allowing. It is not for the offender's benefit, but for our own.

We define forgiveness as a *letting go of anger*. It is a conscious, deliberate choice we make to stop holding onto our rage or the memory of our rage. We have the power of choice and we can choose to let it go. This does not concern the perpetrator of our grievance at all. He need never know what we have chosen to do in our own behalf. It is none of his business. This is between us and us.

After we have confessed our anger and forgiven our perpetrators, what will take its place in our heart? We will find that our anger, with its consequent tension, pressure, anxiety and stress, has been replaced with feelings of relief; openness to life; liberation (*"I have freed myself from the old roles I used to play"*); identity (*"I am the one who made the forgiveness happen"*); living in the present instead of the past and all the other facets of self-respect. We have done another Homework on our own behalf. We have assumed appropriate responsibility for our own emotional well-being and we have given ourselves emotional first aid. As a consequence, we will experience ourselves as the authors of our own lives.

36. FORGIVING OURSELVES

Forgiving others is difficult, but it is even more difficult to forgive ourselves. If we are still angry at ourselves for the stupid things we did as children, we cannot respect ourselves as fully as we need to do to get the most out of life.

We know what we did; we were there the whole time. We do not want anyone to find out because it would be too humiliating. The pain of our guilt would be unbearable and we would be punished severely. We have the attitude that guilty people are worthless. We spend our lives preventing this exposure of our underlying feelings of worthlessness, but it gnaws at our hearts every day.

Much of this scenario takes place below the level of conscious awareness. We must make it conscious so it can be properly drained and healed, like an abscess. It is hard to do for ourselves because we are too close to it. We need the intervention of a competent counselor.

There's the rub. If we tell a counselor what we did, our secret will be out and the wheels of retribution will start to turn. We cannot bring ourselves to set this process in motion; it might hurt too much. This fear keeps many people from getting the help they need.

One response to this resistance to psychotherapy is that we can stand more pain now as adults than we could as children. Another response is that most of this psychic pain is fictitious. We are not guilty. We were merely imperfect human beings then as we are imperfect adults now. Our saving grace is that we are not worthless *because* of what happened. We are worthwhile *in spite of it*.

"Why did I let it happen?" Many of us suffer from terrible guilt over things that happened to us as children. Underneath our feelings of guilt, we are angry at the perpetrators of our victimization. We resist the conscious awareness of this anger because we are afraid of the consequences. We do not know what the consequences might be and we do not want to find out.

Deeper still is our anger at ourselves for letting it happen, as if a helpless child could have prevented anything from happening in the real world. We imagine as children that we are responsible for everything that happens in our little world and that, if something bad does happen, we have no one but ourselves to blame. Not only do we feel responsible, guilty and ashamed, but we are *angry* at ourselves. We cannot respect anyone who fails to prevent such terrible things from happening. We have made the mistake of taking the whole thing personally.

These are all attitudes we have about ourselves. They are mistaken attitudes and they must be replaced with better ones.

We can effect change in our self-attitudes by writing our feelings down on a piece of paper. First, we can write an anger letter to the perpetrator, who will never see it. Then, if we wish, we can write a cleaned-up version that we can send or not. It is our choice. This is called, *"The Second Letter Technique."* (page 171)

The next step is to write ourselves an anger letter. *"If only I had done something else, the whole thing would not have happened. I should have seen it coming, I should have known. Why was I so stupid?"* When we get these childhood misperceptions out where we can see them, we can begin the process of reevaluating them in the light of our adult intelligence and experience. We can see the absurdity of requiring ourselves as children to outwit older, stronger victimizers who should have known better than to take advantage of a situation but did not. We can see that these people did not respect themselves. They were behaving out of their self-contempt, and we hate them for it. But *we* didn't do it. We need not be angry at ourselves.

We can even find it in our hearts to forgive that little child for being so terribly inadequate to cope with a situation that children should not have had to cope with. We need to ask the question, *"What kind of children allow such terrible things to happen? Bad children? Immoral children? Guilty children? Stupid children?"* The answer, of course, is *none of the above.* These things happen to imperfect children in an imperfect world, which is regrettable enough. We need not make it worse by condemning ourselves to a lifetime of grief and self-punishment for something we did not do and could not prevent.

90

Once we have put our self-anger in this new perspective, we are ready to take the last step in the anger management process. We have a choice now: to hang onto our anger or to let it go. Our residual anger at ourself has been keeping us from being as happy as we deserve to be. It keeps us from being as loving as we can be. It keeps us from respecting ourself. And who is it up to make this important, life-affirming choice? It is up to us.

Vignette: It's All My Fault

When Lisa came in for counseling, she and David had just broken up. She felt that her life was falling apart. She was distraught and out of control. She cried all the time. Lisa found herself calling David forty times in one day; she couldn't stop herself.

Lisa was an attractive, successful airline executive, but she could not achieve what was most important to her: a stable, happy relationship. David was number seven in a ten-year succession of emotional disasters. It was all very discouraging. Not only did she feel like a failure at the task of love, but she blamed herself for these disasters, which only compounded her distress.

When we asked Lisa what she would like to achieve most in therapy, her answer was, "People think I'm so good-looking and such a winner, but I feel like a fake. I have no real self-esteem. I'm so depressed and tired all the time. Each time I break up with someone, I just fall apart. I feel so weak and stupid for allowing this to happen to me over and over again. What is wrong with me? Maybe I could feel better about myself if I could just stop calling him."

As the oldest of four children, Lisa played the role of the responsible child and took care of her two brothers and handicapped sister. Lisa remembers that her mother was never there for her, but she had to be there for everybody else. To make matters worse, her mother resented the fact that her father showed Lisa attention.

From this upbringing, Lisa acquired the following attitudes:

- "Helpers are not there to help me, so I conclude I am not worth helping."

- "If my own mother cannot love me, who can? Nobody! I am unlovable. Unlovable people can be abandoned at any time."
- "Nothing I do is good enough."
- "I pretend to be strong but I'm really weak inside. My strongness is a fake and so am I."
- "My hard work is not appreciated and I feel good for nothing."
- "Since I am the responsible one, everything that goes wrong is my fault."
- "When I fail, it proves that my parents were right. I really am worthless and unlovable and there's nothing I can do about it."

We pointed out to Lisa that each time a man leaves her, it confirms her old feelings of worthlessness. This confirmation undermines her feelings of accomplishment in the real world and keeps her from being happy. She holds herself in contempt. The contrast between the reality of her career success and her underlying self-contempt is what makes her feel like a fake. Lisa feels powerless to do anything about her unhealthy family or her role in it. In a crisis, her old feelings of inadequacy come pouring back. She falls apart.

Her heartache in the present is painful enough, but the apparent confirmation of her childhood feelings of worthlessness makes it even worse.

In our problem-solving process, we look for an entry into the individual's constellation of mistaken attitudes, convictions and expectations. Lisa's tale of woe provided us with many such points of entry such as *"The helpers do not help," "I can be emotionally abandoned at any time," "I am inadequate to cope," "I am a fake," "I am unlovable," "My life is out of control and so am I"* and *"I feel good for nothing."* We also know that Lisa is angry at herself for being so inadequate to solve her problems. But we chose to leave that issue for a later visit, after she has done some Homeworks to strengthen her self-respect.

The Blame Game

We felt that Lisa's pain was being compounded by her intense self-blame. She kept saying that everything is her fault. Her efforts to contact David were not so much to win back his love and affection as to relieve the pain of her guilt, fault and sense of responsibility for what happened. She felt she had to do something. She had no choice. Calling David was doing something, even if it didn't make sense.

This tendency to blame herself for what goes wrong has been a recurring theme for the last 28 years. It is instantaneous and nonrational. It is a bad habit. It needs to be replaced with better habits.

To strengthen Lisa's self-respect, we must give her a Homework to do. We do not simply say, "Lisa it is not your fault," because that would just prove to her that we do not understand how guilty and worthless she really feels. We do not point out to her that she gravitates to difficult, irresponsible men to confirm her negative attitudes toward herself. She would hear this as an accusation and would assume responsibility for this negative compatibility. We did not tell Lisa to stop calling David. That is not the issue. The issue was the self-contempt that prevented her from solving her own personal problems and forced her to depend on the judgment of people who were no more competent than she was. We do not do what she expects. We do not give her good advice which she would not take anyway. Instead, we do what she doesn't expect. We take her side. We agree with her:

Maybe you are right, Lisa. Maybe it is all your fault. What do you plan to do about it?

"I have no idea. That's what I came to counseling for."

Lisa, you have a choice now to hang on to this guilt, fault and blame or to let it go. What choice do you prefer?

"I choose to let it go, of course, but how do I do that?"

You are not as powerless and out of control as you think you are. You have the power to stand in judgment on Lisa forever and condemn her for her worthlessness and stupidity, or you can choose to forgive yourself.

"But it is me! I keep doing it. I have no one but myself to blame."

We've already established that. That is not the problem. Would you like to break this cycle of fault leading to fault.

"Of course I would."

What are you afraid would happen if you did?

"I wouldn't know who I was anymore."

That's scary isn't it? And it is going to take courage to let go of the old Lisa and see who takes her place.

"I'm not sure I can do that."

I agree. Of course you are not sure. If you were sure, it wouldn't take courage. You have the power of choice now and you have the power to forgive. You can choose to use these powers to your advantage.

"I'm really tired of doing things for other people. Maybe it's time I did something for myself. Is that selfish? I always thought it was."

It is not selfish at all. It is entirely appropriate that you take care of yourself for a change.

"How do I forgive myself? I just know I'm going to do it again, I can't seem to stop myself. I must be stupid or something."

I agree that 'stupidness' is unforgivable. But that is not what you are. What you are is imperfect, and your attitudes toward your imperfections set you up to make mistakes in judgment that you would not have made otherwise. You are trying to prevent imperfection by striving for perfection.

"But I'm too imperfect."

Our goal is to make you less imperfect in the right way. Can you forgive yourself for being as imperfect as you have been all these years? You will soon learn that you did not get this way all by yourself. You had help.

"Do you mean that it's my parents' fault?"

What if it is no one's fault? What if they were imperfect, too, and taught you things about yourself that were not true? You have been behaving accordingly ever since. You are an obedient child. They ordered you to fail and you've been obeying that order since third grade.

"Maybe some day I will be able to forgive them, but I can't right now."

That's true, but first you must learn to forgive yourself.

"What if I can't? What if I don't?"

With such what-ifs, we predict failure in the future based on our failures in the past. That is your discouragement talking. This is a new ball game. The new Lisa can choose to live in the present and do what reality requires right now.

Lisa did her Homework. She wrote herself a forgiveness letter. As she saw the parade of sins, crimes, guilts and faults marching across the page, she was able to put them into a new perspective. These were not sins or crimes at all. They were no more than human imperfections. She could see that some of her vulnerabilities came from her mother's unhappy example and that she was consistently gravitating to men who reminded her of her father, who didn't have much self-respect. She realized that hanging onto this history of disasters did not make things better. It only perpetuated her negative consistencies.

She had a new tool now. She had the power of choice. She could choose to hang on or let go. She was afraid that if she let these old consistencies go, she would not know who she was any more. But these griefs and regrets were not her identity. They were excess baggage from the past. She could choose to throw them overboard. She chose to let them go.

As she freed herself from these burdens, she felt liberated, independent, in control, appropriately responsible for herself and grown up. She no longer needed to depend on David for the validation of her worth as a person. That was the wrong solution to the wrong problem. It had nearly driven her crazy. Now, the whole problem had become fictitious and it did not need to be solved. The obsessive thinking stopped. The behavior stopped with it. She could validate her own existence now. She had an independent identity of her own. She did not call David forty times that day; she was free of him and of the Lisa she used to be.

As she looked over her forgiveness letter, she saw she was not such a bad person after all, and that people were using her mistaken attitudes, roles and beliefs against her. Hanging onto her old guilts did not make her less vulnerable, as she had hoped; it made her more vulnerable. Respecting herself could make it easier to avoid guilt-producing situations in the future. Lisa was able to replace her guilt feelings with feelings of regret. She was sorry that these bad things had happened, and her regret was appropriate. She was able to let them go.

Lisa saw that blaming herself for everything was mischief — it didn't need to be done and was counterproductive. She was able to disengage from her own self-destructive mischief. Lisa felt like an equal member of the human race in spite of her faults and imperfections. As an imperfect human being, she found forgiveness much easier to do than it was in the bad old days last week. There was nothing to forgive.

37. GIVE IT A PASS

Some people think they have only two choices: to respond to an anger provocation in kind like a stand-up guy or to slink off into the corner like a wimp. There is a Third Choice that we did not know we had: *To give it a pass.*

Curly: "Your wife is ugly."

Moe: Shrug.

Curly: "Your kid is ugly."

Moe: Stare.

Curly: "You're ugly too."

Moe: Shrug. Stare.

This nonsense isn't worth responding to. It is a waste of our time and energy. We have chosen on an adult basis not to dignify it with a reply. We are not suppressing our anger. There was no real grievance here, only useless kid stuff. The anger did not ignite inside of us;

there is no anger here to suppress. We are not letting them get away with murder; there is no murder, only mischief. We have no good intention to improve their deportment. As self-respecting human beings, we can choose not to take mischief personally. It's not a reflection on our worth as a person.

We give them a pass for our benefit, not theirs. When they see that their mischief has failed to produce the desired overreaction, they write us off and find another patsy. We're no fun any more.

38. GIVE THEM A CHOICE

Most people express their anger the same way every time, perhaps with sarcasm, revenge, sulking, pouting or screaming. They do not enjoy expressing their anger in these negative, destructive ways, but no one has ever told them what their options are. They have no choice, and that is frustrating in itself.

We can render a great service by revealing to our friends and loved ones that there are better ways to communicate their legitimate anger. We are not giving them a choice so much as we are revealing alternatives that they had all along but didn't know they had.

Vignette: It's up to You

Clare and Blanche had been friends since third grade. Blanche had always been known for her temper. She was just like her mother. Clare was more the long-suffering type, the pleaser who could not bring herself to tell people the truth about how she felt. In counseling, Clare learned how to tell her friend the unpleasant truth about their relationship. This was not a good intention to straighten Blanche out; she had a real intention for herself.

C: "Blanche, I'm sorry that you were so angry last night. I don't blame you for being angry. That's not the point. The point is the way you express it. For years, I've been telling myself, 'She doesn't really mean what she is saying. That's just the way Blanche is. She can't help herself.' But it hurt my feelings when you blew up like that. How would you feel if I talked to you that way?"

B: "I've never thought about it. It must be hard to take sometimes."

C: "It's hard to take all the time. It's not your fault. I realize now that no one ever told you what else you can do besides blow up all over the place."

B: "But I feel better after I let it all out. Isn't that what I'm supposed to do?"

C: "You don't live on a desert island. There are other people involved, and you need to take their feelings into consideration. You have lost too many good friends already. Besides, your momentary relief doesn't change anything for the better. You will blow up again the next time you get angry."

B: "You're right. I've been doing this since grammar school. The rest of me has grown up, but this part hasn't."

C: "You have choices now that you don't know about. You can choose to express your anger in a less hurtful way."

B: "I don't know if I can change."

C: "It helps if you know what there is to change to. For instance, you can choose to say, 'It makes me angry when you do that,' or 'when that happens.' You can also choose to write an anger letter to the person you are angry at."

B: "What if I am angry at myself?"

C: "You have probably been angry at yourself for years. This underlying anger at yourself blows up in my face when I am ten minutes late meeting you. You can drain it out of your system by writing yourself an anger letter."

B: "That sounds so silly."

C: "It's no sillier than driving your friends away with that out-of-control temper of yours."

B: "What if I don't do it?"

C: "There's no law that says you have to write anger letters. These are choices you have. These are preferences that have been open to you all your life. You just didn't know about them. You are not doing it for me or for our friendship. You are doing it for you. It will give you some relief from your pent-up anger. It is up to you to do it or not. But if things don't get better, I will have to start seeing you less often. My heart can't take it anymore. If you blow up at me next Saturday night, I want you to know in advance that I'm not going to rationalize it away any more. It's just too unpleasant. I will just get up and go home."

B: "Is that a threat?"

C: "No, it's not a threat. It's just my preference. It will be a consequence of the choice you make. I'm not trying to control you for your own good, but I have a choice to stay or to leave. By staying around, I am giving you permission to abuse me, and that's not good for our relationship. I have my choices and you have yours. It is up to you now. I just want you to know in advance so you won't be taken by surprise."

B: "I guess it's about time I stopped putting on a sideshow for everybody. I used to get what I wanted by throwing a tantrum, but I can see now that I have been paying too high a price for it. It's not worth it."

C: "You can choose to let it go and replace it with something more constructive — like asking for what you want, and securing cooperation. As I said, it's not up to me. It's your choice. It's up to you."

"Do we have to eat a whole egg to
know it is spoiled?"

Rudolf Dreikurs

39. GOOD INTENTIONS MAKE US ANGRY

How do we feel when Aunt Birdy pushes more mashed potatoes on our plate and we have to lose six pounds by Saturday night? We feel angry. But we can't very well punch out a sweet old lady who only wants us to live forever.

We have a conflict. It is the same one we have had for years. We either express our anger openly and risk losing an aunt or suppress it again where it will turn into symptoms that we do not need. Fortunately for us, there is a Third Choice, the middle way:

1. We can remember to identify Auntie's unwanted benevolence as mischief. It does not need to be done. She is pleasing us her way, not our way.

2. We can disengage emotionally from her mischief. We can choose not to perceive it as an insult to our intelligence and maturity, which it is not. We do not take it personally. It isn't about us, it's about her. She is not our enemy and we are not her out-of-control victim. She is merely an imperfect human being and her imperfection is making us angry.

3. We have a choice to manage our anger in the new way or manage it the same way we did when we were six. We can choose to Consider the Source and let our anger go: "It's only Aunt Birdy playing the only role she knows."

4. We are now free to do the unexpected on our own terms as independent grown-ups. We can choose to validate the goodness of her intentions, not the content. We can say something like, *"I know that you want the best for me, Auntie, and I appreciate it, but I'll be fine."* We have just told the truth about ourselves and about her. When she hears us talking to her in this new, more mature way, she is more likely to respect us and stop treating us like an overgrown six-year-old.

40. THE "GOOD FOR NOTHING" SYNDROME

When we do good things for people, we expect something good in return, such as a thank you, a smile or a nod. We feel disappointed when we do not get the reciprocity we expect.

Some of us feel more than disappointed. We become angry at the unfairness of this ingratitude. We take the absence of validation as if it were an *in*validation. Our goodness has been all for nothing. We feel we were taken advantage of and played for a fool. We let it happen. We were stupid. We should have seen it coming and we failed to prevent it. Our stupidity makes us angry at ourselves. We feel like a chump, and it's our own fault. We have taken this whole thing personally.

These bad feelings, which constitute the *Good for Nothing Syndrome*, make us feel worthless. They confirm our feelings of inferiority and inadequacy from childhood. We will learn nothing from our setback. We may say to ourselves, "No more Mister Nice Guy," but we will do it all over again tomorrow. Or, we will become mean and cynical.

Our antidote to feeling good for nothing, which means worthless, is our self-respect. *"I am a worthwhile human being in spite of my faults and imperfections, whether you appreciate me or not. I am not dependent on you for my worth as a person. I can validate my own goodness. I know what I did. I behaved appropriately under the circumstances. I would not have behaved any other way. I need not be angry at myself."*

"Neither fight nor give in;
cooperate instead."

Rudolf Dreikurs

41. GRIEF AND LOSS

As Elizabeth Kubler-Ross writes in her book, *On Death and Dying,* there are four stages in the grieving process:

1. **Denial** — "Oh no! It can't be true."

2. **Anger** — "Why is this happening? It's so unfair."

3. **Bargaining** — "I'll do anything if you'll make this stop."

4. **Acceptance of the inevitable.** "Thy will be done."

Many times, the acceptance stage does not take place. Instead, we have a feeling of *resignation* to our fate, which is not a healthy outcome at all. Resignation is malignant, and it will consume us if it is left untreated.

In our resignation, which includes the tendency to withdraw from the world in discouragement and say, "I give up. What's the use?" there is an element of residual anger that has not been successfully worked through. This anger soon turns into depression, which contributes its unhealthy share to the malignant situation.

Anger is our natural response to a grievance, which includes the loss of a loved one. It is important that we apply some of the anger management techniques we have learned in this book, but this is difficult to do because the anger component in our grief is often lost in the mixture of other strong and deep emotions that we have been experiencing. Our anger gets away from us and it prolongs our grief. Even though we are not consciously aware of our anger as such, we need to ask ourselves some focusing questions, such as *"Who am I angry at?"* We never think of asking such questions because we all learned we are not supposed to be angry at a person who has died. That is not acceptable in polite society and is considered unseemly. We would feel too guilty, so we solve the problem by choosing to suppress our anger. Yet we are angry at them just the same, not for dying, but for causing us this bereavement. We are not *blaming* our loved one for dying, but we are legitimately angry that it happened. If we are angry at the deceased for leaving and abandoning us, for betraying our trust that he or she would live forever, we can write that emotion down in an anger letter. It is not a hate letter. We are merely expressing our anger in a mature, appropriate way to save our own sanity.

It is healthy for us to validate our own legitimate anger at our loss. Our focusing question often has the effect of making the facets of our unconscious, unacceptable anger conscious, so we can resolve our conflicting attitudes and experience some relief at last.

The next focusing question is, *"Who else are we angry at?"* Perhaps we are angry at the doctors at the hospital, the drunk driver or some other individual who contributed to this loss. Now the question becomes, *"What can I do about it?"* When we feel that there is nothing we can do because revenge would only get us in more trouble, we feel powerless and out of control. This powerlessness is painful, and it compounds all of the other pain we are feeling. We can relieve this component of our distress by choosing to write the object of our anger an anger letter. This, too, is an action that we can take on our own behalf. It puts us back in touch with the real world. It helps us to break the cycle of negative feelings and emotions whirling inside of us and restores the feeling that we are in control, competent, independent and all the other facets of self-respect. We do not have to mail the letter. It is not for them; it is for us.

What if we are angry at God? We can write the Deity an anger letter, too. What if we are angry at ourselves? We may blame ourselves for failing to prevent it or to get there in time. We may be *obsessing* about these unsolved and, by now, insoluble problems. We are in the throes of, *"If only I had. . ."* and we cannot get out.

Writing ourselves an anger letter often gives us some relief from our feelings that these problems are insoluble and that we are guilty as charged. We are not guilty; we are merely imperfect. The problems are not insoluble. They are, in most cases, fictitious problems that reality does not require us to solve.

The next focusing question might be, *"What angers me the most about this loss?"* The answer often bubbles up immediately. "It is so unfair. This is not supposed to happen to good people." We need to identify our vulnerability to perceive unfairness in situations where

105

fairness is not a relevant consideration. Fairness does not have to do with rewarding goodness or punishing badness. Fairness means *without bias*. These tragedies happen every day in an imperfect world and our mistake is to protest the cosmic unfairness of it all. We can use our adult sensibilities to put our anger in a more bearable perspective. Cosmic rage is unbearable and unmanageable.

The response to our focusing question might be, "Why does this have to happen to me?" This response tells us we are perceiving this regrettable loss as if it were a personal victimization, which it is not. We are not a victim. We are a worthwhile human being in spite of what has happened to us.

We can continue to ask ourselves, *"What else angers me the most about what happened?"* We can use our responses to shed some light on the powerful attitudes that are contributing to our distress and making our grief more painful than it needs to be. We may be angry at the *wrongness* of it all and standing in moral judgment on the party we hold responsible or on the system. We may be angry that all of our goodness in the deceased person's behalf has been in vain and that we have been good for nothing. That is unfair, also. Our anger problem has many facets, and the more aspects of our anger that we can identify and relieve, the better off we will be. We will accept, and recover from our grief sooner than we would otherwise.

42. THE HARVEY WALLBANGER SYNDROME

The Harvey Wallbanger solution to the anger problem involves the perforation of plaster walls, doors, partitions and other structural materials with one's fist, feet, or head. The individual, usually a male, is trying to express his anger without doing bodily harm to his loved ones and other persons who could file charges. He may imagine that these outbursts give him relief from his anger, but such relief from super-anger can only be partial and temporary. The adrenalin will continue to pump, and his anger will continue to build in his psyche until another minor irritant triggers the next eruption. He has not broken his anger down into its components. He has not identified the real object of his anger, which is probably himself. Someone ought to reveal to him that he can make other choices that won't be so hard on the wallpaper.

43. THE HAT TRICK, OR VOTING WITH YOUR FEET

Someone once said that the best way to win a fight is with your hat — grab it and run. There is a certain amount of truth in that unlovely homily, and it is nice to know flight is one of our legitimate options. We are not required to go down with the ship in the name of perseverance or self-righteous indignation.

There is no law that requires us to state our case over and over for the tenth time after our point has been shouted down the last nine. When we see that we are getting nowhere, that both we and our debating partner are temporarily out of control, we have the power of choice: We can choose to say it for the eleventh time or we can choose to grab our hat and run.

When we choose to leave the arena, we are allowing a number of positive things to happen: We are giving our respective wounds time to heal. We are giving all the parties a chance to come down from their highly charged emotional state; and we are allowing our adult competence and judgment to come to the surface in a calmer atmosphere.

This is not "quitting" or "wimping out." This is assuming appropriate responsibility for resolving a problem that was not being resolved any other way. This is not withdrawal in discouragement, but disengaging from mutual mischief. This is not abdicating responsibility, but appropriate responsibility for our own sanity. This is true control. We are making it happen on our own valid terms.

107

Harvey, does that mean you don't want peas with dinner?

44. HOTEL THERAPY

Sometimes partners need a breather from the task of relationship and from each other. Too much togetherness can be suffocating. We lose our perspective and we lose ourselves in the shuffle.

We have a recommendation for female partners, who often work two eight-hour shifts every day. We suggest that they "Take Time Out of Time" (page 198) to treat themselves to a day and/or a night off at a nice hotel with a spa, room service and cable television, or as much amenity as they can afford. They would like to take us up on our suggestion, but their old attitudes rise up inside to trip them up. They may say:

- **"It costs too much."** "It's all right for George to go bowling and beer guzzling three nights a week but it's not OK for me to spend a little of our joint funds on a Mental Health Day.")

- **"It's a waste of money."** ("Spending money on my own pleasure is irresponsible and selfish. It is a waste of hard-earned money that could be spent fixing the toilet.")

- **"It wouldn't be right."** ("It would be wrong to indulge myself when my children haven't had a new toy for three days.")

- **"I wouldn't know what to do with myself."** ("I have had very little practice feeling independent, in control, at peace with myself. I can't get there from here.")

- **"I'd feel guilty."** ("I have acquired the attitude that anyone who fritters away time and money on herself is guilty of waste, self indulgence, displeasing, selfishness, irresponsibility, enjoying happiness I have not earned and do not deserve, and other non-crimes from my childhood.")

- **"It's too scary to even think about."** ("They need me. What would they do without me? Their needs justify my existence. I am dependent on their dependency. I don't have the courage to make a break for the border, even for one night. I have too much anxiety to take the risk.")

109

There is an old Barber Shop Quartet song entitled, "How Can I Miss You If You Never Go Away?" It is also written: "Absence Makes the Heart Grow Fonder." These people behave as if they have never heard of these ideas. They feel that they don't deserve to implement them even if they have.

Such people are *allergic to happiness*. They are not allergic to drudgery, self-sacrifice, deprivation, super responsibility or self-criticism. These are all manifestations of their self-doubt which prevent them from enjoying a respite they deserve as worthwhile human beings in their own right.

Vignette: They Actually Missed Her

Charlene was in a very difficult marriage. Her husband, Phil, was passive aggressive. He drove her crazy with his false promises, excuses, manipulations, exemptions, and all around phoniness. Charlene learned how to use our "Consider the Source" technique (page 40). She stopped believing that her husband meant what he said. She was able to disengage emotionally by reminding herself that, "It's only Phil being Phil." It still made her angry, but she was taking his mischief less personally.

Her children were 8 and 10. Phil began playing his tricks with their minds, too. That was going too far. He was turning them against her, making her the scapegoat for all the marital squabbling in their home. The kids bought into his mischief. He had them convinced that their daddy wouldn't lie. Well, he would.

Charlene saw she was outnumbered. She couldn't use adult logic on her kids. She didn't have an ally in the whole house. She chose to stop fighting it and to begin disengaging from their mischief with her feet. She made her break for the border. Charlene decided to take a night off. She went to the Motel 6 on the outskirts of town. She called home to let them know she was alright and that she'd be home in the morning. She did her toenails for the first time in eight years, she soaked in a bubble bath, she watched TV till it was sinfully late. She was recharging her batteries. This is not self-indulgence; she was taking a well-earned Mental Health Day.

When she got home the next a.m., her loved ones had actually missed her! They never had that experience before. It didn't make them angry; it made them appropriately appreciative of her efforts in their behalf. She told them what she had done for herself and how much better it made her feel. She didn't blame anyone. It wouldn't have helped. Her absence brought them closer together. They shared her happiness. They respected her independence, her self-confidence, her new identity as a human being. This was not a self-indulgent good intention on her part. It was a real intention. It didn't make things worse; it made them better. It was "Win, win, win." Phil got the message. If he started to make her crazy, she was prepared to do it again. She could Vote With Her Feet (page 107). He couldn't argue with that or manipulate it. He wasn't cured of his passive-aggressive mischief, but she had given him dose of reality to think about for two minutes.

45. HOW DOES THAT HELP?

Believe it or not, Trixie's spouse and tormentor, Ralph, may be inflicting his anger upon her for her own good. He is hoping to pound some sense into her thick skull and she doesn't even appreciate it. He only wants her to be better than she is. In addition, he is screaming at their six-year-old daughter to improve her deportment and ridiculing their nine-year-old son to make a man of him. He actually thinks he is helping! He is not thinking at all, of course. These good intentions of his have nothing to do with being rational. They arise out of attitudes that formed in the matrix of his relationship with his own parents and siblings, who didn't know what they were doing, either.

That is why we do not make the mistake of saying, "Stop that! You're hurting Billy's feelings." In Ralph's nonrational view, hurting feelings is supposed to help develop self-reliance, so why should he stop?

No one has ever questioned the helpfulness of these destructive behaviors. We do not attack the behavior because parenting skills is

111

not Ralph's issue. His issue is phony helpfulness to his child as his own ill-prepared father was helpful to him. On a deeper level, he is using this good intention to overcompensate for his painful feeling that he was inadequately prepared for the task of parenting. When his imperfect child breaks a two-dollar coffee cup, it reactivates his underlying conviction that he does not know how to cope with the unexpected. This is painful. Ralph is trying to relieve the pain of this reminder of his own inadequacies at his child's expense. He is trying to help himself, but he doesn't know how to do that, either. He is helping no one. It is all counterproductive mischief.

Our technique here is to zero in on the helpfulness aspect of his mischievous good intentions; not in a threatening or judgmental way nor as a partisan in the child's behalf against his father, but in a conciliatory, thought-provoking way.

Trixie can ask: "Ralph, how does that help?"

He may or may not answer the question. He may not know what to say. That is all right. At least it has started him thinking. In a sense, it is a rhetorical question. We do not expect an answer. This is our way of planting a seed of doubt in his mind and perhaps opening a window to let in the breath of change, the fresh winds of sanity.

46. HUMOR IS A SAVING GRACE

No book on anger management could be complete without at least a mention of humor as an outlet for hostility, which is one of the high-tech names for the emotion of anger.

We understand behavior in terms of its purpose. Making jokes is behavior, and it can have many purposes. Some purposes are negative and some are positive. It depends on the predisposition of the humorist:

- Making a joke is *doing something* when there isn't much else we can do to relieve the pent-up pressure of our anger. It relieves our feelings of powerlessness and gives us a choice we would not have otherwise.

- A joke often represents a compromise between saying something dangerously displeasing and saying nothing at all. It is a liberating third choice.
- A humorous put-down can be a way of setting subtle limits on a mischief maker who cannot be attacked openly.
- Humor is a form of self-empowerment: "I have the power to say this funny thing and you can't stop me."
- Humor may have an element of superiority: "I have the ability to see the absurdity of this situation and you do not."

If we are healthy, self-respecting human beings, our humor will be a *saving grace*, a lightening of the situation for everyone's benefit. However, if we are suffering from unresolved residual anger from the past, our humor may be hurtful and destructive. If we are suffering from extreme self-contempt, we will find our humor only in cruelty and pain.

Humor, like every other human attribute, does not exist in a vacuum; it exists in a human context. Its purposes will be consistent with that context. As people replace their childhood self-contempt with self-respect, they find themselves more able to resist the temptation to say something funny at someone else's expense. They can choose to let the negative opportunity pass.

Vignette: Humor Is in the Ear of the Beholder

Lily and Ron had been going together for a year. Lily's job took her out of town overnight. Ron didn't like the idea of her being alone at night in a hotel full of traveling salesmen. He had been burned many times before. He trusted Lily, but he didn't trust her traveling companions.

Lily had the habit of teasing Ron about his suspicions. She would call from the hotel and make little jokes about male-female goings-on and Ron would bite every time. His old jealousies would rise up in him and he would be in a lot of pain. He told Lily to stop, but she didn't see why she should. When Lily comes home, Ron is not glad to see her. He is still smoldering. Lily's self-serving mischief has turned out to be counterproductive, as it usually does.

The Wednesday before their counseling session, Lily called from Tucson to say that her sales presentation for the regional director was

113

a hit. "It was another notch on my bedpost, I mean, a feather in my cap." She had done it again. Ron's old angers at past betrayals came to the surface. He knew now that the issue wasn't Lily's conduct, but his vulnerability to being provoked. However, he could not sort out his anger at her for doing this to him from his anger at the last three women in his life, or from his anger at his mother. All these women used to provoke him terribly. He always seemed to gravitate toward women who made him angry.

When asked why she made jokes knowing that Ron was sensitive to the issue of betrayal, Lily said, "I just want him to make me feel attractive when I am so far away from home."

This answer tells us that Lily's *joke* has the purpose of relieving her feelings of inferiority and insecurity. It reveals a core of dependency behind her facade of corporate success. Below that is a still deeper — and contradictory — purpose. It isn't that Lily forgets how much she hurts Ron with her amusing shots. She remembers very well. She wants to have it both ways. She wants him to respond to her and to hurt him at the same time. Why does she want to hurt him? She is angry at him for being jealous, which she sees as controlling and demeaning. It is hard for her to express her anger directly, so she uses *innocent* remarks as her way of getting revenge. It works all too well. Ron's anger at these provocations turns into painful expectations of betrayal and victimization. He listens to their phone conversations not to reassure himself that she is all right, but to try to find clues as to what she is really doing behind his back. He feels like a persecuted victim of women, which is a role he learned to play in his mother's house. Her counterproductive mischief is making his jealousy worse. It is turning his anger into paranoia. That hurts everyone.

Lily's Homework is to tell Ron that his insecurities make her angry. She is to catch herself depending on Ron for the validation of her femininity and choose to validate her own worth as a person instead. When she thinks about it, she sees that her jokes never did accomplish their purpose of making her feel more attractive. She can do much better without them.

Ron's Homework is to catch himself falling for Lily's mischief and taking it personally as a confirmation of his old role as a victim.

114

The new Ron is feeling like a worthwhile human being in spite of his imperfections, both past and present. Lily is a worthwhile human being in spite of her imperfections, too. If she makes him angry, he is not to say, "Stop telling me jokes like that," which would be giving orders. She does not submit very well to commands. He cannot secure her cooperation that way. Instead, he can choose to say, *"It makes me angry when you pick my scabs and make them bleed."* There is nothing funny about that.

Ron's additional Homework is to trust Lily. Before he can do that, he needs to trust *himself* more. He is the one who chose her for his companion. He made a good choice. He just didn't make a perfect one. He is worthwhile in spite of it.

Do's and Don't's

Do not cloak your anger in a funny remark. People are not deceived. They are hurt by your anger, whether it is said *in fun* or not. "I was only kidding, can't you take a joke?" Yes, they can, but that was not a joke. If you are angry, tell the truth. If there is an absurdity in the situation, you can comment on that without attacking the other individual personally. For instance:

When they say	You can say
"Don't you know anything?"	"I was absent that day."
"You left a spot on this saucer!"	"You can't get good help."
"You're too sensitive."	"What should I be, insensitive?"
"You're just like your mother."	"Whose mother should I be like?"
"Why on earth did you do that?"	"It seemed like a good idea at the time."

Do not use adult humor or sarcasm against a child. A child looks to you for validation and encouragement. A child is no match for your verbal fluency and can only come out of the exchange a loser, inferior and discouraged. The child takes what you say more literally and personally than you realize. Just because it happened to you in your childhood, you do not have a license to pass the damage on to the next generation. Humor should be a saving grace, not a bludgeon.

47. "I" MESSAGE

When we are angry, we are quick to focus on the person who provoked us. Our attention is directed towards those who caused our grievance. We are predisposed to relieve the pain of our anger at their expense. We are trying to build ourselves back up by tearing them down. We say things like, "You should do this" or "You should stop doing that." Our speech is full of advice, commands, condemnations, and recriminations, none of which is constructive.

We need to be smarter than that. We need to stop sending counterproductive "you" messages and begin to talk about ourselves. We are in no position to read another person's mind, to understand their underlying purposes or to assess this unpleasant situation logically and dispassionately. We feel inadequate to cope with it. When we talk to other people about themselves, we get into deep water we cannot always get out of again.

We are much better off talking about ourselves. We know more about ourselves than we will ever know about them: We know how we feel right now, we know what happened to make us feel that way, and we have preferences as to what we plan to do in the future. We can choose to express our anger in the middle ground between ranting and stuffing. For instance, we can say, *"It makes me angry when you do that. I am very angry right now. If it happens again, I will be angry again. I just want you to know how I feel. If you don't want me to feel this way any more, you know what your choices are. It is up to you."*

"Courage is the willingness
to take a risk."

Rudolf Dreikurs

When we talk about ourselves, we are not moralizing, judging or criticizing. We are not provoking a counter reaction that nobody wants. We are telling the truth. We are creating an opportunity for a dialogue between two imperfect human beings, one of whose imperfections made the other angry. The damage is not irreparable and the mistake was not fatal, so let us clear the air the right way and get on with our lives.

When we talk about ourselves, we are helping the other person to understand us in an appropriate way. We are revealing ourselves in ways that will help them to cooperate with us in the future. We are not giving orders or demanding submission. If we use the right words and the right music, as self-respecting human beings in our own right, we will make the relationship stronger than it was before.

48. I'M SORRY

Some people find it difficult to use the words, "I am sorry." These words seem to imply some sort of guilt, and they are reluctant to make that painful admission. "I'm sorry" is particularly hard for perfectionists to say. It is a painful exposure of their failure to achieve total perfection. They want to keep such failures a secret forever.

"I am sorry" does not imply a confession of culpability or failure at all. It means, *"I regret that this negative thing happened."* Regret is the wish that things were other than they are. You are not owning the problem or assuming responsibility for solving it. You merely feel appropriate regret that whatever happened, happened. You are also expressing regret that the other person is in so much pain. If that is truly how you feel, then that is what you say. (See "TELL THE TRUTH" on page 201.)

When you say, "I'm sorry," it is a way of giving yourself permission to be an imperfect human being — a permission that your parents and teachers may never have given you. You are an adult now and it is time you gave it to yourself. Throughout these pages, it is all right to be imperfect. You are worthwhile in spite of it.

118

I'm sorry is a very effective anger management technique. It takes the sting out of the situation. It is like putting salve on a burn. It focuses appropriate attention on the emotional component of the other person's distress and away from the superficial debate about who did what to whom. Very often, if you do it right, you will get an, "I'm sorry, too," in return. What could be better than that? The above applies to persons who have self-respect. Unself-respecting people speak a different language. Their "I'm sorry" is not an expression of sincere regret. They are sorry they got caught. This is not sincerity. It is mere *sinceritiness*.

49. LET IT GO

Why do we hang on to painful, disturbing emotions and situations that we would be better off without? It doesn't make sense but we do it anyway. There may be a higher principle involved here. We just don't know what it is. It is probably no more than an inappropriate attitude keeping us from dealing effectively with a reality situation, such as,

- "If I let go, I'll lose control totally. There will be a disaster. I can't afford to let go of one inch."
- "If I let go, I'll look like a quitter. What will the neighbors think?"
- "Letting go is irresponsible. I must be perfectly responsible at all times even if it means going down with the ship."
- "My father never let go of anything in his life. It made him miserable. As is loyal, obedient child, I have no choice but to follow him over the cliff."
- "If I stop hanging on, I won't be me anymore. I won't know who I am! I might even cease to exist! It's not worth it. I'll hang on. It's the lesser misery."

As grown ups now, we can use a stressful, anxious situation as an opportunity to replace these inappropriate attitudes with more mature ones such as:

- "As a self-respecting human being, I can choose to hang onto this grievance or I can choose to let it go. Hanging on never helped; maybe letting go will. It's scary, but I am willing to take an appropriate risk in my own behalf."
- "I am not powerless and out of control. I have the power of choice. I can choose to let it go."
- "I do not need this aggravation."
- "I don't need this power struggle."
- "I don't need to control this situation."
- "I don't need to straighten this other person out with my good intentions."
- "I don't need to solve this problem because it isn't worth solving. It is only mischief."
- "These are needs I don't need to need. I can choose to let them go."
- "I have other things to do with my time and energy. I am not quitting or copping out. I am just letting it go. I'm letting it go not from weakness, but from strength."

Very often, when we let go of these worries, doubts and negative expectations, we will feel more in control than we ever did before.

50. LEX TALIONIS

One of the earliest attempts to manage anger was the Lex Talionis or Law of Retaliation: "A life for a life, an eye for an eye, a tooth for a tooth" (Exodus 21:24). To our modern taste, these prescriptions for counter damages seem bloodthirsty and barbaric, but when we compare this enlightened agenda with the unlimited retaliation that preceded it, we can see it was a step in the right direction. It was a daring breakthrough in social engineering. We might even say that the Lex Talionis was an early attempt to replace unbridled, out-of-control revenge with a primitive system of logical consequences. It was a step on the long road towards civilization. Anger management did not end there. It began there.

"You are not required to do it all.
That would be perfection.
Do what you can do.
That often turns out to be
quite a bit."

Rudolf Dreikurs

51. LIGHTEN UP

It is very hard to be jovial when we are angry. When our adrenal glands are pumping adrenalin into our bloodstream, our digestive system shuts down and so does our sense of humor.

Some of us never had a sense of humor to shut down. We go through life as though the present were something to be gotten over with as soon as possible. These people call themselves "serious," while others call them "Party Poopers."

Some people are at the other extreme. They see the humor in life even when there is no humor to be seen. They call themselves "optimistic" or "Susie Sunshine;" we call them "inane." They need to "lighten down." Here again, the goal is to find a healthy balance between too much cheerfulness and too little.

When we are in the grip of an anger attack, we can catch ourselves perceiving the situation as grimmer than it really is. It is helpful if we can find an absurdity both agree on, such as, *"We sound like the second act of 'Aida,' don't we?"* See if that doesn't make the anger more manageable. It is absurd that two people are making each other crazy when, for the same price, they could be making each other happy.

Vignette: Two Agendas in One Kitchen

Mike and Tina were fighting about the mess in the kitchen. Mike was perceiving her criticisms as if they were victimizations and defending himself against her. Tina was defending herself against his defenses. She was feeling unappreciated and unloved. Each was recapitulating the stormy tenor of their parents' marriages and they hated it. Tina saw that she was getting nowhere with her good intentions to teach Mike the niceties of domestic management. He was not a willing pupil. So she decided to lighten up.

In the past, she had tried to end these anger spasms with a cute remark, such as, "You look so adorable when you scootch up your face like that." Mike was not mollified by these peace gestures. Indeed, he took them as further proof of his wife's lack of seriousness.

Tina chose to stop trying to lighten Mike up, which she had no competence to do, and to work on lightening up her own disposition instead. She chose to begin replacing her good intentions for Mike with a real intention for herself. She broke her heaviness down into its components so she could let go of each one in turn:

1. "Here I am, just like my mother, standing in moral judgment on my husband for his wrongness. Who am I to judge another person's worth? Besides, it's hard work. I can choose to stop doing it."

2. "I am trying to improve my husband against his will. I can choose instead to accept him as he is, in spite of the fact that he has a long way to go. Maybe if I get off his back, he will improve himself."

3. "I am saying negative, hurtful things to the man I love. How can I build him up that way? I can choose to say something constructive instead, like, 'I'm sorry I yelled at you. Let's have some hot chocolate'."

4. "I am defending my integrity in ways that do not work. I can choose to accept myself in spite of my unfortunate contribution to this confrontation. As an imperfect human being, I am not required to defend myself. I can stop any time I want."

5. "I am not the powerless victim of this hulk. I am not a pleasing child either. I have the power of choice. I can choose to stop doing what displeases me, like fighting, and to start doing what pleases me, like walking away."

6. "I am trying to wean Mike away from his parents' horrible example. I can't do that by screaming at him. I can do it by setting an example of self-respect for him to follow if he chooses. If I don't set it, he can't follow it. I am not doing this for his good; I am doing it for my good."

Tina said, *"I don't want to fight with you. I'm sorry I made you so angry. I'm going to make something to drink."* Mike yelled, "Come back here, I'm not through with you." *"Well, I am through with this fight. You can carry on without me."*

After a few more moments of grousing for the record, Mike got out the marshmallows and the cups. He cleared a space on the table and tried to remember why he overreacted to Tina's observation about his messiness. He realized he was feeling like a victim, just as he did when his mother yelled at him for the same offense twenty years before. *"At least I'm consistent,"* he mused,

"It's hard to lighten up when you're being victimized. But I'm not a victim, I'm just a slob. I can live with that, but it certainly isn't worth defending or making either Tina or me unhappy over. Like Tina has said, I'm a worthwhile human being in spite of my messiness. I think I'm starting to believe it."

52. LITIGATION

We do not have duels to the death anymore. Instead, we have instituted an even more painful technique of anger management called "the lawsuit." We are the most litigious nation on earth. Our lawyers are the beneficiaries of our inability to solve anger problems like grown-ups. It would be much cheaper for all of us if we could learn to remove the anger component that turns a difference of opinion into a courtroom grudge match. If we can identify our vulnerabilities to taking the ups and downs of life personally, we would be likelier to resolve disputes on a business-like basis in an atmosphere of mutual respect.

Very often the legal issue is not even the issue. The underlying issue may be, "You hurt my feelings. You made me feel worthless and I let you. I took it personally and that hurt. I'm going to get revenge on you for hurting me. My self-deceptive good intention is to change you for your own good so you'll never do it again." Like most good intentions, this one will prove counterproductive. We will spend a fortune we cannot afford to teach a lesson no one will learn.

"The best way to destroy an enemy is to make him your friend."

Abraham Lincoln

53. LOGICAL CONSEQUENCES

When we let our nonrational emotions determine our behavior, there is usually a price to pay. Our actions turn out to be counterproductive. While our emotions are a legitimate part of the human condition, they are not guided by rational thought processes. They are often triggered by carryover attitudes from our pre-rational childhood leaving our fragile adult intelligence trampled in the dust.

Our feelings are important to us and we should know them by their rightful names, but they are not necessarily a reliable guide to taking actions in the real world.

When it comes to anger, we are not the impotent victims of the people who offend us. Neither are we the passive prisoners of our own emotion. We have the power of choice now. We need to interpose conscious thought and ask ourselves a focusing question or two, such as, *"What does the reality of the situation require me to do?"* Reality never requires us to behave irrationally, but we do it anyway. We have never learned how not to. This is especially true when we are angry. We can choose to outgrow the illogical consequences of an anger situation we have been employing since childhood such as:

- Muttering under our breath.
- Nursing our anger in our hearts forever.
- Calling them dirty names.
- Holding our breath until we turn blue.

We did not invent these techniques out of our adult intelligence. They represent childhood solutions to anger problems we did not know how to solve way back when. Our overriding predisposition is to relieve the pain of our anger. We need to replace this mindless, illogical predisposition to react impulsively with a more constructive predisposition. We can acquire the predisposition to replace our current system of illogical consequences such as yelling, screaming, hitting, sulking and so on with consequences that have some logical relation to the grievance in question: the product of our mature judgment and experience. They are appropriate to reality as we see it.

126

Whether we like it or not. They are not childish, self-indulgent or irresponsible. They are appropriately responsible choices we have made to relieve the painful pressure our unresolved anger problem is causing us. Our logical consequence is not a good intention to straighten somebody out. It is not for their good but for our own.

For instance, when our daughter, Susiebelle, spills her orange juice, we can consciously choose not to scold her and send her to her room. Nor do we need to lecture her on the evils of waste. We can say, *"It makes me angry when you knock over your orange juice. Now get a sponge from the sink and clean it up."*

Susiebelle can see the logical connection between the antecedent behavior and its consequence. She is not being held in contempt. She is merely an imperfect child with imperfect small muscle skills. Her imperfection does not make us super-angry. It only makes us angry and we tell her the truth in a way that does not deprive her of her self-respect. This is how children learn the logical connection between cause and effect.

This is how the world works: If we make a mistake, it is our responsibility to repair the damage insofar as we are able to do so. Our worth as a person is not at stake. It is not even an issue.

Logical consequences are not subjective, they are objective. Unlike punishment, they have the following characteristics:

- Logical consequences express the reality of the social order, not solely that of the person applying them.
- Logical consequences are directly linked to the misbehavior.
- Logical consequences involve no element of self-serving moral judgment.
- Logical consequences are applied in a respectful manner.
- Logical consequences are concerned only with what will or will not happen now.
- The person is given a choice to make and is informed of the consequences of his or her decision. The consequence is carried out in a firm but fair manner.

The prerequisite for imposing these logical consequences on our children is our *self-respect*. Self-respecting parents do not take their child's little misbehaviors personally, for they, too, are worthwhile in spite of these lapses on their child's part. Such parents are free to use their adult judgment and their mature creative faculties to devise an appropriate and instructive consequence to impose upon the child. If the child abuses a privilege, the privilege is taken away. Toys left underfoot are put up on the closet shelf for an agreed-upon length of time. We do not deprive the child of our love and affection. That is not logical. Anger is not hate. We can be angry and love our child at the same time.

If we do not respect ourselves as much as we would like, we may use an anger situation as an opportunity to do some emotional growing up. We can catch ourselves about to overreact in an old, destructive way and consciously choose not to. We can catch ourselves in the act, take time out (page 198) and give ourselves an opportunity for something more creative to bubble up. We are not merely counting to ten, but using this interval to solve the problem at hand. To help us in our creative process, we can ask ourselves if the behavior was an honest mistake or mischief. If it is mischief, we can disengage from it, as we have learned to do, and do the unexpected. Our children usually do not expect us to be logical. We can choose to do what they do not expect.

In any case, the old, nonlogical way never worked. We may have thought parental success meant terrifying our children into silent submission or buying their compliance with goodies. This is not positive success but is instead a negative success. We have not solved any problems or even dealt with them intelligently. We have merely postponed them. They will be back, only worse. Tyrannism and overindulgence are not logical.

If we can come up with a logical consequence, such as telling the truth, *"It makes me angry when you do that,"* which is always a good fallback position, we will experience a feeling of relief. We have confronted a problem in the real world and dealt with it constructively. We have earned the right to have feelings of accomplishment, success, competence, trust in our judgment, identity, maturity and control. Each time we do a Homework, these positive feelings about ourselves get stronger. We are not building ourselves up by tearing anyone down. If we do it right, everyone wins and no one loses.

These are some logical consequences we can use the next time we have an anger problem:

- We can tell the truth: "That makes me angry."
- We can write an anger letter.
- We can choose whether or not to deliver it.
- We can deprive the offender of our company for an appropriate length of time, up to and including forever.
- We can tell the offender about our grievance and what it has cost us emotionally and otherwise. We can let him know what he can do to compensate us for our losses.
- We can put a frog in his underwear drawer. It isn't logical, but it always gets a laugh. No one can be logical all the time.

What a different world this would be if all the wife beaters, child abusers, politicians, generals, zealots, judges, managers and motorists on the planet would start using logical consequences every day instead of what they have been using all their lives.

54. MIND READING

Some of us expect our loved ones to read our minds. Rationally, we know they cannot do it but, subjectively, we expect them to just the same. This absurd expectation sets us up for a lifetime of frustration and disappointment. It is especially malignant in the area of anger management.

Vignette: You Should Know How I Feel

Mona and Bill were referred to the Anger Clinic by their marriage counselor. They fought all the time and it was destroying their relationship. It was clear that they could not get to their problems because their fulminating anger always got in the way.

The morning of their third session, they had a typical squabble. Mona said to Bill, "You're brushing your teeth too hard, you'll make your gums bleed." Bill defended his right to brush his teeth as hard as he pleased. The war was on. They had a lot to talk about when they got to the Clinic.

We began our analysis by asking our usual focusing question, *"What angered you the most when that happened?"*

Bill replied that Mona was trying to control him as usual and he resented it. He rebelled against her attempt to change him in ways that didn't make any sense.

Mona was only trying to help Bill and she was angry that he did not appreciate her concern for his dental health. She felt good for nothing. She was angry at him and angry at herself for even trying to make his life better.

Mona, of course, had good intentions and they were an insult to Bill's intelligence. They made him angry.

Our next focusing question to Bill was, again, *"What angered you the most?"*

Bill didn't hesitate for a second, "She should have known I was angry, but she kept going on and on about my gums."

The issue is not gums, is it? The issue is that you were angry at her for inflicting her good intentions you without your permission. What does that mean, 'She should have known I was angry'?

"It means she should have stopped doing what she was doing. She should have seen that I was angry at her."

But she didn't. She had her own agenda. She was not attuned to yours. Where does that come from, this expectation that Mona should know that you are angry and be guided accordingly?

"I don't know."

What is the first thing you remember from your childhood?

130

"My dad was a waiter in a strip joint. Mother hated it. They fought about it all the time. She was jealous. He said he needed the money. I remember one time they were punching each other in the living room. I was in the kitchen."

How were you feeling?

"Frightened and insecure. I couldn't express my feelings. I felt out of control. I remember thinking that if they only knew what they were doing to my insides, they would stop fighting."

Did they ever find out what they were doing to your insides?

"No, of course not."

You never told them, did you? On what day did you stop hoping that people would read your mind and stop misbehaving without your having to tell them?

"On no day, I guess. I never did stop feeling that way."

This morning, you were angry at Mona for her utter failure to read your mind and stop nagging you about your tooth-brushing style.

"Yes, I was. It all came back to me: Feeling powerless and out of control, and still unable to tell her how I felt or what I wanted her to do."

What do you think you might do about it the next time Mona makes you angry with her good intentions?

"I don't know."

You are right. You don't know. It is foreign to your upbringing. You have never seen two mature adults expressing their anger appropriately and solving their mutual problems cooperatively. It is no wonder that you feel inadequately prepared to solve your anger problems with Mona.

"I blame her for starting it, but underneath I know it's my fault."

Does 'faulting' on yourself help? It is not a matter of fault. It is a matter of human imperfection. You were inadequately prepared to cope with these problems. It is not your fault.

"Is it my parents' fault?"

It is no one's fault. We are all imperfect human beings and we make mistakes. Let's find out what they are so we can stop making them.

"All right. What can I do next time?"

The first step is to identify your feeling. You cannot express your feeling if you do not know what it is. You are not 'upset.' You are angry.

"I was angry all right."

The next step is to catch yourself expecting Mona to pick up on your vibrations. That is not her job. She has her own problems. She is not a mind reader. You have to read your own mind.

"I can do that."

The third step is to express your anger appropriately. You can choose to say, 'Mona, it makes me angry when you tell me what to do.' Is that the truth?

"Yes, that's the truth."

Your Homework, then, is to tell the truth about yourself. When you do, you will not feel controlled by Mona. You will be in control of yourself. You will be making it happen.

"Is it all right to tell her I'm angry?"

I'm not a mind reader, either. Why don't we just ask her a relevant question? Then we'll all know.

"Mona, is it all right if I say I am angry?"

"Of course it is. I would understand and calm down. I would know where you were coming from," replied Mona.

"I thought it would make you angry."

"It makes *me* angry when I don't know what's going on. I don't think about your anger. I am too busy thinking about myself."

We need to find out where that predisposition comes from. Tell me, Mona, what's the first thing ***you*** *remember?*

132

"I remember feeling hurt and sad. I don't know why. One afternoon I was in my room, crying on my bed. Mother came in and said, 'What's wrong?' I was so hysterical I couldn't tell her. She said, 'If you can't tell me, I'm going to leave.' I couldn't tell her and she left. I cried even harder."

How did you feel?

"I felt abandoned. It was my fault. I couldn't tell her what she wanted."

Are you afraid that Bill will abandon you too?

"I never realized it, but you're right. That's why I try so hard to please him, so he won't leave me."

You are trying too hard in ways that work in reverse. You are driving him away from you with your good intentions.

"What else can I do instead? I have to do something."

You can replace your good intentions with real intentions. You can do what reality requires, not what you think it requires.

"What's a real intention?"

Telling the truth about your anger would be a real intention. Just like Bill, you cannot express your feelings to this day. You cannot tell people what you want. It sticks in your throat. You hoped your mother would comfort you without your having to risk abuse by asking for it. You have a lot in common. Tomorrow morning, if Bill makes you angry. . .

"I'm sure he will."

I want you to catch yourself swallowing your anger for fear of being abandoned as you were emotionally abandoned by your mother. You have an adult identity now, and as long as you have you, you cannot be abandoned.

"I'm not sure."

I'm glad you could tell me that, Mona. If you don't tell me, I won't know. Sure, it will be scary. You will have to take a risk. What will it take to tell him you are angry tomorrow?

133

"It will take courage."

What does courage mean?

"I don't know."

Courage is the willingness to take a risk.

"But maybe I don't want him to know I'm angry. He might leave."

Bill, when she is screaming in your face, do you know she is angry?

"It's hard to miss."

So you see, Mona, your anger is not a secret. That is not the problem. Your problem is not Bill. The problem is in you. You have an emotion you cannot express appropriately. You had better solve that problem before you worry about Bill's gums.

"What should I do?"

Your Homework is the same as Bill's. You can say, 'I'm angry at you,' or 'It makes me angry when you do that'.

"You're right. We need to communicate more."

Not if the communication is negative and destructive. Then you need to communicate less. You need to replace your negative communications with positive communications. You need to change the words and the music. You need to tell the truth.

"I can do that."

As you do your Homework, you will both be unlearning the miserable lessons that you learned about yourselves as children. You will be replacing your feelings of inadequacy with the feelings that you are competent to take life as it comes and solve problems as they arise. You will feel in control, independent and appropriate responsibility for yourselves. You will even feel relief from the pressure of your pent-up anger. You will feel like equal members of the human race who can cooperate with each other in an atmosphere of mutual respect.

"What if we have no models of cooperation to follow?"

Starting now, you can learn to become your own models.

134

"We can do that."

Don't forget! No more expecting Mona to read your mind and then complaining when she can't. You have a mouth. Use it. It's called positive 'communication.' And it's free.

55. MINIMIZE CONTACT

One very simple-sounding technique for managing the anger in our lives is to identify the people who provoke us the most and stay away from them.

As usual, this solution is not as simple as it seems. Neighbors have been known to shoot each other because of a fence a few inches over the property line. It is hard to stay away from people who live so close to us. We can use the technique of disengaging from their mischief. We can also reduce the time we spend in their company to a bare minimum. We do not have to waste hours of our lives listening to them scream insults in our face. We are in control of our feet. We can use them to walk away.

It is hard to minimize contact at work but, there too, we can choose to minimize our exposure to the boors and fools who clog up the hallways and elevators. We are not required to return insult for insult, nor to make them understand the error of their ways. We can choose to find other things to do with our time.

This is not *ignoring, snubbing, displeasing, avoiding,* or *copping out.* We are using our adult judgment to make appropriate choices in the real world. We can choose to let them go.

The same technique can be applied to relatives. We can see them when there is a family celebration or holiday, but we do not have to overdo it. We need not live in fear of displeasing them or of their gossip about us to the neighbors. We can choose to liberate ourselves from these carryovers from our childhood. We can let them go, too.

In American Psychology, this solution might be seen as "running away from the problem" or "failing to confront the issue head on,"

135

but we would say that every issue does not need to be confronted and resolved. That would be perfection. We can use our adult intelligence to tell us where to best invest our time and energy. We have done our Homework with these people and set an example of self-respect for them to follow if they choose. We can see now that they are not responding to treatment and so we are off the hook. They may be too far gone in their self-contempt to be turned around now. We have reached the conclusion that these mischief makers are not there for us and we are not required to be there for them. There is a limit to our responsibility for the party of the second part.

The Mother-Maker Syndrome

For example, if we have been going back home time after time, spending years of our lives trying to make our female parent into a warm, loving mother, then we need to examine our own motivations. This is a self-serving good intention, and it will not work the way we want it to. We are not accepting our parent the way she is but are trying to improve her deportment for selfish reasons of our own. The same principles apply to male parents and siblings. When we replace our good intentions for these people with more appropriate intentions for ourselves, we will find it easier to minimize our contact with people who take more out of our lives than they put into it.

We are not giving up in discouragement. We are just making more appropriate arrangements for ourselves, which we have every right to do. We are not selfish or negative. We are minusing a minus in our lives. That is not a minus; it is a plus. It is a real intention for our own sanity. (See "FAMILY-FREE DIET" on page 71. See "THE HAT TRICK, OR VOTING WITH YOUR FEET" on page 107.)

"For some people, life is a case of,
'I have cast my bread upon the waters
and it didn't come back toasted.'
It's very depressing."

Rudolf Dreikurs

56. THE "NO ONE CAN MAKE YOU ANGRY BUT YOURSELF!" PLOY

Every once in a while, you'll hear someone say on a talk show or in your kitchen, "No one can make you angry but yourself." This, too, is an anger mis-management technique. It is no more than a good intention on the part of someone who does not know what anger is or what to do with it. It is someone's way of saying, "I can cause you a grievance but it's your fault if you let it make you angry." That way, they win both ways and you lose both ways. It comes out even. Here is a statement you can use the next time someone pulls this trick on you.

"How does saying that make things better, Susie? It only makes things worse for both of us. It makes me angrier than I was before! I didn't get this angry all by myself, Susie. I had help. And you're it. First you keep me waiting forty minutes and then you tell me it's my fault for getting angry! That's not fair and it's not true. People make me angry all the time. They cause me a grievance and my legitimate anger kicks in. It's part of the human condition. Fortunately for me, I have learned to manage my anger like a grown-up. My anger attitudes from the past have been identified and replaced with mature attitudes towards people, towards life, and towards myself. I don't suppress my anger and I don't explode like a hand grenade. I don't get super-angry often. I mostly get angry somewhere in the middle — between the extremes.

"You have just wasted forty minutes of my life because you can't get your act together and that *waste* makes me angry. You *control* me into standing here like a dummy when I could have been doing my income tax. That's *not fair*, either. I don't keep *you* waiting. As an adult, it's my responsibility to show up on time to keep from hurting the people I love. It's the least I can do. Your difficulty in accepting responsibility for your own actions makes me angry, too.

"When I do get super-angry, it's not *me* making myself angry. It's my old attitudes and griefs from the past being triggered and rising

138

up to compound my anger in the present. It's not a matter of guilt, fault, or blame. That's absurd. That's a cop-out on your part. It was my responsibility to identify these old attitudes and put them in a more appropriate adult perspective. If I hadn't, I wouldn't be talking to you like a civilized human being. I'd be screaming in your face like I used to in the bad old days. It wasn't a matter of fault then, either. No one taught me how to express my anger the right way because I wasn't supposed to be angry in the first place. They didn't know how to manage their own anger in the second place. So it's no one's fault.

"There's no cure for fault, Susie. Blame doesn't make people better. It just tends to rob them of their self-respect and make them angrier. Unless they've had the course. It's a good thing I did or you'd be going to this movie by yourself. I just want you to know that if you keep me waiting more than fifteen minutes next time, there will be a consequence of your thoughtless behavior. I have a choice: I can go in by myself or I can go home. It won't be your fault. It will just be a preference on my part to use my own judgment and live my life on my own appropriate terms in the present. So, if you enjoy my company, it's up to you to show up on time or not. What could be fairer than that?"

57. NUMBING OUT

Some people complain of feeling *numbed out, trapped in a void.* They feel *cold* and *frozen.* It is a painful, scary sensation. They feel terribly out of control because they do not know how they got into this state nor how to get out of it. This numbed out state can last for hours, days or weeks. Such people may be able to put on a facade of competence and carry on their normal activities without revealing to others their underlying distress.

Herman is suffering from the Numbed Out Syndrome. His hyper-critical mother ridiculed and scorned everything he did. He was a good boy, but a little uncoordinated. Mother praised his younger brother, Carl, who could do no wrong. Little Herman was in pain from his feelings of inadequacy to cope. He couldn't do anything about anything.

His solution to the problem was to do nothing and feel nothing. His goal was not to achieve happiness, but to prevent further pain. His attitude became, *"Nothing ventured, nothing lost."*

To this day, Herman feels he cannot and dare not confide in anyone. He has learned from childhood that when he is emotionally distressed, the people he counted on to help him — his parents — will turn against him and make his situation even worse. He has acquired the conviction that the "helpers do not help." He may also have concluded that he must be strong and self-reliant. He must work these things out for himself *like a man*, which, of course, he does not have the emotional preparation to do. He is the prisoner of this good intention that he has for himself. Herman has not resorted to alcohol or drugs to relieve the pain of his existence. He is doing it the hard way: Cold sober. He is controlling his way through life, numbing himself out from the inside.

As a consequence of these counterproductive coping techniques, Herman has sealed himself off from other human beings. The worse it gets, the worse he gets. No wonder he feels trapped. He has defined control in terms of hanging on to everything and keeping it all in. He has become a walking Black Hole, letting nothing out and getting no relief from the mounting pressure of his counterproductive efforts to control his situation.

The day may come when the facade cracks. He can't keep it in and he can't let it out. He has an insoluble conflict. He may let go altogether and go berserk. He may kill someone or he may kill himself. His neighbors will say, "I don't understand it. He seemed normal yesterday."

This state can be understood as a consequence of mismanaged anger. The individual who does not respect himself has learned to feel that he is invalid and that his emotions are invalid, wrong and stupid. He has to deny the existence of such worthless emotions for fear of the negative consequences.

Vignette: Feeling No Pain

Herman has spent twenty years learning to deny the validity of his anger. He does such a good job of denying it that he can't find it anymore. It has gotten away from him. He loses sight of the connection between his legitimate anger on Monday, his cold fury on Tuesday and his numbed out feeling on Wednesday. He has an emotion trapped inside of him that will not go up or down. He does not have a handle on it and cannot get one. He cannot manage an emotion he cannot feel. He has succeeded all too well, but it is a negative success. In extreme cases, such as Herman's, the individual has gone beyond suppressing the experience of his painful anger. He has generalized his suppression and invalidation processes to all feelings and emotions. He has numbed himself out across the board.

The antidote to the numbed out feeling is to restore the connection between the individual's present distress and the original precipitating anger. We can do that by asking our focusing questions: *"Who are you angry at?" "What happened to make you angry?"* Since he has lost sight of his anger, he may have to be prompted to remember: *"What happened yesterday? What happened the day before?"* We continue this stimulus until his memory is jogged into making the connection. We need to be patient. His anger has congealed and it will take time to remelt. In the meantime, we are creating an atmosphere in which he feels encouraged to express his anger for the first time in twenty years. We may even have to lead him by the hand by saying something like, *"It must have made you angry when your boss told you to do your whole report over." "No, I'm not angry." Well, I'd be angry if I were you. I'd want to rip his lips off." "You would?"*

After we have succeeded in getting the juices flowing again, the next step is to hear him out and let him vent the anger that was not vented at the time of the grievance. In encouraging him to express his anger in detail, we are overcoming his tendency to deny his rage without even realizing he has done so. It is a bad habit, and he can learn to replace it with a better one.

By our actions and our example in hearing him out in an atmosphere of mutual respect, we are canceling out, to a small extent, the

141

lessons and attitudes he learned so many years ago. He is experiencing healthier, more liberating lessons in the present moment:

- "Some helpers do help."
- "It's all right to get angry and to express it openly."
- "The world will not come to an end if I let my feelings out."
- "Control does not mean suppressing and denying. It means taking life as it comes, and that includes taking anger-provoking situations as they come and dealing with them in the present."
- "I am not alone and abandoned in my time of distress. I have me and I am an equal member of the human race."
- I do not have to solve these problems all by myself to prove how independent and strong I am. I can ask for help when I need it, just like everyone else."
- I am an acceptable human being in spite of my unpleasant human emotions."
- I do not have to prove how strong I am by keeping my emotions in. As strong as I am, that is strong enough. I don't have to be any stronger than that."

Herman is now able to use his anger problems as an opportunity to outgrow his self-contempt and replace it with self-respect. It is hard for him to outgrow his childhood self-contempt in a social vacuum. He needs a self-respecting listener to set an example of moderation and self-acceptance for him to follow.

Among other things, Herman was finally able to admit his anger at God for taking his first wife, Marsha, after only three years of marriage. His anger at this loss was below the level of conscious awareness, but it was ruining his relationship with his new wife, Inga. She is in tears half the time.

After Herman's pent-up anger has been properly identified, expressed and drained, he is in a position to take some positive action in the real world. He has a power now he did not have before: The power of choice. He can write an anger letter to God. He can even accept his own contribution to Inga's distress as a regrettable human imperfection on his part and not as a crime to feel guilty about. He can choose to assume appropriate responsibility for rectifying the situation by apologizing to Inga for sniping at her for every least little thing. He can also choose to catch himself in the act of doing it and decide to stop. He can get closure now and feel relief from his unfinished business with God.

Vignette: I Can't Feel My Life.

Eva was numbed out. She didn't know how she felt and she didn't care how she felt. She didn't even care whether she cared or not. She didn't care about anything — her job, her family, her friends or herself. She didn't feel like living. She felt like quitting by committing suicide. But she couldn't do that, either. She didn't even care about dying.

Eva's Early Recollection #1:

"I was very sick when I was seven. I had an operation. My parents would come and visit me. My mother would try to comfort me, but all she could do was cry. My father got upset with her crying. He would wait out in the hall 'til she was ready to go home."

Attitude Analysis:

- "I have no one to comfort me. I have to comfort myself."
- "I don't want to be weak like my mother. My father despised her weakness and so do I."
- "Crying doesn't help. It only makes things worse."
- "I want to be strong like my father. That way, nothing can hurt me."

Eva's Early Recollection #2:

"After my operation, my mother and father fought, but they never kissed and made up any more. He was mean to her, like he didn't care about her. He called her "stupid." He would slam the door and leave. She would cry for a long time. I was scared he wouldn't come back."

143

Attitude Analysis:

- "Weak people, like my mother (and me), can be abandoned at any time."
- "It doesn't pay to be weak or to care about someone."
- "Someone can hurt you terribly just by leaving. I won't let myself care about anyone that much."
- "Women are out of control. They can be victimized by some-one strong."
- "Anger is painful and scary. It doesn't pay to get angry."

Eva used numbing out as her way of preventing these terrible things from happening to her. She thought she was controlling her emotions. She did not know any other example of control to follow, so she made up her own. It cost her dearly. She had no close friends. She could not feel her life.

She thought she was being strong. She did not know the difference between strength and phony strongness. She kept wondering, "If I am so strong, why can't I solve my problems?" She is now learning how to correct these very basic mistakes.

Eva is replacing these solutions with more appropriate ones. She is learning to control her anger by expressing it appropriately. When her co-worker took credit for a project she had worked on for a week, she said, *"It makes me angry when you do that, Ralph."* It took courage, but she did it. She overcame her scary fears of abandonment, displeasing, weakness and all the other facets of her self-contempt. In that moment, she felt like she was coming out of a shell, a shell she didn't know she was in. She had managed her emotions like an adult. She had taken the first step toward an identity as a three-dimensional, warm-blooded, grown-up human being.

58. THE ONE-TWO PUNCH

Once we tell them the truth about our anger, what do we suppose will happen? Will they kiss us on the cheek? Will they say, "Thank you for calling this to my attention?"

Certainly not. They will probably lash back with something to throw us off balance, to exonerate themselves at our expense, such as:

- "That's your problem."
- "You're always angry."
- "Who cares if you're angry?"
- "You are too sensitive."
- "You're crazy."

. . . and so on.

This is their way of solving the problem we have just created for them. They do not know how to solve anger problems, so they try to invalidate the whole thing out of existence. That way, they won't have to solve it. We call these comeback responses, *deflections*.

Our first step is to identify these rejoinders as mischief. They do not need to be said, but our mischief makers don't know what else to say. They haven't had the course. We do not take the rejoinder at face value as if it made sense. We do not say, "I am *not* always angry." That is walking into their trap. We have just been diverted from our anger path onto a dead-end street on their inappropriate terms. They win and we lose.

We can choose not take these remarks as if they were a reflection on our anger or our worth as a person. They are only firing for effect, to get us off their case. Their hurtful response has nothing to do with our worth as a person. We are worthwhile no matter what comes out of their mouth.

They feel inadequate to cope with our anger. They are seeking to relieve the pain of their own inadequacy by tearing us and our anger down. We do not have to let them get away with it. They wouldn't

145

really feel any better if we did. Nothing would be gained. We would both lose.

We can ask ourself, *"How has this mischief made me feel?"* The answer will come out: Angry.

Having identified their anger deflections as mere mischief, we can now go on to do the unexpected. We can tell the truth for a second time: *"You have just made it worse, Buster. I am angrier now than I was before."* That is the truth, too. That is the issue we need to be dealing with, not their nonsensical, phony deflections.

This technique is called the "One-Two Punch." After we have hit them with our anger in the first place, we are prepared in advance for their snappy comeback with a backup punch of our own.

They will be surprised by our resoluteness, competence and preparedness in these anger matters. They may even come to respect us and apologize for making us angry in the first place.

They may also try to deflect the one-two punch with another jab of their own. "Where did you get that stuff? Did you read it in a book somewhere?" That will make us angry, too, but we are prepared for it. *"You just did it again. You keep making it worse."* In so saying, we are letting them know we have no intention of letting these deflections throw us off course. These people do not usually get past our first backup punch, but we are ready for them if they try.

59. PATIENCE

Some of us want our own way and we want it now. We do not see why life does not give it to us. That makes us angry. Our impatience has several facets:

- "Life is supposed to give me what I want. My mother always did."
- "If I don't get what I want, I won't know who I am."

- "I can't wait. Waiting is a waste of time, and waste makes me feel like I am irresponsible, guilty, and out-of-control."

We are not only angry, we have made the mistake of taking this deprivation personally, which compounds our distress and confuses our judgment.

The antidote to our impatience is patience. If we can put our wants in a more moderate, mature perspective, we are more likely to get them. Not only that, but we will live longer and enjoy the wait a lot more. We can tell ourselves that we do not have to take the disappointment or delay personally. We are worthwhile human beings in spite of it in the meantime. While we are waiting we are not out-of-control altogether. We have the power of choice. We can choose to do something constructive while we are waiting. We can let go of the rope and do what we *can* do.

60. PEELING THE ANGER ARTICHOKE

As we have already discussed, people can learn to use focusing questions to pry off the upper layers of their emotional response and get at the fundamental issues which have been overlooked and neglected. We can learn to stop seeing anger as if it were an unstoppable flow of molten lava and choose instead to see it as an artichoke that can be peeled down with the right utensils and put to constructive, instead of destructive, use.

To peel back the layers of our friend's or loved one's anger, we begin with a focusing question such as, *"Who are you angry at?"* This question focuses their attention on the here and now and gives them permission to be angry. It expresses an intelligent, sincere concern on our part for them in spite of this unpleasant situation. It demonstrates that we are prepared, in control, and competent. These qualities are very reassuring in any crisis.

147

Vignette: The Good For Nothing Syndrome

Our friend Sara is angry about her job.

We can ask,

What happened to make you so angry?

"Sheila told the boss, Judy, I was in the cafeteria when I was really down on the fourth floor trying to trace an order she had lost."

Who are you angry at?

"At Sheila!"

What angers you the most at Sheila?

"Here I am, trying to save her bacon and she rats on me to Judy, who just loves to stick it to me. She knows I should have gotten that promotion instead of her."

That sounds like you are angry at being victimized in stereo.

"Darn right."

What angers you the most?

"That I was trying to help her out and she didn't appreciate it. Judy didn't appreciate it, either. She thought I was lying."

You felt your goodness was all for nothing. What angered you the most?

"It's so unfair. I was doing her a favor and she stabbed me in the back."

You are angry at this betrayal. Sheila and Judy both betrayed you. You are feeling like the victim of this unfairness. Who else are you angry at?

"I'm more angry at Judy. She has responsibilities. She should know how to manage people better than that."

You are angry at her irresponsibility. What else angers you?

"That there's nothing I can do about it."

Now you are angry at feeling powerless and out of control.

148

"I didn't realize that my anger was so complicated."

We're only halfway through. Who else are you angry at besides Sheila and Judy?

"There isn't anyone else. Wait. I'm angry at *myself* for knocking myself out all this time."

What angers you the most about yourself?

"It's that I must be stupid or something. I never learn. I'll probably do it again tomorrow. I'm such a pushover, and it's my fault."

Sara, when your goodness doesn't pay off fairly, you feel good for nothing, stupid and worthless. You are angry at yourself for letting it happen and for failing to prevent it.

"It's the story of my life. I remember taking my little brother to the park. When we got home, my mom bawled me out for not telling her where we went. I really got clobbered."

She didn't appreciate your consideration, did she? This is a recollection of feeling good for nothing, stupid and irresponsible in spite of your goodness in looking after your brother. Now, when something similar happens in the present that reminds you of this pain from the past, you feel your childhood worthlessness has been confirmed.

"Hasn't it?"

Not at all. You were not worthless then and you are not worthless now. You were an imperfect little girl doing what you thought was right. You meant well. It should have been rewarded, but your mother was not a rewarding kind of person, and you got short-changed. You were punished, instead.

"I keep setting myself up for it. That's stupid."

There is another explanation that has nothing to do with native intelligence. You are not doing this consciously or rationally. You are a good person and you do the right thing. But, there are times when people cannot appreciate what you do because they have negative feelings about themselves which prevent them from appreciating you or anyone else.

"That's right. They don't pat anybody on the back. Like it would kill them."

It would be inconsistent with their self-contempt. In the same way, you are consistently behaving in ways that maintain and confirm the roles you carried over from childhood into adulthood. It is not your fault that you do.

"I'm consistent all right. How can I stop?"

By replacing your role as The Good-for-Nothing Child with an adult identity of your own. It is called self-respect.

"I've never had a lot of that, I'll tell you. How do I get in on it?"

You earn it by doing Homework.

"What is that?"

Very often, it takes the form of doing the unexpected on your own terms instead of reacting to someone else's. Tell me, what does Judy expect you to do about your anger at her?

"She expects me to swallow it. That's what I've always done."

That's another role that you play: The 'Pleasing Child' who can never get angry.

"That's true. I never get angry."

Yes, you do. You just aren't aware of it and you don't show it. You suppress it and you never let anyone know it's down there, not even yourself.

"That sounds like me."

Now that you know what Judy expects, you can choose not to do it and do something else instead. What is the last thing Judy and Sheila expect you to do?

"I don't know."

The last thing they expect you to do is to tell the truth. To say, 'I'm very angry about what happened yesterday. I just want you to know how angry I am.'

150

"I couldn't do that."

Why not?

"It's too scary."

What scares you the most?

"They wouldn't like me."

They don't like you now! You are just their victim. Victims aren't very like-able.

"You're right."

What's the worst thing that could happen?

"Come to think of it, which I never did before, nothing would happen."

They wouldn't send you to your room, would they? They are not your mother, and you are not six years old. Can you say that to them tomorrow?

"I'm still not sure."

It's still scary, isn't it? It will be scary until after you have done it. What is it called when you overcome your scary fears from childhood?

"Fearlessness?"

But you are not fearless. You are afraid. It's called 'courage.' If you have no fears, you don't need courage.

"That's what I need. How do I get it?"

Courage is the willingness to take a risk. You don't wait until you get it. You go ahead and do it anyway.

"That's not easy."

Children do what is easy. Grown-ups do what is difficult.

"I'll do it."

Good. Afterwards, you will have feelings of accomplishment, success and the confidence that you can do it again.

151

"Sounds good to me. It's worth the risk. I have really learned a lot about myself from all these questions. They make me think about things I've never thought about before."

You knew the answers. You just didn't know that you knew them. We have used these focusing questions to make your unconscious fears and attitudes conscious. Now you can put your childhood carryovers into an adult perspective. You can see things more clearly now.

"That's how I feel — like I've been liberated from something that's been holding me back."

Liberated from what?

"From the me I used to be."

And what has taken its place?

"A feeling that I have an identity of my own. I can make my own choices now."

That feeling is called self-respect.

61. PHYSICAL EXERTION

Running around the block, punching a pillow, chopping wood, hollering down a rain barrel and throwing a rubber brick at the television set are all tried and true techniques for releasing the pain of your pent-up anger. Sometimes these activities release the energy generated by your adrenal glands as a physiological response to the provocation that made you angry. Your body prepared you for fight or flight. You do not do either one, but the energy is still down there looking for a place to go. For some people, working it off physically, one way or another, is a good third choice.

However, many people mistakenly believe that once the pent-up energy is worked off, the anger problem has been solved. They do not feel so frustrated because they have relieved the *"powerlessness"* component of their distress. They had the power of choice and they chose to pound their pillow or run around the block.

The anger component of their frustration, however, has not been relieved. It has not gone anywhere. That is why we recommend that after your workout, you identify the object of your anger, the nature of your grievance and sort it out as you are learning to do in these pages.

62. POWER OF CHOICE

We all know what frustration feels like, don't we? But we do not know what the word frustration means. They don't teach us this stuff in third grade. Maybe they should. Frustration can be defined as feeling *angry plus out-of-control*. Our anger compounds when we feel powerless to do anything about our powerlessness! We become angry at ourselves for our inadequacy to solve our problem and relieve our pain.

The specific antidote to our feeling of powerlessness is the feeling that we are *not* powerless. There are some powers we forgot we have. It is true that we cannot make our favorite TV star return our phone calls, but we are not totally out-of-control. There are other choices open to us. We can choose to call someone closer to home, to watch a different TV show or to use our judgment and solve our frustrating problem on a mature, creative basis. There is no law that says we cannot live our lives until we solve our frustrating problem perfectly. We can even choose to let go of it and do something else altogether.

Very often, the solution to the problem bubbles up after we have stopped trying so hard. The technique, then, is to stop operating out of attitudes and give ourselves a choice that we forgot we had and see what happens.

"For he who gives no fuel to fire
puts it out, and likewise he who
does not in the beginning
nurse his wrath and does not
puff himself up with anger
takes precautions against it
and destroys it."

- Plutarch

63. PREPARE IN ADVANCE, OR "THE FRONT STOOP TECHNIQUE"

We know what is waiting for us when we get home or to our mother-in-law's place. We can choose to barge right through that front door into a replay of the War of 1812 or we can choose to do something different for the first time in our lives.

For instance, we can choose to catch ourselves about to walk into that trap and decide instead to stand for a minute on the front stoop and collect our thoughts.

Even though we have encountered this domestic barrage a thousand times before, we are always caught by surprise! We will find ourselves saying things that a moment's forethought might have prevented. Now, *before* the barrage begins, we have the luxury of reminding ourselves that there is mischief ahead and that we can choose to disengage from it, that we are worthwhile human beings in spite of the issues that will be raised, and that we can give ourselves Emotional First Aid if the situation requires it, and it probably will.

We can, in addition, refresh our memory as to the life-lines that are available to us: "What Difference Does It Make,"(page 235) "Disengage From the Mischief," (page 53) "Agree With It" (page 29) or whatever techniques we are most comfortable with.

Thus forearmed, we are much better prepared to cope constructively and effectively with the encounter that awaits us. We can remind ourselves that we deserve to be happy and successful and that we can choose not to use this confrontation to bring about the unhappiness that worthless people deserve. We will be shifting gears in advance from the old, vulnerable us to the new, prepared us. Good luck favors the prepared.

64. PUNISHMENT

The word "punishment" comes from the Latin word *poena,* which means "pain." When someone causes us a painful grievance, we feel entitled to inflict pain in return. We justify our behavior by calling it "punishment," the implication being that the experience will benefit the miscreant's character and improve his deportment in the future. This is an overcompensatory good intention and only keeps us from feeling as guilty as we would otherwise.

When we punish children, we are teaching them they are wrong and guilty. They take their punishment personally, as a reflection on their worth as a person. They hold themselves worthless. They cannot respect people who are as guilty and wrong as they seem to be. With repeated punishment, children become convinced of their worthlessness and begin to behave accordingly. Their negative behavior is consistent with their self-contempt. They feel they do not *deserve* to behave positively.

Badness is not always what it seems to be. When there are two children in a family, both cannot be first best. One or the other is left to seek a place in the family constellation as the *First Worst Child.* This child is a magnet for punishment. The more punishment First Worsters receive, the more confirmed they are in their unhappy role.

Roger is not really a bad child. When the good sibling goes to camp, Roger moves into the vacant role and behaves very well. When the good child returns, Roger reverts to his previous role as First Worst. We call this dynamic, *"Musical Chairs."*

Wise parents do not play one child against the other. They do not say to Roger, "Why can't you behave like your sister Shirley?" In a way, this is like ordering the child to continue playing the role of the bad child. We are, in effect, reminding the child that we expect him or her to disobey us. The child obeys our order and disobeys. Punishment, then, like all good intentions, is counterproductive.

Self-respecting parents understand negative behavior as mischief. They do not take it personally and they do not overreact or under react. They understand mischief in terms of its purpose: To gain negative attention, gain power and control, get revenge, or withdraw in discouragement. The parents respond appropriately to the negative purposes and replace them with more positive purposes. For instance, they can give the child a choice between two positive activities. The third choice, making mischief, is not one of the options.

This approach requires time, energy and creativity. Parents who do not respect themselves do not trust their judgment. They do not value their own resources and feel inadequately prepared for the task of parenting. They are angry at their child and at themselves for their generic copelessness. They solve their problems all at once. They punish the child as if it were the child's fault that they cannot cope with the tasks of parenthood. The solution to the problem is not to control our children into mindless conformity, as they do in some cultures, but to replace the parents' own self-contempt with self-respect.

Self-respecting parents encourage all their children to respect themselves as worthwhile human beings in their own right. When Roger misbehaves, his parents institute a system of logical consequences. If Roger refuses to eat dinner, knowing that his indulgent parents will feed him from the refrigerator, they wise up. They disengage from his mischief and take away from him the power to control them. They set limits. They let him know that if he does not finish, there will be no snacks to assuage his hunger pangs later. They give him a choice: Eat now or wait until breakfast. It is his responsibility, not theirs. They involve the child in the procedure so he feels like an active participant, not a victim of unreasonable, all-powerful parents.

If Roger chooses not to eat and tests their resolve, the parents must make good on their agreement regarding snacks. Roger's consequence will be his hunger until the next morning. The issue here is not nutrition or inflicting pain, but securing the child's cooperation in running the household on an appropriate, civilized basis. Allowing children to dictate the rules to grown ups is not appropriate.

Another logical consequence of mischief is our anger. We can manage our child's behavior by saying, *"It makes me angry when you push your little sister down."* Our anger is a consequence that children can understand.

157

Adult Punishment

The punishment of adult offenders is notoriously inefficient and counterproductive. Some people, who are not too far gone in their self-contempt, respond positively to the imposition of fines and penalties. They are not a significant social problem.

People who suffer from extreme self-contempt, however, do not see punishment in the same perspective the others do. Their logic is upside down. They take pride in their negative accomplishments and seek confirmation of their role as First Worst in their families and in the community. Punishment proves they *can take it*, as if such things needed proving. People who feel inferior and inadequate inside need to prove to themselves and others that they are not weak, but strong. The more severe the punishment, the stronger they are seen to be. Self-respecting people are not deceived. We know the difference between strength and this phony, overcompensatory strongness.

These offenders make us angry. We try to make our punishments unemotional through the institution of an impersonal, unbiased judicial system, but that is just a good intention that we have for ourselves. We wish to appear impartial and free of vindictiveness. We have yet to impose a system of logical consequences whereby a thief knows in advance that if he is caught, he will have to make financial restitution to those he robbed. Under our present system of jurisprudence, he gets to keep the money. We do not have a system of active remorse. Victim and victimizer are prevented from seeing each other as human beings.

Offenders are sent to a correctional institution where they are further dehumanized and robbed of the last vestiges of their self-respect. Their perception of themselves as worthless is confirmed and, when they return to the community, their behavior will be consistent with their enhanced self-contempt.

George Clemenceau once said that war was much too important to be left to the generals. We could as easily say:

- The law is much too important to be left to the lawyers.
- Justice is much too important to be left to the judiciary.
- Correction is much too important to be left to the correctors.

158

65. RATIONALITOSIS

Marvin deals with his anger by rationalizing it away: "Oh, I'm sure he didn't mean to kick me in the knee. It was an accident," or "I miss my stereo set, but the man who stole it must have needed it more than I did. I just hope he likes good music."

This is an abuse of one's rational thought processes and a flagrant misuse of the mental faculties we were born with. Marvin does it, not because he is stupid, but because that is how he solves his potentially dangerous anger problem. If he allowed himself to feel his legitimate anger, he might have to do something rash, like stand up for himself. However, if he can deny his anger out of existence by using his "higher mental capacities," he can prevent the scary things that happen to people who expose their secret anger for everyone else to see.

Everyone assumes he is rational. Sometimes (as in Marvin's case), there is no basis for that assumption, but we assume it anyway. The truth is that there are two kinds of people in the world: 1) Those who are sane and rational, and 2) Those who only imagine they are. We need an absurd word to distinguish the pseudo-rational folks in group 2 from the sane people in group 1. Since there is no word in the English language at present that will discriminate between these two categories of mental functioning, we have decided to call the process whereby people diagnose their own sanity without a license, "rationalitosis."

Marvin's rationalizing does not relieve his anger. He only thinks it does. His anger is still there. It is accumulating and making him sick. Someday, he will reach a point where he cannot rationalize it away anymore. They will call it a *"nervous breakdown."* It has nothing to do with nerves. It has to do with faulty attitudes that clash with the demands of everyday living. After years and years of unsuccessful clashing, the accumulation of grief, despair, self-anger and self-contempt cannot be denied away any more. It overwhelms the senses. The faulty coping mechanisms collapse. The system crashes.

Marvin's mistaken attitude is: "Any problem can be solved rationally if I just put my mind to it." But emotional problems, such as anger, grief and guilt, cannot be solved rationally. We are not objective about our subjective feelings. We have feelings about our feelings. We have attitudes and expectations that were formed in our childhood, and they cannot be reasoned away because we are not aware that they exist. It is irrational to believe they can be overcome by our higher intellectual faculties and disposed of. Some problems must be solved subjectively, but the schools do not teach their students how that is done.

Marvin can learn to accept his anger as a legitimate part of his makeup. He can then go on to the next step of peeling his anger down into its many components so he can understand each one of them and relieve them properly. He can learn to replace mistaken attitudes with appropriate ones. These successes will provide him with a way of replacing his self-contempt with self-respect. That is rational problem solving. That is Anger Intelligence.

66. REDUCE IT TO ABSURDITY

Most of the things we argue about are trivial. That is because the subject of the argument is not the real issue. The issue is something farther down in our psyche, such as, "I want my way and you're not giving it to me." It is absurd to argue about issues that aren't even the issue. If you can find the absurdity in an argument, which is an unpleasant waste of time for everyone, you can break the tension with laughter. We aren't laughing at the other person, only at the absurdity in which we find ourselves.

Sam and Janet were late for a doctor's appointment. Sam was barreling down the freeway while Janet was upbraiding him for taking so long to fill up at the gas station. "Let me out of this car, right now," she demanded. In the old days, Sam would have taken this absurd demand at face value, as if Janet expected him to take her overreaction literally. He would have responded with a nonrational retort of his own such as, "Don't be stupid," as if this were a matter of I.Q. This time, he didn't make the mistake of taking her inappropriate demand personally or literally. He was able to shift his attitudinal gears. He chose to reduce her imperious command to the absurdity it was. He said, "Wait 'til I get'er up to 100 miles an hour." They both laughed. The anger bomb was defused. The tension was relieved in a safe way and rendered harmless.

67. RIDING IT OUT

Under the stress of someone else's anger attack, we feel compelled to do something even if it doesn't make sense and makes things worse. We are trying to forestall any accusation that we are slackers or cowards under fire: "What will the neighbors think if I just stand there like a dummy?"

So we go into overdrive and say to the person, "Don't be angry. You'll have a heart attack," or "Calm down. Everything will be all right." Well, it won't. We are not dealing rationally with the real issue, which is that this person has a legitimate grievance and it needs to be addressed. We are doing something about their anger, but it isn't something that needs to be done. We are trying to suppress it because it is so uncomfortable for *us*. It is self-indulgent, well intentioned mischief. Our unconscious motivation to look useful has nothing to do with coping effectively with a person's rage. It has nothing to do with solving problems in the real world. We are solving fictitious problems that do not need to be solved. We are escaping from our feelings of *copelessness* into mindless, counterproductive *busy-ness*.

When we feel inadequate to cope, we feel compelled to say such things as, "Stop that this instant" or "Don't you dare talk to me like that." We give ourselves the illusion of activity although we are doing nothing to make things better. We behave as if such well-intentioned activity were better than no activity at all. It isn't. It is worse. We feel as though we have to do something; we just don't know what. Maybe there is no such have to.

The antidote to our counterproductive strategy becomes apparent immediately. The opposite of doing something is *not* doing something. It is a choice we did not realize we had. Twenty-five hundred years ago, the Buddha told his followers: "Don't just do something, stand there." This is difficult advice for activists like ourselves to take. We are impatient to put the problem behind us, but our counterproductive actions are like pouring kerosene on the flames. They only make the problem worse.

We call this technique of doing nothing, which runs counter to our innermost strivings, Riding It Out. Sometimes we can expedite the healing of an anger attack by listening and by validating the others' grief simply by our unobtrusive presence. We may nod our head in sympathy, empathize with their distress, but we are not jumping up and down like a jack-in-the-box trying to relieve our feelings of inadequacy and copelessness in ways that increase their pain.

Sometimes our forbearance on these occasions allows other people to come up with an appropriate solution to the anger problem sooner than they would have otherwise. We have gotten out of their way. We have created an atmosphere in which problem solving is possible. That is not doing nothing, that is doing something. Their solution to this problem will be better for them than any of our well-intentioned but ill-advised interventions would ever be.

68. ROAD RAGE

Road rage is violence looking for a place to happen. There is no violence without anger. These people are mismanaging their anger at seventy miles an hour. The issue is not speed limits or rules of the road. The issue is high speed mischief on the part of unself-respecting, self-destructive rebels without a cause. Their self-contempt will be the death of them — and the unfortunate family of four that crosses their path.

We understand road rage as mischief. It doesn't need to be done. They do it because they have negative purposes in the service of their self-contempt. They need negatively exciting mischief to drown the pain of their self-anger and self-contempt.

They are fulfilling one or all of the four purposes of mischief:

- They get *attention* from driving crazy on the freeway that they cannot get any place else. It's negative attention, but it proves they exist.
- They get *power and control* over their two-ton vehicle and through that, have power and control over the other motorists who are bullied into pulling over and getting out of their way.
- They get *revenge* by screaming imprecations at the drivers around them, honking their horn, blinking their lights and then pulling away free of guilt, responsibility, or consequences — until someone phones the State Police with their license number.
- This results in enforced *withdrawal* from the adult tasks and responsibilities of life for thirty days.

The antidote is not more Drivers Ed. It is Anger Ed. These people can attend Anger classes to learn who they are really angry at and why. They can learn how to excrete their anger in the right way and spare the rest of us the annoyance and invalidation, the powerlessness, the hurt and the discouragement that their mobile mischief is causing us.

69. SCAPEGOATS

When life makes us angry, we look for someone to take the burden of pain off our shoulders. When we feel burdened by guilt, we displace our painful emotion onto the head of someone who is powerless to do anything about it. When we are feeling both angry and guilty, we must find a scapegoat we can use as an outlet for energies that threaten to blow us up from the inside.

"I can't feel my life."

Carrie Fisher
Post Cards From The Edge

In ancient times, superstitious, societies used to tie their grievances to the horns of a goat and throw it over a cliff. It made them feel a lot better, but it was hard on the goat.

During the dark ages, impoverished individuals would hire themselves out as "sin eaters," consuming food that held the sins of those preparing the food. Having taken on the wrongs of others, they would then be punished by the people.

In more recent years, a modern technological society felt guilty and angry about losing its previous world war. It tied its anger and guilt around the neck of a helpless segment of its population. As a matter of national policy, it threw its own citizens into gas ovens. This advanced society, too, was looking for fast relief from its collective pain in ways that did not work in the long run. This society had failed to evolve. Its veneer of civilization was very thin.

Looking for scapegoats is a syndrome. It is a combination of pathological attitudes that occur together. These attitudes may or may not be conscious, but they determine the scapegoater's behavior just the same. These attitudes were acquired in the past, but they are applied in the present where they do not conform with the demands of reality. They override reality for a short while and the internal pressure is relieved temporarily. However, reality has not been dealt with appropriately and the pressure will build up again. The individual will eventually die without ever having lived.

These are some of the attitudinal components of the Scapegoater Syndrome:

- "I am not a victim anymore. My scapegoat is the victim now."
- "I am the victimizer, which hurts a lot less."
- "I am not powerless, for I have the power to victimize."
- "I am not out of control. I am *in* control. I am making this victimization happen."
- "I am not an inferior loser. I am a superior winner. I am superior to this wretch!"
- "I am not wrong. I am right."
- "I am not worthless. My victim is worth even less than I am."

166

"Don't just do something,
stand there."

Buddha

- "My problem is not insoluble, for I have just solved it."
- "I do not have to change and grow. That is too scary. I can stay just the way I am forever."
- "I am not responsible for my own downfall. Others are to blame. I am exempt from responsibility."
- "I am angry. I need a safe outlet for my anger, and you're it."

What do all of these attitudes have in common? They are all over-compensations for feelings of inferiority and inadequacy to cope. Overcompensation, in turn, is characteristic of people who feel inferior and hold themselves in contempt.

Gloria was the scapegoat in her family. Her father and three brothers were angry at their mother for her cruelty. They didn't dare confront her directly, so they dumped their anger on Gloria, who strongly resembled her. As often happens, the scapegoat turned out to be the strongest member of the family. The other members of the family were enabled to maintain their sanity at her expense. She nearly cracked under the strain, but she did not.

Gloria needed support and encouragement after she emerged from the ordeal of her childhood. She learned she could choose to do Homework in her own behalf. As she did what pleased her and disengaged from the mischief of others, she overcame her fear of expressing her anger. In place of her role as the world's scapegoat, she experienced an identity of her own as a worthwhile human being in spite of her faults and imperfections. Her family members came to see her in this new light. She had independence and courage. They respected her. She had earned it. The scapegoating stopped.

The antidote to looking for a scapegoat is self-respect. Self-respecting people do not have to solve their emotional problems on the backs of people who had nothing to do with the case. They do not deny their contribution to their own distress and do not take their setbacks as reflections on their worth as a person. They can accept their imperfection and learn from their mistakes. Each time they bounce back from a reversal on the basis of new information and insight, they grow as individuals and strengthen their self-respect. They feel competent to solve problems in ways that work.

Do's and Don'ts

- If you seek out scapegoats and wish to outgrow this carryover from kindergarten, remember that you can be angry at what happened or at the individual who caused you this grievance. However, you need not be angry at yourself for being imperfect. You can choose to accept your imperfection. You are worthwhile in spite of it.

- When you make this change in your attitude, your anger at yourself will be released in the right way. If your anger at yourself is not down there, it cannot blow you up from the inside. You will not have to release your anger at the expense of a fellow human being or family pet.

- You can choose to respect yourself in spite of what happened. A mistake in judgment is not a crime. It's only a reflection of your human imperfection. You are not a criminal. You cannot build yourself up by tearing yourself down with self-criticisms or by tearing others down, either.

- Catch yourself about to use your spouse, child or co-worker as a scapegoat and choose not to. Ask yourself a focusing question: *"Who am I really angry at? How can I express this anger in a way that will give me the relief I need?"*

- If you are the scapegoat, catch yourself taking your current setback as if it were a victimization. Victims are inferior and worthless. You cannot respect such people. You can only hold them in contempt. You can ask yourself, *"Am I perceiving victimization where no victimization is required in the real world? This is only mischief. I can disengage from it."*

- Catch yourself taking this negative situation personally, as a wipeout of your self-respect. You are not a powerless, out-of-control victim anymore. It's over. You have the power of choice. You can choose to perceive what happened as one of the ups and downs of life that occurs in an imperfect world. You can say, *"It makes me angry when you dump your problems on me."* This is telling the truth. It takes courage. They respect people who have courage. They will find themselves a safer scapegoat. You're no fun anymore.

169

70. SENSE OUT OF NONSENSE

When we are fighting, we often make the mistake of taking nonsense seriously and trying to make sense of it. "You're wrong." "No, you're wrong." This approach is not productive. We have to be smarter than that.

Smarter often means *hearing the sense behind the nonsense.* "You're wrong," often means, "I am angry at you for what you did." The issue is not rightness or the absence thereof, but the other person's anger. That being the case, it is smarter to address the real issue so it can be resolved: *"I'm sorry you're so angry. Tell me what I did to make you so angry."*

Vignette: I Have To Understand Myself

Carla overheard Jeff and Lorraine talking in the employees lounge. Lorraine was saying, "How can they fire Steve? I can't get my work done without him." Jeff replied, "Never mind Steve. I'd worry about my own job if I were you."

Lorraine got up and stormed out of the room. Carla felt bad for both of them. She does not like to see people unhappy. She was about to go into her old routine of calming Jeff down by explaining Lorraine's underlying motivation to him, so the whole thing would make sense to him.

She caught herself just in time. She realized that Jeff wasn't interested in sense or motivation. He had his own agenda and it did not include rational thought processes. She realized that she didn't understand Jeff's vulnerabilities well enough to explain anything to him. She also caught herself feeling responsible for solving other people's anger problems, which she had no real responsibility to do. Instead, she chose to let Jeff continue to think what he thinks. She didn't feel guilty, irresponsible or out of control. She had made an appropriate choice in her own head. No one knew about it but her, but it was an accomplishment just the same. She had let go of old habits and roles she used to play in grammar school and didn't need anymore. She saw how much nonsense there was in the world around her. She had no obligation at all to make sense of it for anyone but herself. She decided to lay her burden down. She felt relief, independence, security within herself and all the other facets of self-respect.

71. SECOND LETTER TECHNIQUE

We tell people that it helps to make their anger external and visible by writing their spouse, mother, father, boss or child an anger letter. We tell them to let all their old anger out, pull out all the stops, call them all the bad things they couldn't call them at the time. This is relevant *venting* (page 217). It is directed at its appropriate object in a controlled, managed way. Carrying out ones choice to pick up a pen and move it on a piece of paper is a life affirming accomplishment in the real world. They are getting it out of their head and their bloodstream. They are giving themselves permission to make their anger tangible and concrete in the real world so they can get it out of their system for the first time in their lives. We want them to be able to see their angry words in front of them so their higher thought process can comprehend them and put them in a rational perspective.

When we suggested to Blanche that she write her vindictive mother an anger letter, she said, "I could never do that. It would break my mother's heart."

To which we replied:

She doesn't mind breaking your heart three times a week, does she?

"I still can't do it."

What would prevent you?

"I'd feel guilty."

Of what crime?

"I don't know."

You'd feel guilty of the crime of displeasing, which is the greater misery. You prefer the lesser pain of keeping your anger in for a lifetime to the even greater pain of displeasing your overcritical mother who doesn't mind displeasing you at all.

"That doesn't make it right."

It's not a matter of right and wrong. It's not a matter of getting even or beating her at her own game. It's a matter of living on your terms and not hers because her terms aren't appropriate. It's a matter of declaring your independence as a self-respecting person in your own right. That is the third choice.

"I still can't do it. I'd be too scared."

It causes you anxiety just thinking about it. You feel out of control and that's scary. But that is what happens when you live on someone else's invalid terms instead of your own valid ones. Would you like to start living on your terms? It will take courage now.

"I don't have that much courage."

It's not your fault you have been discouraged by your parents since childhood. Who has to encourage you?

"I do, but I don't know how."

*Would it help if you had a **choice**?*

"To write her an anger letter or not?"

That's too hard a choice for you right now. What if there's a third choice?

"I don't see how."

You're too close to it. You haven't learned what your options are as a self- respecting, independent person yet. The third choice is to write your first letter and get it out of your bloodstream. You can then choose to write her a cleaned- up version that you can send her if you wish.

"I don't have to send it?"

172

Do you see that you didn't know you had that choice open to you? Your old attitudes were in the way and you couldn't use your rational thought processes to solve the problem. When you operate out of adult judgment, instead of attitudes, all kind of choices open up.

"Is my time up? I have some letter writing to do. Do I have to send the second one?"

"Have to" is an old attitude. We are replacing it with adult judgment and the power of choice. It's your choice to send it or not. You're living on your own terms. You're not quite used to it yet.

"I'm out of stamps. Have you got any stamps?"

72. SHOULDING

We expect people to do what they should do and we become very angry at them when they do not. We attempt to relieve our anger by reminding them that they did not do what they should have done and that they should do it in the future. This process is called "Shoulding." It is another example of a mindless good intention. It does not work because we neglect to determine the offender's purpose in not doing what should have been done.

Maybe they did not do it because they knew we would erupt like a volcano if they didn't. Well, we just confirmed their expectations. They are making mischief and we are paying off. Telling them what they *should* do is irrelevant to their underlying purpose, which is to get our goat. They have the power to do it and we have given it to them.

Like all good intentions, shoulding is *self-indulgent*. Its true purpose is not to improve the offender's behavior in the future, but to make ourselves feel morally superior to them. This is our way of overcompensating for our own feelings of inferiority. Our anger at the other person has a note of moral indignation and righteousness which is hard for them to refute. It makes positive communication between equal members of the human race impossible.

"I am not required to finish the task;
neither am I permitted
to put it down."

Hillel

Like all good intentions, shoulding is also *counterproductive*. People resent our superior airs and the implication that they are too stupid to know what they should have done or too lazy to do it. This, too, precludes cooperative problem solving.

What does "should" mean? *Should is merely a preference.* Children should pick up their toys so we do not step on them. It is a preference, not a moral crime when they fail to do so. They are not guilty, merely imperfect. It is our responsibility to bring about the desired behavior by securing positive cooperation instead of negative rebellion.

Vignette: You Should Walk the Dog

Marcy loved her dog — she just didn't love to walk it. Her mother kept telling her that she should walk the dog. Marcy already knew she should. That was not the problem. The problem was that she didn't want to. Her mother's nagging did not succeed in making her want to.

Marcy was 18 years old. She wanted it both ways: All the advantages of adulthood plus her exemptions from childhood. She was on the cusp of growing up. She didn't see why she shouldn't have what she wanted.

Her mother learned to stop nagging Marcy about the dog. When Marcy next said, "I don't want to," her mother was ready for her. She used our technique of *agreeing with it* (page 29). She said, "I know you don't want to. *Do we only do what we want? Grown-ups do what is required. Even if you don't want to, do it anyway.*"

Mother didn't get into a power struggle over the time of the dog walking. Marcy could choose when to do it. If she didn't do it, there would be a logical consequence: The dog would have to stay at her married sister's house for a week.

Marcy chose to do what reality requires dog owners to do. She made it a growth opportunity. She assumed responsibility for her pet and for herself. She felt she had made a mature decision in her own behalf. She was outgrowing her childhood exemptions and replacing them with something better: Self-respect.

Do's and Don't's

- Do not stand in moral judgment on people who fail to do what they should do. They are not wrong, merely imperfect. You are no more perfect than they are.

- You have the right to your preference, and so does the other person. Perhaps you need to find out what those preferences are so you can work out a compromise. Catch yourself assuming their preferences are invalid and inferior to your own. Maybe they knew something you don't know. Maybe they are making mischief. Maybe they are operating out of attitudes that need to be identified and changed in the right way.

- Use logical consequences to shape behavior in the desired direction. Catch yourself protecting people from the consequences of their irresponsibility. Let them experience the negative aftereffects. Do not reward them by putting on an emotional fireworks display for them.

- When people *should* on you, do not take it personally. You are a worthwhile human being in spite of what did or did not happen. Your worth as a person is not the issue; do not make it so.

You might ask yourself what your purpose was in not doing what should have been done. Did reality prevent you from doing it or did you have purposes of your own? Were these purposes positive or negative? If they were negative, then you were just making mischief. Mischief making is a preference too, in a way. It just isn't a very constructive preference. Do not be surprised if the outcome is negative.

73. THE SILENT TREATMENT

The *Silent Treatment* is not to be confused with the techniques of *Riding It Out* (page 162) or *Admirable Restraint* (page 27). This technique, unlike those, is not appropriate for the reality of the situation. The Silent Treatment is immature, inappropriate and counterproductive. It is not positive communication, but negative communication.

Dan's silence is sending Florence a message, "I won't talk and you can't make me." Florence is getting it loud and clear.

When Dan gets angry, he goes into his *control mode*. He shuts down and clams up. Florence used to pound on his chest, "Speak to me, Dan." His lips were sealed. He was a fortress under siege. He would not crack.

In the second grade, we used to call this "sulking and pouting." Over the age of twelve, it is the "Silent Treatment" or the Big ST, as we call it for short in the anger biz.

Dan has found that he cannot control very much in this world, but he sure can control his lips. As a kid, he could hold his breath until he turned blue. His mother caved in every time. Now it is Florence who is under his power, pleading for mercy, putty in his hands.

At the same time he is accomplishing his power and control purpose, he is also punishing her for offending him. He is getting revenge on her in a way that leaves no visible scars. If she were to complain about his immature anger management technique, he can say, in all innocence, "What did I do? I didn't say anything!" Maybe that is the problem. Maybe he should have said something.

Florence has learned to take away from Dan the power to drive her nuts with his mischief. She knows now that her life will go on whether this bozo talks to her or not. She can now say, *"Could it be that you will talk to me when you are good and ready? That's all right I am going to the movies. Maybe we can have a chat when I come back. Or not."*

She can also choose to tell Dan the truth about herself: *"It hurts me when you clam up like that. If you continue to hurt me like this, there may be a consequence that you will not care for. It is entirely up to you."* This technique is called "Giving Him a Choice."

74. SOMATIZATION

We all know what happens when Uncle Harry gets angry. His face turns beet red, his eyes pop out, the vein in his forehead starts throbbing, he stutters and sputters. That is somatization. His anger is manifesting itself somatically, that is, physically. "Soma" means "body," and our anger affects our body more than we realize.

When we become angry, our body prepares itself for a crisis. We prepare for fight or flight. Our adrenal glands start to secrete energy-giving adrenalin, our digestive system shuts down, and our heart pumps faster to get blood into the extremities where it is needed. We are all afraid that Uncle Harry is going to have a cardiovascular accident some-day if he doesn't calm down. We used to call these accidents "apoplectic strokes," which heightened the association between the somatic event and the strong emotion that precipitated it.

Heart researchers at Duke University recently discovered that it isn't only the erupting volcanoes like our uncle who die of anger-related physical disorders. People who silently fume over their griev-ances are doing themselves in as well. In fact, the researchers are now saying that mismanaged anger ranks with cigarette smoking, obesity and high-fat diets as a major factor in fatal heart disease. They found from standardized tests that women who showed signs of suppressed anger were three times more likely to die over the 18-year study period as women who did not show high anger levels.

Another study, with lawyers, showed that only 4% of the easygo-ing subjects died by the age of 50, while those who ranked in the upper 25% of the hostility chart suffered a mortality rate five times as high: One in five subjects died. In 1988, almost 100,000 Ameri-cans died of cardiovascular diseases. How many of them might have been saved by teaching them how to express their anger in the middle ground between erupting and suppressing?

Researchers have found that college students with high anger scores tend to have elevated levels of low-density lipoprotein, the "bad" cholesterol; and abnormally low levels of high-density lipoprotein, the "good" cholesterol. This imbalance increases the risk of cardiovascular disease in later years. The arteries grow stiffer, the heart muscle weakens, the liver and kidney are damaged, and too much fat is released into the bloodstream. The system cannot tolerate this internal abuse, a weak spot ruptures, and the individual suffers the consequences of fifty years of mismanaged anger. Death from a heart attack is the ultimate somatization.

Dr. Bernie Siegel has written about the effects of the mind on human physiology. As a cancer doctor, he sees malignancy as "partly a reaction to a set of circumstances that weaken the body's defenses." He describes two kinds of depressed patients: Those who give up and withdraw from normal activity and those who "continue with their routines" and put on a "show of happiness, when on the inside their lives have come to lack all meaning."

Both types of depressed patients have one thing in common: They are both mismanaging their anger. They are keeping that energy inside instead of letting it out in appropriate, healthy ways. In most cases of depression, the individuals are angry at themselves and they do not even know it. When they say they do not feel angry, they are telling the truth. That's the problem. Their anger has turned to depression.

Dr. Siegel describes a typical cancer patient as experiencing "a lack of closeness to his parents" (unbelonging, abandonment); a lack of the kind of unconditional love (I am unlovable) that could have assured him of his intrinsic value" (I am worthless); and an inability to overcome challenges (I feel inadequate to cope). Such people tend to view themselves as stupid, (Stupiditude) clumsy, weak and inept despite real achievements that are often the envy of classmates (Whatever I do, it isn't good enough).

These aspects of the typical cancer patient are all facets of self-contempt. When we have the twin determinants of mismanaged anger at the self plus a context of self-contempt, they place our organism under severe stress. We can see how this stress would, after many years, result in a breakdown of the body's defenses. The resulting malignancy is, in a way, an outcome of the individual's lifelong, self-destructiveness, which arises out of the conviction that "worthless" people do not deserve to live and be happy; they only deserve to suffer and die. They are arranging to fulfill their prophecies of disaster.

Do's and Don'ts:

- Do not live on other people's terms. Live on your own terms as a worthwhile human being in spite of your faults and imperfections.

- Do not live in fear of displeasing other people. That is dependency. Do what pleases *you* for a change.

- Do not store up your anger until you explode. Express your anger appropriately at the time, one way or another.

- If you cannot tell the person who caused you the grievance that you are angry, tell someone else whom you can trust.

- Do not use euphemisms for your anger. You are not "bothered" or "upset." You are "angry."

- If you cannot express your anger orally, write it out in the form of an anger letter (page 32), draw an anger picture (page 66), or talk into a tape recorder.

- Do not suppress your anger for fear of being called "weak." Emotions are not a weakness. We are not made of stone. Emotions are a legitimate part of the human condition and they need to be managed constructively.

- Do not let your anger control you. You can choose to manage it in positive ways. Your anger has no brains. You do.

- Be open to risks. It takes courage to overcome the fears of a lifetime. Courage is the willingness to take a risk. After we take the risk, we often find it wasn't so scary after all. If we don't take it, we will never know.

- Write *yourself* an anger letter. You are angrier at yourself than you realize. You may not feel angry, but it is down there below the level of conscious awareness. Sometimes it helps to just start writing to yourself about some of your childhood "sins" of omission and commission. Not only do you feel guilty, but you are angry at yourself for *allowing* these things to happen — as if

181

you could have prevented them. Once you start writing in this frame of mind, a process of association begins and one thing leads to another. Get it all out. If you get tired, you can stop for today and write some more tomorrow. You do not have to do it perfectly. It will be good enough as it is.

75. SORTING IT OUT

When people get angry, they often do things that do not need to be done, like yelling, screaming, cursing, hitting, abusing, threatening, stabbing, shooting and so on. Some of this mischief can be very scary indeed. With practice, serious students of anger management can learn to disengage emotionally from this useless flak so they can intervene appropriately and effectively. This does not mean they are ignoring the mischief. Not at all. They know exactly what is going on and they are choosing to focus their efforts on the kernel of legitimate anger that triggered this attack in the first place. They know there is a grievance down there somewhere. It is their task to cut through the barrage of mischief and get to the real issue so they can put it in perspective and relieve it. They can say, *"You must be very angry. What happened to make you so angry?"* (See "PEELING THE ANGER ARTICHOKE" on page 147.).

76. SPANKING

Parents have been spanking kids since time began. Here again, there are two ways of doing it: The wrong way and the right way.

These are some of the wrong ways:

- Spanking a child as a release for your pent-up anger.
- Spanking a child indiscriminately for no reason that he or she can see.

"Do we only do what is easy?
Children do what is easy;
grown-ups do what is difficult."

Rudolf Dreikurs

- Waiting for father to come home six hours after the fact, which creates unhealthy anxiety in the child.
- *Pounding sense* into a child for his or her own good.
- Spanking a child to teach him morality. "Spare the rod and spoil the child" does not mean "beat the tar out of him for his spiritual well-being." That is bullying. That is cowardice. That is overkill. That is an immoral good intention.

We must not victimize our children for our own unhealthy purposes. Children have a way of paying us back when they are six feet tall. They might repay us by brutalizing our grandchildren or not calling us on our birthday — or any other day. Another way is to self-destruct. That will teach us a lesson we will never forget.

We define spanking as *a swat on the behind*. Spanking a child to set limits on out-of-control behavior is the right way. Giving them a choice between behaving and misbehaving, with its consequent spanking, is the right way. If the child tests us to see if we mean it, we must not flunk the test.

Spanking should be a *logical* consequence (page 126) of the child's own behavior, but if we are angry at what happened, we are not going to think in terms of logical consequences. We are going to overreact out of our own inappropriate anger attitudes disguised as good intentions, such as, "I'm doing this for your own good. Some day you'll thank me for this!" We need to manage our own anger before we make this decision to intervene negatively in our child's life. We want to teach them the right lessons, not the wrong ones.

When we are illogical and punitive, we teach our children that people are unreasonable and unpredictable. They cannot trust such people and they have no effective defense against them. We cannot improve their behavior by betraying their trust.

When we give our Susiebelle a swat for running out into the street, she gets the connection between her behavior and the consequence. We are not victimizing her or making her feel worthless. We are trying to get her attention. This is not negative attention. It is not our self-serving good intention. It is a real intention on the part of a self-respecting concerned parent. We want to change the behavior, not destroy her self-respect. If we tear down her self-respect, she will hold herself in contempt and behave accordingly. Our efforts will be counter-productive. We will find ourselves doing more spanking than we had planned to do.

77. STAY ANGRY

After a few seconds or minutes, anger can begin to transmute into unhealthy by-products, such as depression, anxiety, obsessing, paranoia, eating disorders, suicidal impulses, substance abuse, etc. We are then stuck with these by-products, for we have lost sight of the anger we had ten minutes before. This Stay Angry technique reminds us that our original anger was a healthy, legitimate emotion. If we can stay angry and manage it properly before it goes sour, we can spare ourselves the pain of these self-destructive derivatives. We can choose to stay angry until our anger dissipates, as healthy anger does after a short while. Then we don't have to stay angry anymore. We can let it go. This is called: Riding It Out (page 162).

78. STRESS

We define stress as *the consequence of exceeding our ability to adapt.* We try to do too much too soon. We try to go higher, farther and faster while sitting in our office or raising our child.

There are two obvious ways of relieving stress. Pretending it is not there is not one of them:

1. We can manage our external environment so it does not exceed our ability to adapt to it. For example, we can chose to play eighteen holes of golf instead of thirty-six.

2. We can improve our ability to adapt to the experiences of everyday life. We can start by identifying the attitudes and convictions from

185

childhood that are still impeding our competence to cope, and getting rid of them. We can get out of our own way.

"Stress" was invented in 1946 by Dr. Hans Selye at McGill University in Montreal, Canada. Before that we did not have stress. We had aggravation. Aggravation was a much more descriptive word than the current terminology, which is more clinical and sterile. Aggravation means weightiness or heaviness. It also implies an anger at having this weightiness on our backs or in our stomachs. It connotes a grinding and gnawing that eats us up alive. The new nomenclature is more attractive and it protects us from such unpleasant, earthy associations. Stress is high tech while aggravation is no tech at all.

We see stress as arising out of frustration, which we define as *anger plus powerlessness to do anything about it.* This fits our definition of stress as the consequence of exceeding our ability to adapt. When this happens, we cannot solve our problems. When we are *angry,* we have a painful problem. When we do not know how to solve our anger problem because anger is unacceptable in polite society, our original problem compounds. When we take our failure to solve our anger problem as a *reflection on our worth as a person,* our original anger problem is compounded still further. The stress mounts.

When we feel inadequate to cope with a problem that seems for now to be insoluble, we painfully confirm our underlying feelings of copelessness and inferiority. The original issue is no longer the issue that is killing us. It is this painful confirmation of our personal worthlessness as a human being that does the damage. This is a paradigm of aggravation. It is very stressful.

Our feelings of inferiority and inadequacy are personal vulnerabilities that predispose us to being more stressed by life than we need to be. They are *internal* stressors. We try to fight these stresses in the wrong way by overcompensating for them. We do too much in order to prove we are not weak, little or stupid any more. These overcompensatory solutions work in reverse. They make things worse and the negative outcome is that we *prove* to ourself we were right the first time: We are as useless and inferior as we felt ourselves to be. That

186

state of mind is very stressful. We are not aware that this silent stress is down there. We can't relieve it until we find out.

Do's and Don'ts

- Catch yourself trying to prove you are not worthless. That is negative ambition. It can't be done. Your feeling of worthlessness is a fictitious problem and it does not have to be solved. Your antidote to feeling worthless is not to climb mountains, but to accept yourself as a worthwhile human being in spite of your faults and imperfections.

- Catch yourself trying to adapt *perfectly*. That is the ultimate over-compensation, and you cannot do it. It is a set-up for failure. You are not required to adapt perfectly. You are required to adapt well enough, and that does not require any proving or demonstrating at all. You will accomplish a lot more with a lot less stress if you can manage to put these extreme attitudes from childhood into a more mature, appropriate perspective. Your stress level will come down considerably and so will your blood pressure.

- Do not fight the stress. Fighting stress will only make it worse At the other extreme, do not go along with stress to find out how much of a beating you can take before your heart explodes. In finding out, it may be too late. In Japan, they call it *"karoshi" or "death by overwork."*

- Ask yourself, *"What am I trying to prove and to whom? Who cares? Can it be proven? Does it work? Can I choose to stop overcompensating? Can I let it go? How good is good enough?"* The answer is, *"As good as I am right now, that is good enough. I will be a lot better off if I can let go of these bad habits from third grade. In the meantime, I am good enough as I am."*

- Replace your feelings of inferiority with feelings of adequacy and competency by giving yourself some simple Homework to do. For instance: If you consider yourself too busy to think about making your spouse happy right now, do not put it off until you retire. Make it happen in the present, of your own free will and volition.

187

"I wouldn't belong to any country
club that would have me
for a member."

Groucho Marx

- Or, catch yourself having impossibly high standards for your child or your co-worker and feeling anger at their failure to live up to your attitude-driven expectations. You can choose to let your self-serving expectations go.

You will feel relief from your anger and from the excessive, inappropriate responsibility you have been assuming for a fellow human being. The next Homework would be to do the same thing for yourself: to accept yourself as worthwhile right now, as you are in the present, not as you will be in the future after you accomplish some external goal. On the basis of realistic self-acceptance, you will live to accomplish more goals in the long run and you will enjoy them more.

- Recognize that a major source of stress comes from trying to control in negative ways that we learned in childhood. For example, you can catch yourself controlling to prevent disasters in the future. Choose instead to live in the present and do what reality requires you to do, no more and no less. If you take care of the present in a mature, appropriate way, your future will have fewer disasters than you would have the other way around.

79. SUBSTANCE ABUSE

We do not usually relate alcoholism, drug addiction and chemical dependency to anger, but there is often an anger component in these disorders. If we can identify and relieve the anger issues, the individual experiences a feeling of accomplishment, success, self-understanding and encouragement that other problems can be solved as well.

Substance abusers may not even be aware they are angry. That is part of the problem. Their addictive behavior has not succeeded in solving their anger problems. It has merely numbed them out (page 139). This is not success. It is suppression. The anger problem has not gone away. It remains down below the level of conscious awareness. It continues to go undiagnosed and untreated. It cannot get better and will only get worse.

Anger is an energy. It is not static, but dynamic. When we feel inadequate to cope with our anger problems, we try to stuff this anger down inside ourselves and to keep it there. We get it down there, all right, but it isn't standing still. It is turning into physical and emotional symptoms that are worse than the original anger problem ever was. These anger-born symptoms often give rise to depression and anxiety, which means that the substance abusers now have two problems and they must be *dual* diagnosed by a medical professional to identify mental illness underlying the addictive behavior. Both maladies must be treated, not just the surface mani-festations to receive proper treatment.

It is safe to assume that these addicts are angry. They may deny they are angry; they are just "hurt." We can expose their anger by asking a focusing question: *"How do you feel towards people who hurt you?"* "Angry!"

In dredging this anger up into the sunlight, we are accomplishing several positive purposes. We are relieving the pressure it takes to keep the anger down there, freeing this energy for more productive purposes. We are calling this anger by its rightful name and giving people permission to have this human emotion that they were told as children they weren't supposed to have. In addition, we are validat-ing them as worthwhile human beings in spite of it. No one ever did that for them before. They have consistently done the opposite.

After we have established the fact that they are angry, and that their anger is legitimate and permissible, we need to ask another focusing question: *"Who else are you angry at?"* They are often angry at themselves, but this anger is inaccessible. It is buried under the more obvious anger at the other people in their lives, but it is this self- anger that creates an insoluble problem: "How can I relieve my anger at myself for all the stupid things I have done in my life?" Since this question is unanswerable, these individuals feel inade-quate to cope and out of control. These feelings are painful, and the task of relieving this pain becomes still another problem they cannot solve.

190

Their substance abuse can be understood, then, to some extent, as their way of solving insoluble problems and numbing out the pain of their existence, which they do not know how to relieve in any other way. They hold themselves in contempt, and their self-destructive but negatively exciting behavior is their way of bringing about the fate that worthless people deserve. Their self-destruction, then, is the ultimate solution to the ultimate problem.

By respecting these people in spite of their unpleasant anger problems and setting an example of competence and self-respect for them to follow, we can begin to replace their underlying self-contempt with self-respect. They will begin to see that they were not *stupid, guilty* or *worthless*. They were merely imperfect human beings who grew up under difficult circumstances. They need not be angry at themselves, then there will be no self-anger to suppress. If we can relieve the pain of their existence in the right way, they will be free to stop trying to relieve it in the wrong way.

80. SUICIDE

We do not usually think of suicide as an anger mismanagement technique, but, in a way, that is what it is. We understand suicidal impulses as a function of depression. Depressed people are often angry at themselves for all sorts of reasons, none of which are rational. These "reasons" often have to do with a problem they feel unable to solve: such as a lost love, a lost job or the death of a loved one. They may be angry at a totally humiliating loss of their innocence, their self-respect.

These losses are not the problem. The problem may be that the suicidal individuals are *angry* at themselves for their failure or inability to *solve* the problem. They can never forgive themselves for a lifetime of imperfections. They do not respect inadequate, incompetent failures who are out of control, who fail to prevent bad things from happening. Such people are worthless. They are worthy to die.

191

When this self-anger occurs in a context of self-contempt, these people have no resources with which to counteract their impulses to self-destruction. They cannot bear the pain of their existence, which is another problem they cannot solve. They feel powerless, but there is one power that they have left, the ultimate power: The power of life and death. Self-murder is their way of overcompensating for their feelings of powerlessness. That is one purpose of their self-destructive behavior. At the same time, they can get revenge on the people who have hurt them by depriving them of their company forever. A third purpose served by their suicide is the withdrawal from the tasks of everyday life with which they feel inadequate to cope. These are all negative purposes, and suicide comes under the heading of mischief: *That which does not need to be done*. These negative purposes are consistent with their self-contempt. They are not consistent with self-respect.

We can learn how to give suicidal persons emotional first aid when they need it. We do not debate with them over the relative merits of life versus death. These purposes are not rational, and they cannot be reasoned out of them.

Instead of reacting to them on their territory, we can bring them over to ours.

We can control the interchange. We can choose to ask a focusing question: *"What happened to make you angry?"* This question distracts them from insoluble problems of life and death and gives them soluble problems they can talk about sensibly. Their depression changes back into anger, which can then be managed and disposed of. Moreover, when they hear themselves being spoken to with respect for their legitimate griefs, their self-contempt loses its grip on them. Its place is often taken by self-respect. Sometimes they continue to deny their unacceptable anger. We can give them permission to have this legitimate emotion by modeling it for them. We can say, "I'd be angry if I were going through what you're going through." When both of these aspects of suicidal feelings are relieved, the pain of their existence goes away. They are free. They often come out of their crisis stronger than they went in. The depression lifts. The sun comes out.

192

81. SUPPRESSION

We have been taught by nonexperts in the field that anger must be controlled. This too often turns out to be *suppression*. We are taught by our anger-illiterate elders to fear our anger. We are a nation of angerphobics. We live in fear that an outward expression of unpleasant emotions will have scary consequences. We are afraid of:

- Displeasing people.
- Being abandoned as a consequence of our displeasing.
- Losing control.
- Being victimized.
- Being annihilated as a person in the world.

We are not consciously aware of these fears. We have suppressed them, too. Yet, our fears determine our behavior just the same. When someone wakes us at three a.m and asks, "Did I wake you?" we do not even think of expressing our anger. We lie and say, "No, I wasn't sleeping – just dozing a little." We are so well trained that we cannot even feel the anger that this intrusion must have caused us. Our anti-anger attitudes have kicked in and saved us the trouble of having to solve this problem for ourselves. We arrange to forget painful, anger or guilt-provoking memories from our childhood.

We are older now. We can tolerate pain that we could not under-stand or tolerate as a vulnerable child. We need forget neither our anger nor our memories.

Sometimes an event in the present causes our clients to become angrier than they need to be. We suspect that the source of their excess anger maybe a repressed event from the formative stages of their personality. We can ask, *"What did this event remind you of?"* As adults, clients can tolerate the pain of the recollection. If they cannot, if they experience anxiety, we can ask another focusing ques-tion: *"What are you afraid will happen if you bring it up?"* They can identify these scary consequences and put them in an adult perspec-tive.

193

They may wish to finish the recall process in private. They can choose to go home and begin writing their thoughts down on paper. They begin a process of association that dredges up the secret source of their super-anger and anxiety.

They can write a letter to the person or thing that caused the grievance. They can write an anger letter to themselves. They can write a forgiveness letter in the present. They find that when they are in control of these operations, their anxiety is relieved, depression lifts. They feel liberated from the heaviness of a lifetime.

A Pain We Cannot Feel

Fear and anger are painful. We feel inadequate to cope with these emotions. They create problems for us we do not know how to solve. We try to dispose of these painful problems by suppressing them down below the level of conscious awareness. We coat them over like an oyster with a grain of sand, but the problems are still down there. Their pain has not gone away. We just can't feel it anymore. It sounds like an oxymoron to say we have a pain we cannot feel, but it is the truth. We can tell that the pain is still down there by the shadow it casts over our lives. It keeps us from being as happy and successful as we have the right to be. It interferes with our relationships and makes us abandon people before they can abandon us, which makes no sense at all. Our pain predisposes us to be on constant guard against further pain, and it seduces us into living in the future so we can prevent disasters from happening in advance. These are just a few of the absurdities of everyday life, and they all derive from this pain of our existence, which is unfelt. Our silent attitudes towards anger have created emotional problems we are inadequately prepared to solve.

When we replace our painful feelings of self-doubt and inadequacy to cope with feelings of self-respect, these fears are overcome. We have the courage to take the risks that life requires us to take. This includes the risk of expressing our legitimate anger appropriately. It takes courage to say, *"It makes me angry when you do that."* When we make it happen, we feel in control, independent, mature and competent, all of which are facets of self-respect.

When we write an anger letter to someone who has caused us a grievance, we may tap into the pool of residual anger that goes back to our earliest years. It starts to pour out on the page in a tangible, concrete form. At last, our anger is manageable; we have the adult resources to manage it. As we do this anger Homework in the real world — not the world of attitudes or overcompensations, we begin to undo the effects of a lifetime of suppression. We have earned the right to feel secure within ourselves, confident we can succeed again and liberated from the frightened, inadequate roles we used to play. We learn to trust our ability to cope with strong emotions with which we could not cope in childhood.

82. SWEARING

Swearing is an immature anger management technique we acquired in second grade and carried intact into adulthood. People are rarely impressed by the swearer's sophistication, intelligence or command of the English language.

Excessive swearing is a symptom of self-contempt. When people use scatological language, they are holding their mother tongue in the same contempt that they hold themselves. They are revealing their personal and linguistic bankruptcy.

The antidote to this lingual abuse is self-respect. Self-respecting people do not use language that demeans their hearers as well as themselves. They do not sink to using lowest common denominator vocabulary nor do they strive for overcompensatory verbal pyrotechnics. They communicate in the middle ground between these extremes, even when they are experiencing strong emotion. They respect their hearers as well as themselves and choose their words accordingly. They get relief from their pent-up anger that swearers do not get. Swearers only think they get relief. Someday they will bust a blood vessel, but then it will be too late to correct their mistake.

Do's and Don'ts

- When your children begin using words they learned in school or from their Uncle Bucky, you can choose not to overreact. This phenomenon is not a reflection on your parenting skills or your worth as a person. When you overreact, you are rewarding the behavior and guaranteeing it will happen again very soon.

- Instead of focusing on the child's mischief, you can focus on your anger. When you say, *"That word makes me angry,"* you are not paying off this mischief, but using a logical consequence of the child's misbehavior. Your child does not want you to be angry. The child knows now what will happen the next time: you'll get angry again. That it is no fun at all. If the child tests you again later, you must pass the test. If you overblow, it means that the child has succeeded in getting to you and you will lose leverage. You may up the ante by using a stronger logical consequence, but erupting like a volcano is just paying off the mischief. When you express your anger like a grownup, you are using a real life anger situation as an opportunity to set a positive example for the child to see and follow. See how quickly he uses it on his cousin. Be sure to validate his success when he does.

- You can reveal to the child that he or she has other choices open to them. There are other words they can say that will give them relief without the negative consequences. You can even ask them, *"What word would you rather say when you are angry?"* "Can I just say, 'I'm angry.'" *"That would be a very good thing to say."*

This is not to say that we expect parents to stop erupting immediately and forever. That would be perfection. Imperfect parents erupt from time to time. Our hope is that, as your self- respect increases, your eruptions will come farther apart and end sooner each time. That is a sign you are healing. You are a worthwhile human being in the meantime, and so is your child.

"No matter how cynical I get,
I can't keep up."

Lily Tomlin

83. TAKE TIME OUT OF TIME

We all suffer from time poverty. There is always too much to do and not enough time to do it. We don't even have time to get angry, so we just stuff it down until we can get home and displace it on the dog or whoever we see first (See "DISPLACEMENT" on page 55.).

We learned as children to put other people first and ourselves second. We have no time for our own legitimate concerns. We run ourselves ragged until we burn ourselves out. Then we stop running around permanently. We do all this running and chasing because we think we have to. If we sit still, it is a waste of productive time. Someone will catch up to us and pass us by, or someone will say we are lazy. All our goodness will be for nothing. These are just a few of the mistaken attitudes that propel us into perpetual motion. We are playing an endless game of Beat the Clock. The antidote is to *back off and take time out of time.* That is very hard for us to do, which is why hardly anyone does it.

Vignette: Be My Guest

Nancy was having a thirtieth birthday party for her husband, Matt. Sister-in-law Greta was there a half hour early, as usual, wanting to know where the spoons were and who is going to bring the cake. Before counseling, Nancy would have said, "Get out of my kitchen. Go out there and enjoy yourself." Instead, Nancy chose to take time out of time. She was not interested in a power struggle with Greta over who was going to be boss in whose kitchen. She let it go. She agreed with Greta, *"Here, take this ladle and stir the soup."* She took off her apron and went outside to play ball with her two boys and their father, who did not remember ever seeing her out of the kitchen before. She had a relaxing hour before the party instead of playing her usual agonizing role as the Uptight Perfectionist. Greta was feeling no pain either. She was in total control of these pots and pans. It was a win-win situation and a good time was had by all.

84. TALK IT OUT

Before there were psychotherapists, there were priests, poets and philosophers trying to teach us the truth about the human condition. One such truth was, *Confession is good for the soul.* Confessing our private thoughts and fears is hard to do. If it were easy, we would not need constant reminders to do it.

There are several impediments to talking our anger out:

- Emotionality is seen as weakness or a loss of control.
- Anger is unpleasant, and we fear disapproval, rejection and abandonment.
- We have no parental example of appropriate anger expression to follow. We are predisposed to follow the example our parents set.
- We have not acquired the appropriate verbal terms for the negative feeling in our hearts. We call it "hate," "irritated," or "bothered."
- Our priorities are backwards. Instead of talking about our legitimate anger, we wallow in the pain it is causing us. We use our pain to get attention from others or to revenge ourselves upon them. We make verbal mischief instead of talking sense about our human emotions like grown-ups.
- Our own personal reason. Ask yourself the focusing questions: *"What is the worst thing that would happen if I talked out my anger? What am I afraid would happen if I did?"* Write your reason here:

"_____."

Brain architects tell us males have fewer links between their left and right hemispheres than females. This is their explanation of the difficulty left-brain-dominant men have articulating feelings, which arise in the right hemisphere. Women are said to have more neural connections between left and right brain hemispheres so thoughts and feelings can pass back and forth more easily.

Regardless of neural connections, our experience is that self-respecting people feel freer to talk things out than people who hold themselves in contempt and who feel they must overcompensate by playing the role of the Tough Guy or the Stoic or the Silently Suffering Martyr.

Unself-respecting people do not respect their feelings and emotions any more than they respect the rest of their personhood. They have the conviction that their feelings are not worth expressing and that their concerns are unimportant to the significant others in their lives. They cannot risk being invalidated. It would hurt too much, so they keep it in. They do not see why they shouldn't. It is the misery they prefer to the even worse misery of taking the risk and being humiliated again as they were in childhood.

Do's and Don't's

- Encourage people to express their anger in an atmosphere of mutual respect. It helps if you can put the word "anger" in their ear: "That must have made you angry. I'd be angry if it happened to me."

- When they express their anger at you, do not take it personally. They are only saying you are imperfect. You can say, "Good! I'm glad you can tell me that you're angry." You can then use focusing questions to find out the rest of the story.

- The antidote to fear is courage. Self-respecting people are willing to take the risk. Be self-respecting. Take appropriate risks. Never pass up an opportunity to affirm life.

- Talking it out does not mean using your negative emotion to get attention, pity or useless advice from your well-intentioned resources. If you have no intention of taking their advice, save everyone the time and trouble. Instead of being dependent on the judgment of people who were not even there when it happened, practice trusting your own judgment. It isn't perfect, but it is good enough. You will never be independent until you do.

- Find out why you cannot talk it out. Ask yourself, *"Where does this fear come from?"* Very often, a recollection will pop into your conscious mind that will answer the question.

Another way to find out is to ask yourself, *"How would my life be different if I overcame my fear of talking it out?"* Maybe you would feel guilty of disobeying your parents. Maybe you would be happy, which you have never deserved to be before. These are not crimes, merely attitudes from the past. You can choose to let them go. You're a grownup now.

85. TELL THE TRUTH

Do you see yourself as an honest person who tells the truth?

Of course you do.

It is so easy to tell the truth when nothing is at stake.

You can tell your seven-year-old child that his room is a disgusting mess, but you cannot tell your Aunt Celeste that her moustache is growing in again. It would be too unpleasant and it could get you beaten up or, worse, humiliated in the eyes of your family forever. No, there is too much at stake.

We cannot tell the truth if that truth is inconsistent with the role we have been playing all our lives. If we are the Victim of our family, we cannot tell any truth that would bring about the scary, painful victimization we are trying so hard to prevent. If we are the disgruntled Rebel of the bunch, we cannot say, "Thanks, I love this sweater," because it might give the Oppressors an iota of satisfaction if we did.

This is particularly true of our anger. We are so well trained to deny the truth of our anger that, when the opportunity for truthfulness arises, we cannot do it and we let it pass us by. Often, we are not given another chance.

When we are angry, it would be appropriate and therapeutic for us to say, *"It makes me angry when you do that."* That is the truth, but

201

we cannot say it. Our relationships would be more solid and mature if we did, but no one believes that and hardly anyone does it. Instead, we say things like, "You're the dumbest person I've ever seen in my life." That is not the truth, but we are stuck with it.

It takes courage to tell the truth. That is why we cannot do it when the chips are down. As children, we lacked the courage to overcome our fears. We are adults now, and if we wish to outgrow this baggage from our childhood, we need to make appropriate choices. Courage is *the willingness to take a risk*. If we can take that risk and tell the truth when we are angry, the truth shall make us free. Instead of saying, "I hate you," which is not true, we can say to a loved one, a friend, a co-worker, *"It makes me angry when you do that"* or *"I am angry at you."* That is the truth. We are not "upset" or "bothered." These are euphemisms that water down the truth of our emotion. As adults now, we can use our adult judgment to determine when it is appropriate to "Tell the Truth" (page 201) or "Give It a Pass." (page 96). We are not perfect and are not required to tell the truth perfectly every time.

We can choose when and to whom we express our anger. This power of choice is an anger management technique called, "Discretion" (page 50). Self-respecting people use their discretion in a crisis. They do not abuse the privilege. They know what the reality of the situation requires them to do and they do it.

86. TEMPER TANTRUMS

This is the first entry that most parents will turn to. It is the most common anger management problem parents have, and most of them feel woefully inadequate to cope with these very unpleasant anger attacks.

On one level, it is very frustrating to be two or three years old and not be able to solve most of your problems. A majority of these problems come under the heading of, "I want my way but I can't figure out how to get it. I am feeling powerless to solve this problem."

202

"I was angry with my friend;
I told my wrath,
my wrath did end.
I was angry with my foe;
I told it not,
my wrath did grow.

William Blake

The child's anger is painful in itself. It has many components:

- He confuses his parents' refusal to give him his way as a loss of love.
- He feels it is his fault he is unlovable.
- He feels he is worthless.
- He blames himself for being unable to solve all these problems.
- He has taken the refusal of his desire personally, as a wipeout of his fragile personhood.

This spiral of pain is too much for the child to handle. The temper tantrum is the manifestation of his pain and his powerlessness to do anything constructive about it.

The last thing he needs is to have his all-important parent compound his grief by treating him like the enemy. Some children pick up this unhappy role and run with it ever after.

Parents have feelings, too: Feelings of anger, powerlessness, shame, and guilt. They feel inadequate to cope with the child's inadequacy. Parents do not appreciate being put in a situation which threatens to expose their short comings for all the neighbors to see. Under these circumstances, the parents are liable to react to the problem by throwing a counter-tantrum.

The child, then, has one agenda; the parents have an entirely different one. Parents cannot cope with the child's pain if they are the out-of-control prisoners of their own.

On another level, a temper tantrum can be understood as mischief. It doesn't need to be done.

Why do they do it? "Why" here does not mean, "for what reason." Reason has nothing to do with this situation. Our "why," means, "For what Purpose?" We need to identify his negative purposes so we'll know what we are dealing with.

One purpose of this mischief is to get *attention*, and it works. The attention is all negative, but it proves to the child that he still exists.

A more significant purpose is *power and control*. The child feels powerless to do anything constructive about his situation, but he

204

sure has the power to provoke his parents to madness. When he succeeds, it relieves the pain of his powerlessness. It has a high price, but he seems willing to pay it.

A third purpose is revenge – to get even with his parent for causing him this grief.

A fourth purpose is to *withdraw* into a tantrum from a universe of overwhelming problems he is totally inadequate to identify, let alone solve.

Antidote

To save our own sanity, we must first identify the child's negative behavior as *mischief* and disengage ourselves emotionally from it. It helps if we can identify our personal vulnerabilities to being sucked into the child's propellers:

- "I am taking this tantrum *personally*, as if it were a reflection on my parenting skills, my competence as a parent and my worth as a human being. *I can choose to remind myself that I am still a worthwhile human being in spite of this regrettable happenstance.*"

- "I am feeling out of control because I have mistakenly defined control in terms of shutting this kid up instantly and perfectly. *I can remind myself that I have the power of choice. I can choose to be in control of myself. I certainly cannot control him if I am not in control of me.*"

- "I want my way, my child is not giving it to me, and I cannot make him. I'm as immature and out of control as he is. One of us has to grow up now and it isn't going to be him. *I can remind myself that I am a worthwhile human being whether my child obeys my commands instantly or not.*"

- "I am feeling totally responsible for my child and I am doing a lousy job. I feel guilty of the crime of irresponsibility. I have allowed this catastrophe to happen. It is all my fault. *These mistaken attitudes are painful. It's hard for me to solve problems when I am in pain. I can put things in a more manageable perspective by reminding myself that it is not my fault. It is no one's fault. My imper-*

fect child is having a fit, just like everyone else's imperfect child. He is worthwhile in spite of it -- and so am I."

- "I am vulnerable to worrying about how this looks to the neighbors. I feel like I am being disgraced forever in their eyes. *I need to remind myself that my child is more important to me than those people I don't eve know. I can choose to live on my terms, not theirs. I can free myself to do what the situation requires me to do."*

After sorting out this welter of feelings and attitudes, we are in a much better position to solve the problems than we would have been in the old days.

Do's and Don'ts

- Do not get into a power struggle with your child over who can make whom stop doing what. Catch yourself taking his behavior *personally* as a reflection on you. Do not worry about the neighbors' opinion of you. They have their own problems.
- Do not have a *counter-tantrum*. That just prolongs the agony.
- Do not let him play one parent against the other.
- Remind yourself that you are not out of control. You have the power of choice. Use it.
- Choose to exert firm but gentle restraint on your child. You can put your arms around him to show him you are in control, that you are on his side and that you are not going to make his pain worse by abandoning him.
- Choose to ride out the anger storm without overreacting to the provocation.
- Reveal the power component of the tantrum by asking, *"Could it be that you will stop kicking when you are good and ready? Well, that's all right. I can wait."* It will end a lot sooner this way than if you try to shorten the attack the old way by saying, "Stop that this instant." This just gives him more power to defeat you. On this new basis, you are not out of control. You are living on your terms, not his. When he senses that you are in control and refusing to pay off his mischief, he will calm down sooner.

206

Send him to his room, not as punishment, but as *quiet time* so he can cool down his sensory overload. It breaks the cycle of frustration. You can say, *"We will talk about it when you feel better."* Later on, you can ask the focusing question:

What angered you the most when I wouldn't buy you the ten-pound choco-late bar?

"You never buy me anything."

It seems that way sometimes, doesn't it.

"You don't love me."

I'm sorry you feel that way.

"I don't love you."

I don't blame you for being angry.

"You hate me."

What you do makes me angry sometimes, but that isn't hate. It's just anger and it goes away.

You are not required to defend, explain, account for or justify. You are validating the child's worth in spite of his faults and imperfections, one of which is that he hasn't yet learned how to manage his anger. You can use this painful episode as an opportunity to teach him what he needs to know about anger:

The next time you get so angry at me, I want you to say, 'It makes me angry when you don't do this for me.'

"Is it all right for me to be angry at you?"

Yes. It isn't all right to get upset in the Wal-mart where people are trying to do their shopping. You have a choice now. Can you remember to say that next time?

"If I forget, will you remind me?"

I'd be happy to.

This is not controlling or suppressing. This is revealing to him that he has choices. This is empowering the child to solve his anger problem. This is the antidote to his powerlessness.

87. THE THIRD CHOICE

When we feel frustrated, we feel *powerless and out of control plus angry*. We feel trapped, like there is no way out, with no solution to our problem in sight. We have no choice or, what is worse, we have two choices and we hate them both. If our boss, Harry, makes us angry, we can choose to explode in his face and get fired or we can stuff our anger inside our chest as we usually do.

We are not really powerless and out of control. We just feel that way most of the time. We have a power called the "Third Choice" technique. Instead of tearing our brains in half over two unacceptable options, we can use our adult creativity to give ourselves a third option. *"I know. I'll write Harry an anger letter and then tear it up. I can even choose to write a second letter that I can put on his desk."*

When we have two unacceptable choices, we have an insoluble problem. We turn the problem around and around in our mind trying to solve it. We call this mental merry-go-round *obsessing* and we will never solve the problem that way. We need some new input. We need that Third Choice.

Vignette: Solving the Insoluble Problem

Mary Lou and Zack were having a quarrel. Zack had forgotten his keys again and had to wait an hour for her to come home. He had even forgotten that the spare key was hidden in the mailbox. When Mary Lou drove up and saw him sitting on the doorstep like a forlorn puppy, she blew up. "That's the third time you've locked yourself out of the house. You are so irresponsible. You were the baby of your family and you're still the baby. You just can't cope. You can't solve problems."

"Never pass up an opportunity
to affirm life."

Rudolf Dreikurs

As usual, Zack began defending himself at her expense. He pointed out her recent lapses and faux pas at the top of his voice. This was his approach to problem-solving: drown it out so he couldn't hear it. Mary Lou opened the door and they went in, but their evening together got off on the wrong foot, and it stayed there.

In counseling, Mary Lou admitted she was at an impasse. She knew criticizing Zack only made it worse, but she could not keep her anger in, because it would make her sick if she did. She would have a splitting headache in the morning.

Mary Lou began saying, "I am angry at you, Zack," and he began to take her more seriously and to cooperate with her. She was pleased with her progress and did not want to derail it. She did not want to wear out her "I" Message technique.

First Choice **The Lesser Misery**	**Second Choice** **The Greater Misery**	**Third Choice** **No Misery At All**
Pleasing everyone so they will like me. Living on their terms not my own.	Displeasing everyone and being rejected.	Being an independent person on my own terms and pleasing myself as a worthwhile human being.
Preventing disaster by controlling. Living in fear of impending doom at any minute.	Letting go of control, which is scary.	Taking life as it comes and doing the best I can with it.
Submitting on my knees, like a victim.	Rebelling and being shot down.	Cooperating as an equal member of the human race.

First Choice The Lesser Misery	Second Choice The Greater Misery	Third Choice No Misery At All
Not wanting to be like my mother, a negative ambition that precludes a positive outcome. A counter-productive good intention I have for myself.	Painful anxiety that I will go to the opposite extreme and fall over the edge.	Living in the middle ground between the two extremes as a self- respecting human being.
To keep trying harder and harder.	To stop trying altogether and give up in discouragement.	To stop trying so hard and just do what reality requires no more and no less.
To keep proving that I am always right and never wrong, living in constant stress, never able to let my guard down.	To admit I am wrong and give up the fight.	To accept myself as an imperfect human being as I am right now and do what needs to be done.
To live in fear of abandonment, unable to enjoy the luxury of happiness in the present.	To get it over with sooner by abandoning others before they can abandon me, fulfilling my own prophecy of disaster forever.	To respect myself as a worthwhile human being with an identity of my own. As long as I have myself, I can never be abandoned. I can choose to stop worrying about it.

First Choice The Lesser Misery	Second Choice The Greater Misery	Third Choice No Misery At All
To keep trying to make them understand me, feeling misunderstood and rejected in the meantime.	To keep looking for someone new who might understand me better and being all alone until I do.	To begin learning how to understand *myself* in spite of my faults and imperfections.

Do's and Don'ts

- Do not fight against two conflicting choices, which are based on attitudes from childhood. You cannot fight them or reason them away. You can break their grip on you by replacing them with healthier choices based on judgments that derive from a mature, independent perception of the requirements of the real world. As you succeed in doing your Homeworks, the old conflicting attitudes are replaced by more realistic appropriate ones. You can ask, "What does reality require me to do right now?" It never requires that you do anything perfectly.

The Oppositionality Syndrome

Luckily, there was another choice open to Mary Lou. She saw a pattern of irresponsibility in Zack, but she also saw a pattern of defensiveness and opposition to whatever she said. When Mary Lou confronted Zack about his "againstness," he simply said, "That's just the way I am," which was his way of saying he had no intention of looking into his own motivations or changing himself to accommodate her. It was another example of his *oppositionality.*

The truth is that this is not the way he is at all. This is just a role he has been playing since he was two. He never outgrew his terrible twos oppositionality because it kept working. It kept his parents hopping and now it is doing the same thing to his wife. He thinks he

212

is in control and that he is winning these battles, but it is only mischief.

We can choose to stop focusing on Zack's regrettable irresponsibility and to stop trying to make him agree with us. We cannot force him to see things our way. He is afraid he would lose his shaky identity if he did.

We decided to focus on Zack's oppositionality-for-the-sake-of-being-oppositional. Mary Lou learned how hard it was for Zack to let go of his own position, even if it was absurd. His position in the argument was not the issue. His worth as a person was at stake. That was the issue and neither of them knew it.

That night, Mary Lou and Zack were having a conversation between two grown-up human beings when Mary Lou mentioned the key incident. *"You must have been very angry at being locked out."* She was trying to validate his anger and encourage him to express it in more productive ways. Zack's fragile veneer of maturity cracked and he went into his role as the oppositional child, "You're nuts. I wasn't angry. It didn't bother me at all." Here is where the third choice comes in. Mary Lou could have chosen to rebut his absurdly false statement or she could have chosen to bite her tongue and suppress her feelings. She chose a third course, to change the subject: *"It's hard for you to agree with me, isn't it, Zack?"*

"No, it isn't."

"There, Zack. You just did it again. You can't even agree with me that it's hard to agree."

She had *caught him in the act* (page 37), which made it hard for Zack to deny that he had just done what he did. She was not criticizing or forcing. She was just talking to him in a new key, as one equal member of the human race to another.

"It's always been hard for me to agree with people and I've never known why," said Zack.

"What's the hardest thing about agreeing, Zack?"

"I feel like I won't be myself if I take someone else's side. I'll be giving up something of myself."

"Do you define yourself in terms of your position on these matters? I don't define myself that way. I am a worthwhile human being in spite of my faults and imperfections, whether people agree with me or not. I am even worthwhile if I agree with them. Maybe they know something I don't know. I trust them and I trust myself. I don't have nearly as many battles as you do."

"Isn't that giving in?"

"No. It is cooperating with my fellow human beings in getting the job done, whatever it is. I do not confuse cooperation with submission. I do not rebel. I am a worthwhile human being either way. Isn't that a better basis for getting along with people: As an equal?"

"It's hard to say it, but maybe you're right."

"That's good, Zack. I'm glad you feel that way. That makes me happy. Was it as hard as you thought it would be?"

"No. It wasn't. Maybe I can do it again sometime."

"Who made that happen just now?

"I did."

"So you didn't lose yourself, did you? In fact, you found yourself. That is a feeling of identity, maturity and independence. You are liberating yourself from your childhood roles. You have the power of choice now. You can choose to agree or disagree. Before, you only had one choice."

"You're right. I feel better now."

"You just agreed with me again. What did it cost you?"

"Just the excitement that I used to get from stirring up things. I don't need that any more."

"That's right, you don't. You never did. It doesn't cost you anything that you really need. Can you do it again?

"Sure I can."

"That is called confidence. You cannot have confidence if you are always playing a role opposite some one else's role. Isn't this a pleasanter way to live your life?"

214

"Yes, it is."

"You see? You just agreed with me again. You're getting good at this. You could learn to love it."

88. TURN THE OTHER CHEEK

"If an evildoer smite thee on the cheek, turn the other to him also, for a soft answer turneth away wrath." (Luke 6:29) (see also: Proverbs 15:1; "DISCRETION" on page 50; "DISENGAGE FROM THE MISCHIEF" on page 53; "DO THE UNEXPECTED" on page 57; "THE THIRD CHOICE" on page 208; "THE COMPONENTS OF SELF-RESPECT" on page 290).

89. UNDERSTANDINGNESS

We are all in favor of improved understanding, and we all imagine that we understand ourselves. But what is it called when someone who does not understand another person's attitudes and predispositions tries to make that person understand something they do not want to understand for their own good? This absurd good intention on our part can be called *understandingness*.

Very often, when Herbert and Edna are fighting, their anger attack consists of two parties each trying to pound sense into the other's skull at the expense of the other's self-respect. Herbert is implying that, until Edna understands the truth as he has defined it, she is a dummy. He cannot improve his partner's receptivity to his ideas by placing her in this painful one-down position. She will try to relieve the pain of her inferiority by doing the same thing to him in the name of justice and fair play. An amicable exchange of views is impossible under these conditions.

A good technique is to catch ourselves trying desperately to make the other person understand us by yelling in their ear. We can choose to stop in our tracks. We can choose to replace our self-serving good intentions with a real intention that makes sense. We are now free to do something else — something that might work better. We can disengage from the others' mischief and our own. Trying to make someone understand against their will is mischief; it does not need to be done.

Instead of waiting for people to *understand* the error of their ways, we can tell the truth right now: *"It makes me angry when you do that."* This is a simple, declarative sentence. They can understand it immediately. We can choose not to elaborate, account or explain ourselves to them. We can set an example of constructive, appropriate behavior for them to see and follow. They may not understand in their head why they are following our new example. Maybe they will just understand in their hearts that the new way is a lot more productive than the old one of butting heads. Maybe their attitude toward us has changed for the better. In any case, our life will go on. We are worthwhile either way.

90. VALIDATE, VALIDATE, VALIDATE

One of the purposes of this book is to show how we can use an adverse, unpleasant situation like an anger attack to earn for ourselves the feeling that we are worthwhile, competent human beings. If we work it right, an anger problem can be an opportunity to heal and grow, not just on the outside or for the sake of the relationship, but inside our own selfhood, which is where we live.

First: We validate the other person's *anger*: *"I am sorry you are so angry."*

Second: By saying that, we validate *them* as worthwhile, acceptable human beings in spite of their faults and imperfections, one of which is that they get angry from time to time. We are telling the truth. We are expressing sincere regret that they are having this unpleasant emotion. We are not using euphemisms; we are calling their legitimate emotion by its appropriate, grown-up name. We are,

216

in a way, giving them permission to have the emotion that they have and not water it down or try to deny it out existence.

The third "validation" is for *ourselves*. We have solved the problem constructively. We have put our money where our mouth is and we have had the courage to reach out and intervene effectively. We have earned the right and the joy of feeling like a self-respecting human being. We have used an anger situation constructively. We have treated our partner with respect under difficult circumstances. We have solved an interpersonal relationship problem that we could not have solved before. This successful accomplishment gives us confidence that we can do it again. We were not playing a role. We had an independent, mature identity of our own.

This is what we call Emotional First Aid™. Not only have we relieved the other person's pain, but we have relieved our own. We have had a real intention and did what reality required. We have overcome our self-doubt and replaced it with self-respect. We have stopped the bleeding.

91. VENTING — POSITIVE AND NEGATIVE

No book on Anger Management would be complete without a few words on the subject of venting. For centuries, we were told to keep our anger in; it is unseemly, rude and low class. Since the 1960's revolution in our outlook on these matters, it has become popular to go to the other extreme: to let it all hang out in the name of honesty and truth to oneself as a manifestation of our liberation from the inhibitions of our strait-laced, up-tight grandparents.

Recent research has shown that venting is more beneficial than non-venting among college student test subjects. The researchers evidently believe that the only two variables to be controlled were venting and non-venting.

We would nominate a third variable for their consideration, one that might yield more useful results. The current bias is that there are many modes of venting: hitting pillows, wielding battacas or baseball bats, socking punch 'em dolls, and so on. In one university Psych Department experiment, subjects were told that one of the research examiners had given them a negative test result. They were allowed to vent their anger by sending a loud noise into the examiner's head phones. There was no fear of being identified or punished. These students uniformly felt *good* after venting their anger in this vengeful way. These students were learning that it is commendable to build themselves up by tearing other people down, that it is healthy to use a cowardly attack to vent ones anger. This is not what we should be paying colleges to teach our children.

We would say that their revenge gave them relief from the pain of their frustrated anger. They were in control at the time and place of their revenge, but it was negative control. They had succeeded merely in overcompensating for their feelings of inferiority by victimizing their alleged victimizer. In their constellation of attitudes from childhood, "That's fair."

This is not positive venting. This is mischief and counter-mischief being measured scientifically to the third decimal place. Any bully knows that it feels good to get revenge. Our unmeasured observation over the years is that all ventings are not created equal. Our approach is that there are *two kinds* of venting: one that scratches where we itch and one that does not. We prefer the one that does. We recommend the kind of venting that addresses specific grievances by specific perpetrators. We recommend breaking these painful internal emotions into their components and then externalizing them in mature, constructive ways, such as writing an Anger Letter. This kind of venting uses our higher faculties, not our lower ones. It makes our internal griefs visible in the real world where they are accessible to our higher thought processes.

We choose to vent positively in ways that:

- Identify our anger as a valid emotion,
- Identify the loss of our self-respect in taking the grievance, real or imaginary, personally,
- Relieve the pain of our anger in healthy, constructive ways,

"Like all mischief, good intentions are
self-indulgent, counter-productive
and self-destructive."

Rudolf Dreikurs

- Will help us replace our painful self-doubt with appropriate, well earned self-respect,
- Replace our self-serving good intention to get even with a real intention to strengthen ourselves as persons in the world by assuming appropriate responsibility for ourselves.

If we were the designer of this experiment, we would have dug a little deeper into each student's response to the grievance. Our approach would include asking a focusing question or two such as, *"What angered you the most that the examiner gave you a lower score than you deserved?"*

They would have been able to identify such component attitudes as, "It wasn't fair. I deserved a higher score," or "I felt cheated, victimized," or "I felt Good for Nothing. I went along in good faith and he low-balled me." Each of these attitudes, once brought to the surface, can be discussed and put in a more moderate, less personal perspective.

We might also ask, *"What is the first thing you remember from your childhood?"* The recollection might be one of a similar victimization or betrayal by an authority figure. Such an event would leave unre-solved residual anger that unconsciously compounded the subject's experimentally induced anger in the present. The test subject might have become angrier than the grievance in the present warranted, the excess being explainable in terms of super-anger that could then have been identified and relieved appropriately on an informed basis.

Our approach to venting makes our specific issues real and manageable. It makes our mistaken attitudes and childhood vulnera-bilities apparent to us so we can evaluate and outgrow them if we are ready to do so. It gives us the power of choice. We can choose mature, appropriate modalities over immature hollering and scream-ing from our playground days.

For many people, this mature modality is intimidating, even daunting. Their attitude is, "I'm not ready, coach." It takes courage, which is what discouraged people do not have. Many people are impeded by old attitudes from making the choice of expressing their forbidden emotions like a grownup. We are giving them the opportunity to make a responsible choice in their own behalf, to affirm life instead of evading it. It takes courage to make life affirming choices. It takes no courage to remain the prisoner of outgrown and inappropriate attitudes, to hit a pillow with a stick, or to deafen one's adversary from behind a shield of anonymity.

When our subjects succeed in using their adult courage to break through their childhood attitudes, and vent their anger in an effective way, they earn the right to feel relief, accomplishment, maturity, sanity and all the other components of self-respect. These are the tangible, identifiable rewards of constructive venting.

92. THE VICTIM

As children, we were vulnerable to perceiving the bad things that happened to us as if they were personal victimizations. We took our deprivations and grievances personally, as a loss of our self-worth.

Now, as adults, we have the same predisposition to play the Victim role when there is no victimization. For instance, when we do not get a promotion, we feel unfairly deprived, victimized, and out of control. This unfairness makes us angry, but our definition of unfair is not objective, it is subjective: "Fairness means getting my way. Life is unfair to me when I don't get my way. How can they do this to me?"

The managers feel they have promoted the better employee on the basis of objective considerations, but we, as victims waiting for a place to happen, are not interested in objectivity or real fairness. We have our own private considerations, grievances and anger. The victimization has just happened. This negative situation has confirmed us in our unhappy role. This is not living. This is merely existing from one painful victimization to another.

The tip-off to *The Victim Syndrome* lies in the words: "To me." That is the victim in us talking. Our antidote to playing this childish role from kindergarten ("The teacher held up everyone's picture but mine. Why did she do that to me?") is our self-respect. We can replace our unhappy role as the victim with an identity as a worth-while human being whether we get our way or not. We can say to ourselves, *"Could it be that I am perceiving victimization where no victim-ization is intended? Even if it is intended, I am still not a victim. It is regret-table, and I wish it hadn't happened, but I am a worthwhile human being in spite of it, no more and no less than anyone else."*

Coping With The Victim

When people are angry at us for causing them a grievance, being late, divorcing them or firing them from their job because the plant is closing, we can assume there is an element of victimhood in their rage. If there is not, there is no harm done, but there usually is. This perception of personal victimization makes their pain worse than it needs to be and more difficult to deal with.

We can relieve their painful overreaction to the reality situation by identifying the victim component for them. They are not aware that they are playing this role. They have been doing it for years. It comes naturally to them now. We can say, *"I am sorry you are feeling victimized by all this,"* and that is true. We regret that it is happening. This does not mean we caused the victimization.

Or, we can say, *"Could it be that you are perceiving this as a victimization? Well, it really isn't. It's regrettable. I wish it weren't happening, but you are not a victim. You are a worthwhile human being in spite of it. On that basis, you can get on with your life and do even better than you have done before."* That is emotional first aid. We haven't cured them of their predisposition to feel victimized, but we have treated them with respect in spite of their imperfections. We didn't take their unpleasant imperfections personally. We did not allow them to victimize us.

Vignette: Victim Of Waste

Penny knew her husband Dick had been victimized as a child. She knew he was still predisposed to perceive things as victimization when they were not.

She was twenty minutes late for a rare lunch date with him down-town. He was furious when she got there. Wasting Time makes him angry, feeling out of control makes him angry, and perceiving himself as the victim of her tardiness makes him the angriest of all. She didn't defend herself because she knew she was not the issue and time wasn't the issue. His anger was the issue. She had learned to say, *"I'm sorry you are feeling victimized by my lateness, but that was not my intention. I don't blame you for being angry."* She did not say it in a patronizing, pseudo-clinical way, as if she were talking to a problem child. She had the right words and the right music. She had disengaged from Dick's mischief, but not from him. She spoke to him as one imperfect human being to another.

Dick was able to let go of his anger and fear of being hurt by someone he loved, as he had been hurt so many times when he was growing up. His anger subsided and he felt understood and validated. With Penny's help, his role as his wife's victim was being replaced with an identity of his own as a worthwhile human being. They went on with their lunch.

Vignette: Victim Of A Victim

Gina met Woodie at a single's dance. He was charming. They seemed to hit it off from the very start. He had moved from out of town and had no family here, just a few friends. For the first few months, everything was fine. Then they started to argue, as couples do. After a few more months, he began beating her. Gina didn't think too much of it because she had seen her father hit her mother plenty of times. "That's what involved people do. They hit each other."

The beatings got worse. She lost her feelings for him and wanted to break up. He stalked her on her way home from work. She became afraid of him. She was not his lover anymore. She was his victim.

In counseling, Gina learned to see Woodie as someone who perceived himself as Life's Victim. In his eyes, everyone was against him and for no good reason. He was perceiving her ending the relationship as a deprivation. He wasn't getting what he wanted when he wanted it, which was instantly. This loss of her availability was a grievance. He did not appreciate grievances. They made him angry. His anger was not accessible to him. He could not identify it as such or relieve it. He could never see how he contributed to the negative things that happened to him. It was never his fault.

That weekend, he called her on the phone for a date, as charming as he was the night they met. Gina had learned to identify this tactic as The Old Charmeroo and she knew how dangerously deceptive it was.

She arranged to see him so she could tell him in person that it was over. That was her first mistake. She should have told him right then on the phone. He insisted on changing their rendezvous from a neighborhood café to a fancier restaurant out in the country. She went along with it to avoid displeasing him. That was her second mistake. She should have stayed with her original agenda instead of surrendering control to him. Her pleasingness set her up to be victimized by this self-preoccupied "victim turned victimizer." He was in control and he was going to use his control destructively. This is the only way he knew how to use it. It was consistent with his self-contempt.

Woodie got her out in the country, away from everyone. He was angry at her for not giving him his way, for depriving him of her company, and for inconveniencing him. In his eyes, these *offenses* constituted victimization and he felt entitled to punish her for her *crimes* against him.

He hit her harder than he ever had before. She was truly frightened and she knew she was in big trouble. Fortunately for her, she had learned to disengage from such mischief and to do the unexpected. Instead of yelling and screaming, which he would see as another rejection, another *victimization*, she asked herself, *"What is the last thing he expects me to do?"* He expected her to accuse him of hurting her, to order him to stop, or to threaten him with the law, which she knew was a joke. She did not do any of these useless things. She talked about herself, not in a self-pitying way, which could only invite more abuse and scorn, but in a new way, as a person in her own right. She was making it happen, *"I'm all right. It's OK. I'm fine."* She was reassuring him that she was not going to get revenge on him and that he wasn't going to succeed in provoking her into doing anything that would give him an excuse for escalating the madness.

224

He pushed her out of the car and drove off. She walked to a gas station and called a cab. She never saw him again. She knows he is still out there, working on his next victim, but there is nothing she can do to prevent it. Some problems cannot be solved. That is regrettable. But she is alive and out of harm's way. She is not a pleaser anymore. She is no longer a victim looking for a place to happen. These roles have been replaced with a well-earned identity as a worthwhile human being in her own right. She is not compatible with victimizers anymore. She went through the fire and came out stronger than she went in. She is compatible with self-respecting human beings.

93. VIOLENCE

What was the scourge of the twentieth century? Not cancer, AIDS, drug abuse or heart disease, but violence. More people died violently in that century than in any other. There is no basis for assuming the 21st century will be any less violent because we are not taking any informed, appropriate steps to make it so. Our good intentions along these lines will turn out to be counter-productive.

Every year, there are a 1.25 million reported acts of violence. Some result in permanent injury or disfigurement. Others are fatal, ending in the orphaning of children and the widowing of spouses. There are public and private agencies attempting to deal with the plague of violence in our country, but their focus seems to be on the overt act, such as firing handguns or battering a spouse or a child. If they can prevent these acts, they feel they will have prevented violence. The underlying issues that predisposed an individual to solve problems violently have not been identified or addressed. They have not even been sought out.

There is no "instinct" for beating up first-graders. If there were, everyone would be doing it, not just bullies. Civilized human beings take the time and trouble to learn how to manage their emotions. The problem is that hardly anyone is teaching this skill to the people who need it. We should be teaching young people how to express their anger appropriately in the middle ground between too much and too little. We should teach them how to identify the underlying attitudes that predispose them to taking grievances more personally than they need to be taken.

A mistake we make is to treat violence and aggression as if they were irresistible natural forces — animal instincts over which mere mortals have no power. Bullies have been using this excuse for years. It exempts them from the consequences of their self-indulgent behavior. We have seen such *irresistible forces* turned off like a light switch by a phone call from a good buddy down at the saloon. We need to stop taking these self-serving attitudes at face value if we hope to break the cycle of violence leading to violence.

The cycle is not transmitted by our genetic inheritance from the lower orders. It is modeled for us by the significant people in our young lives. Some of us have learned to accept brutality as an efficient problem-solving technique. It requires no cerebral exertion at all. When we grow up, we can hardly wait to pass it on to our children. We feel justified in doing so. "If it was good enough for me, it's good enough for them. That's fair." We cannot argue with this infantile logic. It is not rational, but the nonrational logic of attitudes and convictions from childhood.

It should be noted, however, that this learning by example is not absolute.

Some children of nonviolent parents become violent on their own. Conversely, many children of violent parents reject their brutal example. Some go to the extreme of crusading actively against violence, while others find the middle ground between the extremes where they can solve interpersonal problems cooperatively as equal members of the human race.

Still other adult children of emotionally or physically violent parents would like to choose the middle ground between excessive violence and grim repression, but they do not have the freedom to do so. These individuals have a pool of forbidden rage that is out of their conscious control. It erupts unpredictably and controls their relationships, their jobs and their lives. It provokes them to behave in ways they despise. The outburst can last for hours. We call these aberrant rages, firestorms.

After each firestorm, they feel sincerely guilty and ashamed. They feel weak and worthless. They beg for forgiveness and another chance. They resolve it will never happen again, only to feel desolate when the next attack overcomes them. Nothing has changed. They are Angerholics

Their anger seems to have a life of its own, but it does not. These people must be prepared to endure the pain of resurrecting their subterranean anger. When this anger is brought to the surface and drained properly, not just papered over, the energy that was bound up becomes available for more productive purposes. The wound is allowed to heal cleanly, and the unbidden anger attacks cease to recur. The cycle is broken.

We all have buttons that can be pushed, such as:

- "I want my way and you're not giving it to me."
- "Your unfairness makes me angry."
- "Your wrongness makes me angry."
- "You are going to abandon me."
- "You do not appreciate me. I feel good for nothing."
- "You are victimizing me."

These attitudes from childhood make us vulnerable to becoming angrier than we need to be. We call this state, *super anger*. If these attitudes can be identified and put in a more moderate perspective, we will be less vulnerable to overreacting and our violence statistics will come down. As it is now, we are not well educated in these matters because we are denying that we have an anger problem. We prefer to call our problem "violence," "frustration," or "disgruntlement." As a consequence of our denial, we are a nation with a high rate of anger illiteracy.

The Real Issue

The issue, then, is not violence or aggression. The issue is mismanaged anger. There is no violence without anger. Violence is an emotional response to a grievance, squared or even cubed. Mass murders and serial killings are not *senseless crimes*. They are anger crimes. Most of the perpetrators have been through the medico-legal system, which keeps turning them loose with their anger undiagnosed and untreated. They have even warned their psychiatrists that they will become violent again, even kill again, but the system spits them out anyway. The present system refuses to hear their cries for help. It does not seem to know what to do about anger except to dope people up or wrap them in cold wet sheets until their anger subsides. Nothing has been learned by anyone.

Many experts see a connection between substance abuse and violence. It may be true that these chemicals stimulate the part of the brain that mediates emotion and that depressants temporarily suspend inhibitions against acting out. It is our conviction, however, that substance abusers were filled with unresolved rage before they became intoxicated and that their anger could — and should — have been worked through and relieved beforehand. Mismanaged anger is painful, and these people are trying to relieve their pain by escaping into temporary anesthetics.

We recommend that as many students as possible be given fifteen minutes each week in their Social Studies class for the study of anger. Teachers should be given in-service training on how to teach anger management skills. This will prepare them in advance to cope with anger situations when they arise. After they arise, it will be too late. We think this is a better solution to the violence problem than metal detectors and armed guards in the hallways, which do not relieve the student's super anger, but merely push it further down.

It is unresolved anger in the classrooms, halls and on the playground that make the educator's task more difficult and painful than it needs to be. Unprepared teachers feel inadequate to cope with student anger, and angry students can sense their vulnerability. Through anger training, the teacher's feelings of inadequacy can be replaced with feelings of competence to cope with anger situations. When students see teachers coping effectively with their problems, they are more inclined to respect what the teachers have to say, and classroom management problems in general decrease.

229

Do's and Don't's

- If you have a violence problem in your home, classroom or place of business, do not let yourself be drawn into a power struggle over who can or cannot hit whom.

- Overt violence is a symptom of anger. Do not deal with surface symptoms. They just tell us there is something wrong farther down. Do not protest the unfairness of an assault or defend your innocence. These are not the real issues. The issue is that the assaulter is angry.

- Validate the anger by saying, *"I'm sorry that you are so angry"* or *"It makes you angry when that happens, doesn't it?"* or *"I don't blame you for being angry."*

- Ask a focusing question: *"What happened to make you so angry?"* Even if you do not get an answer right away, you have validated the anger and the individual. You have done the unexpected, which disrupts the assaulter's scenario. Ask the next question: *"What angered you the most?"* These questions are relevant whether the violence is directed outward against others or inward against the self.

- Give the individual an alternative outlet for the out-of-control anger. You can even ask, *"What would you like to do instead?"* Let them tell you what their choices are. Often, if they can talk it out, they will not have to continue their violent behavior. The antidote to their frustration is the power of choice. It is liberating. We can give them that gift for the first time in their lives.

- Using your focusing questions, peel the individual's anger artichoke all the way down if you can. After you have focused on their anger at those who caused the precipitating grievance, you can ask, *"Who else are you angry at?"*

In almost every case of violence, the assaulters are angry at themselves for some perceived failure or weakness for which they blame themselves. This is their self-contempt. The formula for violence, then, is *unmanageable self-anger in a context of self-contempt.* The antidote consists of replacing the self-contempt with a feeling of self-respect as a worthwhile human being in spite of one's faults and imperfections.

230

At the same time, mismanaged anger at the self is tamed and replaced by appropriate anger expressed appropriately.

- Sometimes the violence is due to a brain tumor or other organic cause. The individual who is chronically violent without a precipitating factor should be seen by a competent neurologist. Your responsibility is to make an appropriate referral and to follow up on it.
- Do not take the anger personally, as if it were a reflection on your worth as a person. That step makes you vulnerable to being victimized. Self-respecting persons who are in control of themselves and confident in their ability to cope are less likely to be victimized than people who doubt their self-worth.
- Do not protect violent people from the consequences of their negative behavior. That is a good intention. Do not make excuses for them. That is *enabling*. They behave violently because they can. Someone is letting them. Use a system of logical consequences, "If this happens, then that will happen," and make it stick. It takes courage because violence is scary. If we give in to our fears, the violence will win and everyone will lose.

94. WALK AWAY

Walking away from anger sounds easy enough to do, except that there are many wrong ways to walk away and very few right ones. Walking away the wrong way means that someone took it personally and suffered a loss of self-respect. They are walking away too late. The damage has been done.

Walking away in self-righteous indignation is one of the wrong ways, as is slinking away like a thief in the night. Walking away with a harpoon through your gizzard means you forgot to disengage from someone's mischief. They have already zinged you. Moping like a naughty six-year-old means you have taken someone's angry accusation more personally than you needed to take it.

We are not impressed by these performances, these over-compensations or undercompensations which reveal the individual's obvious lack of preparation for the task of coping with someone's unpleasant anger. Self-respecting people know how to validate anger and solve the problem. They do not have to walk away in these counterproductive ways.

The right way to walk away is to disengage from someone's mischief. If the other person's anger is couched in mischief, such as criticizing, complaining, judging, accusing and so on, we can remember that we are under no obligation to stand there and *enable* them to abuse us. If they are prepared to express their grievances in a mature, businesslike way, we will be glad to hear them out and cooperate with them in resolving our differences. But if they are only interested in building themselves up by tearing us down, we are free to make other arrangements. We can say, *"I'm sorry you're so angry. I have to leave now, but maybe we can talk about it later when you are feeling better."* If they never feel better, then we are off the hook. In any case, it is our right and responsibility to declare our independence from their immature shenanigans. We are not walking out as a reaction to their offensive terms; we are walking out on our own valid terms.

They can tell the difference. They will respect us more if we do it the right way. The door to a successful resolution is still open.

95. WEATHER-PROOFING YOUR BRAINS

When we buy a new car, they tell us to protect the undercarriage so salt and moisture will not get in through the cracks and rust our car out from the inside.

The mischief makers in our life are a lot like road salt. They are corrosive, persistent and merciless. They will seek out our weak spots and infiltrate our lives. They will use our vulnerabilities against us and destroy us from within. They will do it all without even being aware that they are doing it. Maybe we need to undercoat our brains so these people cannot eat us up alive with their nonsense. We call this undercoating process, "Disengaging from the Mischief." It

233

begins with the awareness that the other person is doing something that doesn't need to be done, such as criticizing, judging, condemning, ordering, manipulating, intimidating and so on. The person is throwing up a smoke screen to knock us off balance and provoking us to make countermischief that we would not be making if he or she would leave us alone.

Once we have identified this unpleasant behavior as nonsensical mischief ("It's only kid stuff"), we can begin the process of taking away from them the power to make us crazy, bring us down to their level, or make us do things we don't want to do. We can do this by correcting our two fatal mistakes:

1. We can learn not to take mischief personally, as if it were a reflection on our worth as a person. For instance, if three-year-old Josh says, "I don't love you," we do not take his little jab, painful though it might be, at face value, as if he really meant it and were making sense. He is not making sense. He is merely making mischief to accomplish some post-toddler purpose of his own, such as getting revenge on us for not giving him a fourth cookie. It is not a reflection on our parenting skills or our worth as a human being. If we take it personally, we will overreact nonrationally and try to pound him back into loving us as he apparently used to do just ten minutes ago. It is important that we understand that this is how little mischief makers try to solve their problems at our expense. It doesn't work, of course, but it is all they know. We can teach them better solutions to the problems of living together, but not if we have already made the mistake of taking their nonsense to heart and jumping down the tubes with them. Our antidote to doing so is our self-respect. We need not make the mistake of defining our personal worth in terms of our child's love in the first place. We are worthwhile human beings in spite of our faults and imperfections, whether Josh loves us at every moment or not.

2. We can learn not to take their mischief *literally*, as if it made sense or was even intended to make sense. Sense has nothing to do with it. These people are not making mischief with their higher cognitive powers. They are reacting to the pain of their unsolved life problems. Their negative behavior arises from

234

nonrational attitudes. We must not debate the validity of their mischief, as if it were worthy of serious consideration and rebuttal.

Disengaging from the mischief means catching ourselves about to make one or both of these two mistakes and choosing consciously and deliberately not to. Having so chosen, we are now free to respond on our own terms instead of merely reacting to theirs. They are no longer in control of us. We are.

96. WHAT DIFFERENCE DOES IT MAKE?

This is a quick and easy focusing question we can ask ourselves to sort out anger sense from nonsense. Most of us react to an anger provocation as if it made a difference in our lives, when most of the time it is only kid stuff that doesn't amount to a hill of beans. If it makes a difference, that is one thing. If it does not, it is an entirely different matter and our response needs to change accordingly.

97. WHAT WILL THE NEIGHBORS THINK?

One of the oldest, and worst of our current anger mismanagement techniques is a particularly insidious good intention that we call, "What will the neighbors think?" We all remember being told, "Stop screaming. The neighbors will think we're killing you." Or "How will it look if you walk around with that grumpy face?" Or, "I can't take you anywhere."

It is one thing to have a decent regard for the opinion of others. That is a characteristic of a sane, civilized society. It is another story altogether when we are set up to:

- Live our lives on other people's terms,
- Have no way of finding out from these people what their terms are,

- Pretend to ourselves that we can read their minds and behave accordingly,
- Base our behavior on determinants that are unknown, unknowable and therefore, totally beyond our conscious control.

When we ask our child to live as if he knew what the neighbors were thinking about him, we interfere with his independence of thought and action. We discourage him from acquiring the skills he will need to live an authentic, valid life of his own in the future. We are predisposing him to suppress his negative, unseemly thoughts and actions in deference to people who do not know he is alive or care much either way. These suppressed materials cannot be worked through and managed in a way that will give him relief and enable him to solve his problems.

This scenario creates problems that the individual may react to by:

- Resigning himself to a lifetime of living on everyone else's terms but his own (dependency, pleasing), or
- Rebelling and doing just the opposite of what he thinks they think, or
- Striving to achieve perfect acceptance and shooting for the moon and then despairing of ever attaining this absurd goal, or
- Alternating between these miserable extremes forever, giving up in discouragement and sinking to the bottom.

These non-solutions to the problems of living are a formula for depression, anxiety and obsessive thinking. They preclude happiness.

Such people will need help replacing this second hand, derivative life style with a mature, responsible identity of their own. We bring about this result by giving people specific Homeworks to do which will have the effect of replacing this constellation of self-defeating attitudes with a more congenial set. One such Homework assignment is called, "Do What Pleases You." Many of us have never had experience pleasing ourselves. We were taught, with the best of intentions, that self-pleasing was faintly obscene and unacceptably selfish. By default, we end up trying to please everyone *but* ourselves. Since we do not know how these people wish to be pleased, we doom

236

ourselves to an unpleased and unpleasing existence. Such a life is not worth living.

When we do an appropriate self-pleasing Homework, we experience liberation, identity, equality, trust in our judgment, belonging and all the other components of self-respect. We are allowing our neighbors to do the same. We have an appropriate concern for their opinion and we have no intention of behaving in bizarre, unacceptable ways. Our intention is to cooperate with them in doing what reality requires mature, civilized people to do, not because we live in fear of ostracism, but because it makes our own life less problematic and more enjoyable. We are able to control our lives positively, not negatively. When we respect ourselves on this new basis, the predisposition to depression, anxiety and obsessive thinking are replaced with a predisposition to take life as it comes and enjoy the ride as best we can.

Vignette: What Will the Neighbors Think?

A suburban couple with two young children were eating Sunday dinner in their favorite restaurant. Scott, the youngest, began to sort out his lima beans from his corn so he could eat each vegetable separately at his leisure. He had been doing this since his high-chair days, which ended more than four years ago. His mother, an otherwise sensible and competent young woman, let out a blast that could be heard in the parking lot. "What are you doing that for? Didn't I tell you to stop playing with your food! Why can't you just eat your succotash like a normal person?"

Being allergic to child abuse, a diner at a nearby table arose and offered the distraught parent his assistance. *"I know his behavior bothers you, Madam, but please tell me this: What difference does it make if he eats his succotash all mixed together or separated into its respective components?"*

"It will take all night. We can't sit here forever."

"Ah! Do you have a pressing engagement later this evening?"

"No. We're not really going to do anything, just go home."

"Then I repeat, what difference does it make?"

237

"I feel like everyone in the room is watching this kid sort out his beans and corn and I just can't stand it."

"May I say, Madam, that no one in this restaurant gives a rap about your child's succotash but you. They are more perturbed by your reaction than by anything your child is doing. I hate to disappoint you, but your child just isn't that important to them."

"I don't want him to grow up playing with his food like that."

"Do you imagine that you can prevent this regrettable outcome by screaming at a six-year-old child?"

"No. I guess it doesn't work."

"What difference will it make if he grows up to be a confirmed food sorter?"

"His wife will think I did a terrible job of training him."

"You are worried twenty years in advance about the opinion of a woman who may not even have been born yet?"

"It does sound pretty silly when you put it that way."

"What difference will it make if she thinks you did a poor job of raising her husband?"

"She won't like me."

"She won't like you if you have driven her partner nuts with your screaming. In any case, it will be her problem from then on, won't it."

"Yes, and I wish her all the luck in the world with his succotash."

"The truth is that it doesn't make any difference at all how he eats his side dishes. The child cannot control very much in his little world, but he certainly can control his veggies. If you leave him alone, he will come to replace this infantile form of carbohydrate control with more mature, appropriate forms of control in the real world."

"What if he doesn't outgrow it?"

"What difference will it make? What is more important, preventing this absurd disaster 20 years from now or having a pleasant dinner with your loved ones in the present? The issue is not table manners. The issues are control, perfectionism, living in the future, fear of failure, and feelings of inferiority. You are trying to relieve your own painful self-doubts at your child's expense. Your good intentions for him cannot make things better, only worse."

"What can I do?"

"Now that is a good question. You can exercise your power of choice. You can choose to let go of your child's eating habits. You can choose to accept him as a worthwhile human being in the present, in spite of his little faults and imperfections."

"How will that help?"

"It will give you some relief from the pressure and stress that you are putting yourself under. You will set an example of self-acceptance and self-respect for your child to see and to follow."

"Then what?"

"Then your pain and unhappiness in the present will be replaced with feelings of identity, maturity, appropriate responsibility, independence and all the other components of self-respect."

"Will that make a difference?"

"It will make all the difference in the world."

98. WHEN IN DOUBT, ASK

When we think someone is angry at us, but we aren't sure, we are often reluctant to find out. We are afraid that asking will only make things worse. So we tiptoe around, hoping it will all go away. This is not a good technique.

Telling people to communicate their concerns to one another is good advice.

The question is, why don't they take it? If they took it, we wouldn't have to keep telling them to communicate.

The answer is that sometimes communication takes courage and many people are too discouraged to break the sound barrier in their own homes. They take the easy way out. They walk on eggshells forever. They may never find out that it would have been easier to do it the hard way.

Vignette: The Silent Insult

Ron and Grace were expecting company that evening. Ron suggested that Grace straighten out the kitchen, fix lunch and vacuum the living room while he got the recreation room ready.

A half hour later, Grace looked up to see Ron plugging in the vacuum cleaner. "He did it to me again," she thought. He gives me a list of chores to do and then does them himself if I'm not quick enough to suit him." She was sure Ron's behavior was a silent criticism of her housekeeping skill and that he was angry as usual at her slowness.

This time, however, she didn't suffer and stew in silence. Instead of trying to guess at Ron's motivation (See "MIND READING" on page 129.), she had the courage to ask him what was really going on. Her hurt and anger showed in her voice. Ron did not take her hostile questioning personally. He realized that there was a misunderstanding somewhere. He did not defend himself against her implied accusation that he was silently finding fault with her. He just told the truth about himself, *"I got through early, so I decided to do the vacuuming myself."*

Grace was glad she had asked. She wished she had been a little less intense, but it could have been a lot worse. They could have had a screaming fight over something that had not happened in the real world, only in her head. Ron was glad, too, that he didn't overreact to this potential provocation. He chose not to say, "You're so sensitive!" It never helped before and it wouldn't have helped now. Grace's question cleared the air, it relieved her pain and she felt in control of herself again. She thought to herself, "I ought to do that more often."

99. WHERE DOES THAT COME FROM? (How to Break the Transference)

Many of our grievances arise out of a transference from some negative person in the past to someone in our present who may not be negative at all. For instance, Jane may remember her father scolding her terribly for losing a dime when money was tight. Now, Sam is complaining about the cost of her gall-bladder medicine. Her old money attitudes and fears come to the fore and she behaves now as she did then: By crying, defending and generally overreacting to the provocation. He cannot understand where this emotionality comes from, and neither can she.

When this happens and neither party can see any basis in the present for an exaggerated anger attack, it is helpful to ask a focusing question such as, *"Where does that come from?"*

Very often this question will evoke a relevant recollection in which the answer to the mystery is embedded.

"Oh, I don't know," said Jane. "Wait! I remember one time when I was seven, my father sent me to the store for a quart of milk. On the way home, I dropped a dime. It rolled into the grass. I got down and looked for it. I was afraid of what my parents would do if I came home without it. They'd think I had stolen it. I didn't realize that it had gotten darker. My father came looking for me. I was still down on my hands and knees. He dragged me home, as I knew he would, scolding me all the way. When I got home, mom took over. The issue wasn't the money. They were trying to teach me responsibility, but they only taught me to hate myself for being so stupid. Now, when you talk about the money I have to spend on myself, all these feelings of irresponsibility, guilt and worthlessness come flooding back."

241

"Now that you know where your feelings are coming from, what can you do about it?"

"I can catch myself going back to being a seven-year-old child again. I can choose to remind myself that I am a grown-up now and that I have adult judgment and competencies. I can remember to feel like a worthwhile human being in spite of my faults and imperfections, one of which is that my gallbladder acts up from time to time. Another is that I have an imperfect husband who has control issues about money. I can choose not to take them personally. I can agree that he is angry, calm him down, and then do what I have to do."

The act of verbalizing early events in our lives gives us a chance to reevaluate their significance to us. As a child, these events may have been very impressive, and we never forgot them. As an adult, we can now use our mature intelligence and experience to put these events in a more moderate, manageable perspective.

This experiencing of past attitudes and fears in the present is called *"transference."* Once you have caught the transference and made it conscious in the present, you can choose to break out of it.

Vignette: Breaking the Transference

Leslie and Bill met at a party and fell head over heels in love. Their first few months together were pure enchantment. Then some of their respective mannerisms began to come out of the woodwork.

Leslie noticed that Bill became upset whenever she said "no" to one of his suggestions for the evening's activity. Bill, noticed that whenever he started to defend his preference for one movie over another, Leslie became agitated and very counter-defensive.

In counseling, Leslie and Bill learned that these out-of-line reactions may have had their origins in each of their childhood pasts.

The next time Leslie became agitated, Bill was ready with a focusing question — *"Leslie, where does that come from?"* He had caught her in the act, while she was still in the throes of a transference from the past. She coughed-up the answer immediately. "When my father got angry and raised his voice, I knew I was in for a beating that would

242

leave me half-conscious on my bedroom rug. Now when you raise your voice, it's just like the bad old days and I can't take it."

Having identified the origin of her defensiveness, Leslie was able to begin breaking the connection between Bill and her father, and between her six-year-old victim role and her self-respecting adult identity in the present.

The next time Bill overreacted to Leslie's "no," she turned the tables on him.

"Where does that come from?" she asked. Bill said, "When my father said no, it was like a red flag. He was trying to control me. It didn't make any difference what I wanted to do, he'd just say, "No." I couldn't rebel against him. It wasn't permitted. I didn't break loose from him until I was 26 years old. Now, when you say, "No," I feel like you are trying to control me the way he did, and it makes me very angry."

Leslie and Bill are still catching themselves in these transferences, but they are no longer being defeated by them. These attacks from the past are coming farther and farther apart. They are taking them less personally each time. They are not dependent children anymore. They are independent adults with minds of their own. They are not perfectly in control, but they are not out of control, either.

100. THE WRONG PARENT DIED

Most of us could not bring ourself to say that we wish it had been our wretched father who died instead of our only ally in the family, our mother. We are angry that our father is still alive. We keep this guilty thought locked inside us. What would the neighbors think of us if we told the truth? We would feel painfully guilty and ashamed. It's not worth the pain. We keep it in forever.

Mary lost her mother, Gina, when she was 18. Her father, Max, had been cruel to Gina and the children for years. But she died and he lived. On the one hand, Mary was glad her mother's pain was

243

over at last. Her father couldn't hurt her anymore. But Mary had to live with the unfairness of this loss. She didn't deserve this grief. She had lost two ways — the absence of her mother's love and support, and the continued presence of a negative father. There was nothing she could do about either one. Ten years later, there is still nothing she could do about it. Her father now lives four states away, but he is still controlling her with his power struggles and manipulations.

Mary was aware of her resentment of Max's mismanagement of her mother's estate, his shameful behavior with other women, and his continued abuse of his three adult children, but she couldn't understand why she was still grieving the loss of her mother after all these years. She still feels guilty of rebelling years ago against her mother's request that she come home at ten p.m. instead of three a.m. She had said things she never should have said. It was too late to go back and repair the damage. The problem seemed insoluble. She regretted that her mother didn't enjoy the happiness she deserved and now she never would. There was nothing Mary could do about that, either.

Talking it out helped Mary relieve some of the internal pressure, tension and stress that these unresolved problems were causing her. Her obsessive thinking about it died down but didn't stop. She was still depressed.

Mary was not aware how *angry* she was at the sense of unfairness that her mother's death created in her heart. She had not allowed herself to wish her father dead in her mother's place; that was too irresponsible and too displeasing to bear. So she kept that secret suppressed inside herself where it turned into symptoms she didn't need. It kept her from being happy in her relationships. Her attitude was, *"How can I be happy when this unfairness is going on and there's nothing I can do to right this wrong."* That attitude has set her up for a lifetime of frustration. Her frustration had turned into joy-killing obsessing and anxiety. It was unnecessarily prolonging her grief and it was killing her relationship with herself.

In counseling, we were able to identify this forbidden anger for her and give her permission to bring it into the light of day. Her anger wasn't a crime or a sin at all. It was unpleasant but very

244

human. To give herself relief from the pain it was causing her, we gave Mary a choice she didn't know she had. She could choose to write an anger letter to her father for still having his life and wasting it in irresponsible foolishness. She could also write a letter to herself for wasting so much of her life in this useless depression, for being so inadequate that she couldn't even identify this stone in her heart let alone remove it. While she was at it, she wrote an anger letter to God for taking the good parent and leaving the bad one down here to continue making her miserable. It was so unfair and she didn't deserve this unfairness.

Writing her anger out gave her some relief from her feeling there was nothing she could do about this insoluble problem. She read her letter over and tore it up. The problem wasn't her mother, her father, herself or her God. The problem was the painful, unresolved anger in her heart. No one had ever told her it was down there or how to relieve it. She was finally able to let it go, to let her mother rest in peace, and to take life as it comes in the years ahead. The grief left with the anger.

101. THE WRONG QUESTION

There are two kinds of questions, the right kind and the wrong kind. The right kind of question leads to resolution of a problem. The wrong kind leads to a dead end and makes things worse.

One such wrong question is, *"What am I doing wrong?"* If you knew what you were doing wrong, you wouldn't be doing it. This is our old feeling of inadequacy to cope coming to the fore. We are condemning ourselves without even knowing what we have done. It's hard to think straight after we have just torn ourselves down. There is no cure for the retroactive wrongness. It's a self-defeating negative attitude. It isn't a matter of right or wrong. It is merely imperfect and inappropriate. We can respect ourselves in spite of it. We can now use our adult judgment to find out what reality requires us to do so we can do it. We are worthwhile human beings in the meantime.

Another example of a wrong question is, *"Why did I let it happen?"* This question implies we are specifically guilty of the crime of *failing to prevent it.* In addition, it implies that we are responsible for preventing bad things from happening and, when they do, we are guilty of the crime of irresponsibility.

These mistaken questions arise out of our childhood attitudes toward control. We have learned as a child that "Bad things happen when I lose control." To five year olds, it appears reasonable to conclude that they can keep themselves from being hurt by preventing these bad things from happening. They appoint themselves the sole responsibility for doing so. Then, when something bad happens, they have no one but themselves to blame. They let it happen. If they only knew how, they could tighten up the controls and prevent it from happening again next time. They are seeking to improve their technique, if you will.

In the meantime, they are feeling victimized by this bad thing, and they compound their distress by faulting their strategic defense system. They are blaming the victim: themselves.

This is a whole constellation of childhood attitudes that we should have outgrown but did not. It is a mistake to define control as preventing bad things from happening. It is a useless good intention that we have for ourselves. We are so busy controlling in this absurd and inappropriate way that we are, in effect, out of control in the real world.

It is nonsense because in an imperfect world bad things happen every twelve minutes. They cannot be prevented by standing sentry duty at the front door. That is not living. That is a substitute for real life that we call *preventation*. It is a full-time job. We put ourselves on guard duty twenty years ago and forgot to take ourselves off. In the meantime, we are not fully alive. We are merely existing.

Self-respecting people do not make these mistakes. They take reasonable, realistic precautions, of course, but they do not devote their lifetimes to such negative, life-destroying ambitions as preventing bad things from happening. They take the ups and downs of life as they come and do the best they can with them. That is a healthy, appropriate attitude. They do not imagine they have the power to prevent a child from skinning his knee or a spouse from falling ill. Their worth as a person is not at stake, so they do not take such misfortunes personally at all. These events are regrettable, but they didn't let them happen. They had no power to prevent them in the first place.

Vignette: I Should Have Known

Tina was having anxiety attacks in the morning. They started four years ago.

"What happened four years ago?"

"I was raped."

Tina's morning anxiety can be understood as anger that has been mismanaged and turned into a symptom. Tina was aware of her terrible anger at the rapist and at her then boyfriend, who failed utterly to cope with her crisis. She had worked through these angers with a rape counselor.

She had not, however, worked through her anger at *herself*. She kept focusing on her wrong question. "How could I have been so stupid to go out jogging so late? I should have known better. It's like I let it happen."

It is this so-called stupiditude that was keeping Tina angry at herself so long after the fact. This anger at herself was below the level of conscious awareness. It was beyond her conscious control. Her out-of-control anger was making her feel she was out of control, that something else terrible was going to happen, and she couldn't prevent that, either. That feeling manifested itself as anxiety. Tina wrote herself an anger letter so she could see her thoughts and fears in front of her and manage them using her adult intelligence.

Tina saw the fallacy of blaming herself for her own victimization. It was not her fault at all, and she was guilty of nothing. She merely used a public area for her own purposes, as is her right under the Constitution. She is not stupid for not knowing the future in advance. She is not guilty for failing to prevent it from happening.

247

Tina understood all of this intellectually, but she didn't fully integrate it emotionally until she remembered meeting a woman at her group who had been raped in her own kitchen. She hadn't "let it happen" at all! She was minding her own business at the time and still it happened. Tina was able to put this issue of "letting" into a more realistic, regrettable perspective. "Letting" had nothing to do with it. She had no power to "let" or "not let." She chose to stop living in the past and live in the present instead. She resolved to take life as it comes and do the best she could with it. She had replaced her wrong questions with more appropriate attitudes toward herself, toward others and toward life.

One of these others was her current boy friend, Brad. Tina had been displacing her many angers onto Brad, who, of course, made the mistake of taking her anger personally and feeling compelled to defend his integrity. Tina hated these fights and blamed herself for "letting them happen." Her wrong question was, "Why am I still doing this, when I should know better by now?"

Tina was shoulding on herself. In so doing, she was setting herself up for more guilt, self-recrimination and self-anger.

Tina is learning that there is no such "should." Should is merely a *preference*. True, it would be preferable if she were strong enough in herself to catch herself about to displace her anger on Brad and choose not to. With practice, someday she will be. In the meantime, she is a worthwhile human being in spite of these imperfections. As she does her Homework day by day and validates her worth as a person, these regrettable lapses will come farther apart and, one day, they will cease. She is learning that negative things happen to imperfect people in an imperfect world and that she can gradually replace her inappropriate feelings of guilt with appropriate feelings of regret when they do, but "letting" is the wrong question. It does not have to be answered.

102. YELLING AND SCREAMING

The *Yelling and Screaming* technique is quite popular with parents of younger children, older children and middle-aged children. This technique is not successful in the long run because it teaches the children to yell and scream back. This becomes their anger management style. This is how they then solve problems in their house.

Out-of-control yelling and screaming is not a terribly sophisticated technique because it requires absolutely no brains. It is not a civilized technique. In fact, it is a *de*civilizing technique. It does not make the children better, only worse. They learn nothing from screaming except that their parents are out of control. Children resent their parents' unfair abuse of their power. When we scream our anger at a fellow human being, it is an indication we do not know what else to do. It is a declaration of emotional bankruptcy. Children are not inclined to hold such bankrupt persons in high regard.

For many parents, teachers, managers, politicians and others, screaming seems to be a short cut to solving problems. It's a great little time saver. Instead of taking the time to express their legitimate anger appropriately like grown-up ladies and gentlemen, they scream it out. It's easier that way. Some day they will learn what many of us already know: It is really easier to do it the hard way.

The Nonscreamers

Some of us never learned the Yelling and Screaming technique from our anger illiterate parents. We were not allowed to express any anger at all, let alone to yell and scream. We learned we would be beaten and shunned if we broke the Code of Silence. We learned that children who express anger outwardly are unlovable and worthless. Under these circumstances, the expression of anger was a luxury we could not afford. Some of us had to acquire the "Yelling and Screaming" technique in later life. Others are still screaming without knowing they are doing so. These are *Silent Screams.* These suppressed screams tear us up from the inside.

"You cannot build yourself up by tearing others down."

Rudolf Dreikurs

Vignette: An All-Time First

As a child, Ivy was not allowed to scream. She had health problems, and screaming was considered to be dangerously stressful for her. One day, when her dolly's head fell off, she yelled and screamed her impotent rage. Daddy beat her with a belt to discourage this stressful behavior in the future. This was his good intention. It was self-indulgent and counter-productive.

Ivy learned her lesson well. Now she does not express anger — or any other emotion. Her fear is that if she expresses any emotion, even a happy one, the dam will burst and she will get another beating. She imagines she is controlling her anger in a mature, appropriate way. However, she learned this technique of suppressing her anger when she was four years old. There is nothing mature or appropriate about it.

After a period of counseling, Ivy's Homework was to write her anger down in the form of an anger letter to her misguided father and her copeless, hand-wringing mother. It took a while, but she managed to do it. It took more courage than she thought she had, but she worked up to it over time.

This accomplishment prepared her for an even more radical break with her tormented past. Her next Homework was to express her anger openly. She was able to do her anger Homework the following week. Her friend, Annie, canceled a dinner date at the last minute. Instead of swallowing her anger, as she usually did, she had the courage to tell the truth: *"It makes me angry when you stand me up. What am I supposed to do now? I am very disappointed in you, Annie. That hurts my feelings."* Annie apologized, which she had never done before. Moreover, she arranged to make it up to Ivy by taking her out to dinner Sunday night. Ivy felt validated and vindicated. She had affirmed herself as a person in the world. This was not aggressiveness or bitchiness. It was appropriate responsibility for her own sanity.

Soon afterwards, life presented Ivy with an opportunity to do some Homework on still another plateau. Ivy worked in a flower shop. She delivered a bouquet to Mrs. Preston, a long-time and difficult customer. As usual, Mrs. Preston refused to pay the thirty dollars

251

on the bill. "Here's ten dollars. Take it or leave it." Ivy had a difficult decision to make. She was angry at Mrs. Preston for putting her in this ridiculous position of having to haggle on the front porch over a measly twenty bucks.

All of a sudden, Ivy let loose! She yelled and screamed at Mrs. Preston, using words that she had never been allowed to use, not even in her dreams. She yelled and yelled. Mrs. Preston's jaw dropped, but she said nothing. After she was through yelling and screaming, Ivy grabbed the ten dollar bill and drove back to the shop. She poured out her story to her boss, Harry, who had been through this with Mrs. Preston many times. He could take it, but it made him angry that his nonrational customer was taking her frustration out on a vulnerable shop assistant. He called her up and told her to come over with the other twenty dollars, which she did.

In the meantime, Ivy was evaluating her strange performance on the front porch. For the first time in her life, she had let her anger out in this unseemly, out-of-control way. Yet she was not out of control. She was just angry. She let her anger happen, and when she was through, she stopped. She was not paralyzed with fear of what the neighbors or her parents would think if they found out. She was not terrified of displeasing people who had no problem displeasing her. She felt good. In fact, she felt triumphant. She had vented her anger and lived. She felt all the facets of self-respect including: identity, maturity, appropriate responsibility, liberation, independence, equality, security and even trust in her judgment. She hadn't lived on Mrs. Preston's absurd terms, but on her own imperfect but valid terms. She had a feeling of accomplishment, success and confidence that she could do it again.

For the first time, she had the power of choice. The yelling and screaming option had never been open to her before. Now it was. It was her right and her responsibility to use this choice constructively and not destructively. She had the adult judgment now to tell her where and when this technique was appropriate. When it was not, she had other choices to fall back on. She could tell the truth, write an anger letter, walk away, or give it a pass. She was not her father's daughter anymore. She was Ivy's Ivy.

We debriefed Ivy's success in her counseling session. We helped her to make the fine distinction between out-of-control yelling and screaming with this constructive but unpleasant use of anger.

This was not destructive on Ivy's part because:

- She was not trying to build herself up by tearing her customer down,
- She was not trying to control Mrs. Preston into doing what she wanted her to do,
- She didn't have good intentions for herself or her boss money-wise,
- She wasn't taking Mrs. Preston's stingy mischief personally.

From our point of view, Ivy:

- Was telling the truth as she saw it,
- Had a real intention to relieve the pain of her frustration in the only way open to her,
- Was assuming appropriate responsibility for her half of the conversation,
- Was setting limits on her customer's mischief,
- Was doing what it pleased her to do instead of living in fear of displeasing,
- Was declaring her independence from a lifetime of overdriven attitudes — loud and clear.

Yelling and screaming out-of-control is a snit. This was not a snit. This was telling the truth. The truth hurts sometimes. We don't say it is pleasant. We don't say you have to like it.

It is true, Ivy was a little over the top, which is understandable considering she had been in the anger closet for twenty years. Her technique needed a little refining, but that would come with practice.

- She was not guilty of a crime, it was merely *regrettable* that she had to be as forceful as she was.
- She is working toward finding the middle ground between too little anger and too much. It is a process.

253

- She had the courage to tell the truth about how she felt, even though it was unpleasant.
- She was living in the present instead of trying to prevent (control) disasters in the future.

Afterwards, her anxiety came down, her depression lifted. Her obsessive thinking settled down. She had begun the process of liberating herself from the old Ivy. We do not advocate yelling in someone's face. It just turns out that way sometimes. If we feel vindicated, relieved, independent, in control, mature, equal and appropriately responsible for our own sanity, then it's a Homework.

"Freedom is never free
and there are no rights
without responsibilities."

Charles August Jordan 1867

Appendix A

ANGER LETTERS

To A Dead Husband

Anne had been a widow for thirty years. Her life had been very hard. She would talk to her dead husband in the evening and pour out her grief at being abandoned at such an early age with two small children to raise all by herself, having to support herself in a job she didn't like. Her out-pourings seemed to help each time, but the feelings kept coming back. Nothing was changing. Anne came to the Anger Clinic. She learned that she was angry at life for what it had done to her, and angry at George for leaving her. It didn't make sense at first to be angry at someone who didn't want to die, but she went home and wrote her anger letters anyway. The nightly harangues stopped. Anne's physical health began to improve after she relieved her store of suppressed anger. She later wrote anger letters to herself and to God. It seems to be helping.

Dear George:

How dare you die on me and leave me without an identity. I had a role as Mrs. George Drago and now, to this day, I still do not have an

257

identity. My brothers never allowed me a role. I'm angry and am suffering with the following diagnosed symptoms due to your death:

1. Spastic colon and uncontrollable bowel

2. Hiatal hernia

3. Diverticulitis

4. Hypertension of the bowel

5. Ulcer

The hiatal hernia leaves me with terrible pain and heart-burn that comes up to my throat. It's hard for me to get my words out. Maybe that is why. Now I can see that writing is much easier for me than talking to you without my thoughts written down. No wonder I get the flu and sore throats so often — yet another symptom of not expressing words on how I feel. There is a great fear that you left me with when you died. I was a victim of your loss and grievance. I thought you married me for better or for worse, for a lifetime, but you died after four years and two children. You made me feel like a victim.

I hate you and am still angry at you for leaving me at the age of 33 and forcing me to stand on my own two feet and raise two small children all by myself. My happy memories to you ended in disaster. I was forced to build my confidence and become more self-sufficient, stronger and more responsible, which made me grow up and mature before my time. I no longer had a post to lean on. But most of all, I lost my feeling of belonging and security and was alone having to find my place in society. I felt I did not belong to anyone any more, not even myself. I felt like a victim of insecurity and abandonment. As a child I was abandoned and you abandoned me a second time. My fear is that I will be abandoned again. I have not found another relationship because of that fear.

You made me lose my self-respect. I felt like a nobody again with no identity and no longer a worthwhile human being. I was in the prime of my life. Your sisters were a thorn in my side because, while they helped me financially when the children were small, I had to account to them for every move I made. I felt like a prisoner in my own house. When your sister, Marge, died, I felt freed from my prison. I went back to college to learn how to manage my money.

On the day of your funeral, your best boyfriend, Jim, told me that you took pills in the service which were as big as a half dollar, in order to dissolve your kidney stones. These kidney stones finally killed you, but I never knew how serious your problem was. This statement just devastated me. To think that you didn't have the courage to confide in me. How could you do this to me? I felt betrayed. To this day I am still angry at you for not confiding in me and for all the suffering I am still going through with my poor health, which is due to your death thirty years ago.

You did an injustice to me by dying and today I'm still angry at you for using me and lying to me.

Anne Drago

To an Alcoholic Friend

Beth and her group are very close. They have been good friends since high school. The five of them talk on the phone each day (frequently making use of "three-way calling") and basically are there for each other through thick and thin. Proms, weddings, in-law problems, first baby deliveries, moving days, house fires and Christmas, they were there for each other. It is a really successful support system. Even their husbands didn't break them up. They joined in and became close friends themselves.

Yet all was not perfect. Group members had their problems individually and collectively, but the girls could usually see each other through and ride it out. But there was one problem that was the vexation of them all. It was insidious and getting worse as time went on. Tina had begun to drink and, slowly over the years, like a dysfunctional family, the group was deteriorating. The five were being involved in crisis after crisis. It was like quicksand. Like many alcoholics', Tina's behavior was often out of control and the girls would be called on to help her. They often realized that they didn't know how to help.

Tina had always been the leader of the group. She was the strong one, and they all loved her. This made it harder for them to cope with her negative behavior.

Beth had even moved in with Tina and her mother when, as a teenager, Beth and her mother weren't getting along. Beth felt she owed Tina and her family a lot. Yet, Beth and the other girls were finding it harder and harder to ignore Tina's actions. Her neglect of her children, verbally abusive phone calls, and frequent trips to the emergency room were becoming just too stressful

To confuse the issue further, Tina was in denial. No one could even mention her drinking or she would fly off the handle and wreak havoc with counterattacks and other mischief.

Beth and the others truly loved Tina. They were worried about her and wanted desperately not to lose her friendship — or her. Even though Tina was very protective of her drinking, the girls knew that by being quiet and pretending it wasn't there (as Tina preferred), they were only enabling her to continue this destructive lifestyle. They did not know what else to do. They felt trapped and powerless.

Finally, Tina caught wind of some talk about her condition. She went out of control, accused them of mutiny and of being malicious behind her back. She blamed Beth for being the instigator. Tina further responded by telling tales on each one of them, some true, some not true. It didn't matter to Tina what she said as long as they started turning against each other and taking the heat off her. She created a smoke screen, a distraction. It was negative excitement and, for awhile, it worked.

One day, Beth couldn't take it anymore and came to the Anger Clinic. She was hurt and confused. Where had all the love and support gone? Fifteen years of friendship were being shot to hell. She didn't know what to do. It was such a mess. Shortly into her therapy, we advised Beth to write an anger letter to Tina. It was suggested that she use the ancient technique called "Telling The Truth." (page 201)

Here is Beth's letter. Notice how Beth:

- Kept it simple
- Told the truth
- Came from a position of love and respect.
- Spoke only for herself, not confusing the issue by speaking for three other people.
- Stuck to the main point and addressed only the main issues.

Beth decided that the main issues that she needed to address were as follows:

- She truly cares for Tina and values their fifteen-year friendship;
- Tina has a drinking problem;
- Tina needs help;
- She will no longer accept Tina's drunken behavior. In the future she will not expose herself or her children to Tina when she has had too much to drink.

Dear Tina:

I am writing this letter because I love you and care for you very much. We've been friends for half of our lives and that's saying an awful lot. There aren't many people who can say that they've had friendships last so long. I am really angry and hurt that you would think that I would ever maliciously hurt you in any way. What I am doing right now is not talking to you while you are drunk.

The last time you called me you were drunk and I will not talk to you when you're in that condition. I never said I wouldn't talk to you at all. As a matter of fact I said, "Call me when you are sober."

Tina, you have a drinking problem. You have had a drinking problem for quite some time. This is not the first time you've had this problem and if you don't get some help it will destroy you. Yes, Tina, you need some help. I know that you are probably in shock right now because I have never come out and said this so blatantly before.

I have asked myself why the "A" word, "Alcoholic," has always been so taboo. Why was alcoholism a "sensitive" subject — your "trigger" spot? There is only one answer and that is that deep down inside you know you are an alcoholic. This wasn't a problem for you when we were in high school or even in college, but it became a problem later on. I have tried to figure it out and I think it was after you and Steve broke up.

Actually, I can remember the first time you got angry with me for talking to Jeff (Tina's husband) about your drinking problem. That made me angry, but I never had the courage to tell you. I am telling you now. I am angry at you for what you are doing to my friend, Tina. You are killing her and depriving me of someone who used to make me happy. I am angry about the loss. I am hoping that my anger will get through to you so that you will start to take my concern seriously.

Anyway, my point is that you have a problem with your drinking. Even though you told me not to worry when we talked about this a few weeks ago, I am worried and I will continue to worry about you because I do love you and care for you. I know you've got your share of problems. So do I, but I do feel that you don't value our friendship. Tina, there is no conspiracy. I am not trying to hurt you. I am only trying to help you. That is what friends are for. You may not need or want my help, but I am your friend. I do care and I am sincerely worried.

You know, we've been estranged, in a way, for the last year and a half. Part of the reason is because after you gave birth to Tommy you started to drink heavily again. Because there was such a taboo on the subject, I never said anything to you or to anyone else until recently. It has taken me a long time to finally confront you. It has always been difficult for me to confront you, but that is another issue that isn't important right now.

What is important is that I am confronting you whether you like it or not, and I will continue to confront you as long as we maintain a friendship. Tina, I wish you could see it. I wish you could look at yourself in a magic mirror and see deep down inside. But there is no magic mirror. This letter is the closest I can come to showing you how you look to a fellow human being.

I wish you would stop blaming your drinking on your problems. See that your drinking is only making your problems worse and please realize that they aren't going away or changing every time you try to escape.

I have so much to say to you, so much more I want to resolve with you, but this isn't the time. I won't play tit for tat. The point of this letter is to let you know that I am here for you and I always will be. But I cannot be there for you when you are drunk. I am sorry that things aren't the way you want them to be. But I have realized that life just doesn't always go the way you plan. In life, you need to adapt and adjust. There are so many things in my life that weren't "in the plan." I have had to adjust and when I can't, I get some help.

Please, for your sake, for Jeff's sake and for Tommy's, but most importantly for your sake — get some help. You know it's O.K. to get help. You've done it before and you can do it again. If you need me, I am here for you.

Love,

Beth

Beth sent her letter to Tina, who called her as soon as she received it. Beth used the techniques she had learned:

She validated Tina's anger: "I don't blame you for being angry." She did not defend her position on this matter. She required no defense. She set an example of sanity for Tina to see and follow if she chose. She was assuming appropriate responsibility for herself, not Tina. She was hurt and angry, but she did not take Tina's raging personally. It was not about her at all. It was Tina's sickness talking and it had to come out.

After the storm passed, Tina calmed down. Beth had passed the test. It was clear to Tina that Beth had real intentions, not phony good intentions like her family members. She felt encouraged by Beth's willingness to go through the fire for her, to stick with her and not abandon her like her loved one's always seemed to do. She felt that Beth had earned her trust by staying the course, riding it out to the bitter end. They talked about some of the options that were open to Tina, but the responsibility for making a choice in her own behalf was hers.

Tina felt respected in spite of her many imperfections. She felt validated. She felt encouraged, which is the antidote for her lifetime of discouragement. They agreed that when they went out next time, they would all order non-alcoholic drinks, and that Tina would enter therapy to find out how to relieve the pain of her existence in the right way. They hung up. They were friends again. They both had been through the fire, and they were both changed. This was not the end of anything. It was a beginning.

Appendix B

THE COMPONENTS OF
OUR CHARACTER

Dr. Rudolf Dreikurs, a student of Alfred Adler, defined self-respect as "the feeling that one is a worthwhile human being in spite of one's faults and imperfections."

This definition is not expressed in terms of "knowing," but of "feeling." It is not based on objective conditions. It is a subjective experience. It is not conditional and does not depend on external indicators of achievement. It cannot be given or taken away by external agencies.

The therapeutic process consists of replacing a client's underlying self-contempt with self-respect. This is not done by bolstering self-esteem with pats on the back or empty shouts of encouragement. We see self-esteem as an estimation or *opinion* of oneself. If this estimation is based on false premises, parental indulgence or mistaken logic, what is it worth? Nothing! People who swagger and strut do not have high self-esteem, as their admiring, naive subjects seem to believe. Their posturing is mere arrogance and bravado. We understand their

veneer of superiority as their way of relieving the pain of feeling inferior and inadequate to cope with the adult demands of real-life. They
are overcompensating for their underlying convictions that they are
not good enough. This is their way of keeping their secret inferiority
from leaking out. They are preventing the painfully humiliating
exposure of their worthlessness

They are not worthless. They just *feel* that way and overcompensate accordingly.

This feeling of self-contempt is below the level of conscious awareness. It is an *attitude* they have towards themselves. It is the task of
therapy to replace this negative attitude with a positive one. This
positive attitude is called self-respect.

Self-respecting people do not have to overcompensate for
anything because there is nothing to overcompensate for. They do
not have to anesthetize the pain of their existence because it isn't
there. They feel good enough as they are. This is not a prescription
for stagnation, but an invitation to do as much with their lives as
they can and to make a positive contribution to their community
instead of a negative one. They are not dependent on others for the
validation of their contribution; they are capable of validating their
own accomplishments. They do not have to live on other people's
terms because they have independent, valid terms of their own. They
are free to live their lives in cooperation with their fellow human
beings as equals.

The goal of psychotherapy is often expressed as relief from anxiety
or depression which is often experienced as insecurity ("I feel so
vulnerable"); lack of identity ("I don't know who I am"); indecisive-
ness ("I can't make up my mind"); or lack of control ("I can't stop
eating"). As we will see from the following lists of facets, these qualities do not exist as entities in themselves. As negatives, they are all
elements of self-contempt. Their antidotes are the corresponding
components of self-respect. When the primary goal of replacing self-
contempt with self-respect is achieved, it is our experience that all of
these component treatment goals are achieved at the same time.

Self-contempt generalizes from individuals to their families, cultures and communities. Unself-respecting people can not aspire to high achievement. They can only sink to the lowest common denominator of personal and group performance. Anyone in their circle who achieves success is looked on as a show off to be brought down to the lower level where he or she belongs. Anyone who is happy is seen as a deviant from the general atmosphere of misery and a way is found to destroy such happiness, which is inconsistent with the prevailing self-hatred. People consumed by self-contempt cannot enjoy happiness. They can only escape from their pain into negative excitement, which is always self-indulgent, counterproductive and self-destructive. It is mischief.

It is our belief that many social problems arise from feelings of self-contempt which predisposes individuals to take without giving, to cooperate negatively instead of positively, to succeed at failing, and to bring about their own destruction as well as that of their loved ones.

The antidote to this epidemic of self-contempt and self-anger is self-respect.

The Components of Self-Contempt

Self-contempt is a complex constellation of negative attitudes and emotions, including the following facets:

1. **Feelings of Pressure, Tension, and Stress** – These feelings arise from our attempts to live on other people's terms, especially when we don't know what those terms are. These negative pressures arise from our need to:

- Please others not ourselves;

- Live up to externally imposed standards and ideals;

- Be responsible and never irresponsible;

- Avoid displeasing others by failing to live up to their expectations;

267

- Control others so that nothing bad will happen;

- Control life for the same reason, and

- Be right and never wrong.

Anger creates a pressure of its own. For example, it threatens to expose the underlying fraudulence of our pleasingness and super-responsibility, which are merely overcompensatory roles we have been playing since childhood. We respond to the pressure of this threat with counterpressure for the purpose of stuffing our anger back down where it can't blow the lid off our pretensions.

Tension is often created when there is a gap between the demands of reality and our feelings of inadequacy to cope with those demands. Tension arises out of not knowing what we think we should know. For example, our tension at a party may arise from our perceived need to do the proper thing, our anger at our ignorance as to what the proper thing might be, and our inability to find out! The tension is compounded by our striving to prevent the humiliating exposure of our ignorance on these occasions. Tension also arises when we try to prevent disasters from happening in the future without knowing what the disaster might be or when it will happen.

We define stress as *the consequence of exceeding one's ability to adapt*. When we feel inadequately prepared to cope with the external demands of everyday life, we experience external stress, with which we are all familiar. We are not so familiar with internal stress, which arises when our attitudes and emotions create problems we can not even identify by name let alone relieve in effective ways. Internal stress includes:

- Trying to maintain a facade of self-confidence and success to keep people from finding out how insecure we feel inside;

- Trying to keep up external appearances when our internal realities are in despair;

- Trying to be happy while suffering from the conviction that we do not *deserve* to be happy;

- Striving to be better than we are when we do not know what *better* means or how to achieve it;

- Striving to relieve the pain of our existence (self-contempt) in ways that do not work.

2. **Feeling out of Control** – In our self-contempt, we feel we do not deserve happiness and success. We feel unworthy. All we deserve is unhappiness and failure, and that is all we have to look forward to. We proceed to prophesize a lifetime of unhappiness and failure for ourselves. We predict disaster. These negative, mistaken attitudes towards ourselves, toward others and towards life set us up for a lifetime of internal pressure, internal tension and internal stress.

Unhappiness and failure are very painful. As part of our self-contempt, we have a tendency to exaggerate the pain of these eventualities by taking them personally. At the same time we underestimate our ability to tolerate the pain.

Under the influence of these two tendencies, the prospect of disaster becomes overwhelming. We cannot cope with the ordinary disappointments of life. Our only hope is to control our existence to prevent these bad things from happening. That way, we won't have to cope with them. We soon find that we cannot prevent bad things from happening in an imperfect world. We are the prisoners of our mistaken definition of control, our inappropriate attitudes, and our negative expectations. As a consequence, we feel out of control most of the time.

3. **Lack of Identity** – When we do not respect ourselves, we tend to play roles as an adult that we acquired in childhood. In the absence of a well formed adult identity of our own, we tend to live our life on other people's terms — that is, we avoid displeasing people, we try to live up (or down) to their expectations of us, their preferences become our preferences, their judgment is our judgment and their scenario is our scenario. Our lives seem hollow and pointless.

4. Feelings of Immaturity – When we carry childhood attitudes and convictions about ourselves into adulthood, such as "I am a Pleaser," or "I am a Victim," we understandably feel less mature than we would otherwise. We maintain and perpetuate these negative roles and attitudes by comparing ourselves unfavorably to the more competent, self-confident adults around us. We may feel faintly ridiculous and we fear that our ridiculousness will be found out. We may feel we will grow up someday in the indeterminate future, perhaps after we get our Master's Degree, only to find that a Master's Degree is no guarantee of maturity, either.

5. Feelings of Not Unbelonging – Many of us feel we do not deserve to belong. We may also feel that we do not know how to belong and, therefore, we cannot ever come to belong. Our problem seems insoluble. This perceived insolubility is a contributing factor in depression, loneliness and social phobia.

We may seek to relieve the pain of our nonbelonging by becoming a joiner, only to find that we have contempt for any organization that would have us. We drop out, feeling worse off than we did before. The Joiner is a role like all others — the Victim, the Rebel, the Pleaser, etc. We cannot relieve the pain of our outcast feeling by replacing one role with another. Even the Crown Prince role that is played by the spoiled brat who seems so superior to everyone else fails to assuage the pain of his not belonging. The Crown Prince has "solved" this problem by turning it upside down and saying, "I don't have to belong to them; they have to belong to me, and I won't let them! I belong up here and they don't."

We may have the feeling that we do not belong in our marriage, in our home, in our work unit. We may think something like, "The boss's pet belongs, but I don't." Teenagers who do not respect themselves may find a group of nonbelongers like themselves and form a gang. Together, they will make useless, destructive mischief which will give the participants a feeling of negative belonging, which to them is better than no belonging at all.

Our feeling of not belonging predisposes us to play certain peripheral roles, such as The Spectator or The Passive Observer of the Passing Scene. Some of us have the feeling that we are in limbo until we belong and that we are still waiting for our lives to begin.

6. Feelings of Insecurity – We feel unsure and vulnerable to the painful vicissitudes of life. We doubt our capacity to defend ourselves successfully. In the absence of an internal sense of personal security against the ups and downs of everyday life, we buy extra locks for the doors. We try to make our lives predictable. We look for ways to exempt ourselves from the pain of failure by not trying in the first place. But the origin of our insecurity is internal. External measures do not address or relieve the pain of our vulnerability to the disasters we predict for ourselves.

7. Distrust – If we don't respect ourselves, we will have trouble trusting others. We may have seen our parents betraying each other or we may have a personal recollection of a painful betrayal by someone we loved and trusted. We may have concluded we can prevent the pain of future betrayals by trusting no one. For us, there is no middle ground between total trust and total distrust.

8. Feelings of Inequality – When we are small, we compare ourselves unfavorably to our older siblings, cousins and playmates. In our naive system of measurement, older is more desirable and younger is less desirable. Bigger is better and littler is worthless. We define our personal worth in such simplistic terms. The trouble is that some of us never outgrow this attitude toward the self.

Even as adults, we are sensitive to these hierarchies of who is better and who is worse, as if these rankings determine our worth to ourselves or others.

We also compare our group to other groups — whether it is our family, work group or bowling team. When we feel unequal, we may feel that our group is unequal. We resent the unfairness of this ranking, whether it is deserved or not. What prevents us from changing bowling teams? We do not deserve to belong to a winning team. We might fail. Our inferiorities might be exposed. No, it is safer to remain loyal to the Chickadees than risk everything by transferring to the more competent Bluebirds.

What prevents us from making a new friend? If the new friend is more popular than we are, we will find a way to put them off. We may fail to return phone calls or "forget" a date. The friend drops us and looks elsewhere. If he or she is less popular, we dump them because they drag us down. Or, we affiliate with them, not as friends, but as fellow sufferers. That is not friendship; that is mutual misery.

Our self-contempt predisposes us to behave in ways that are guaranteed to maintain the consistency of our inequality, and we hate it.

9. Feelings of Guilt – When we have contempt for ourselves, we tend to feel like worthless failures. We feel we have failed to live up to the standards and expectations that have been held out for us. We don't question the validity of these unrealistically high standards; we only know we aren't good enough. We compound our despair by assuming this painful failure is our fault. It was our responsibility and we failed. We have no one but ourselves to blame. We are guilty. We do not know what we are guilty of or how our guilt can be relieved.

In addition to these generalized guilts, the individual may be susceptible to specific guilts, such as the failure to be pleasing enough at a dinner party or responsible enough to prevent a child from being injured. Some of us feel guilty of the crime of failing to be sufficiently unselfish. For instance, Rose, for the first time in her life, insisted that her husband not buy a new bowling ball for Christmas. There were some things she needed for the house that would make them both happy. She knew that her priorities were right, but her old attitude from childhood would always catch up to her and prevent her from asking for what she needed. She would think, "Giving to others is good, taking is bad, i.e., selfish." This year, she learned to see her priorities in a new light. She was not taking anything away from her husband that he really needed. Instead, she was securing his cooperation in the resolution of a domestic situation for their mutual benefit. That is not selfish at all.

Another client, Edith, could not allow her date to pay for her dinner. She insisted on being fair, independent, liberated and mature.

Underneath these high-sounding ideals was her fear of being found guilty of the crime of selfishness. She felt she was taking without giving. It was pointed out to her that this was not the case. She was giving her escort her time and the pleasure of her company and this was his way of reciprocating. There was no selfishness, crime or guilt, only cooperation between two equal members of the human race.

10. Feelings of Oppression and Slavery – We go through life feeling inferior to others who are bigger and stronger than we are. Since we cannot afford the luxury of kindness ourselves, we cannot imagine that others can be kind. They can only be cruel and we expect them to use their superiority over us in hurtful, degrading ways. We become Professional Oppressees, seeing oppression at every turn, even where no oppression is intended. When someone asks us to cooperate, we confuse cooperation with submission and we balk. The relationship suffers.

Since we cannot trust our own judgment because it isn't good enough, we have difficulty in solving problems and making decisions. We tend to make inappropriate choices which tend to confirm our conviction that our judgment isn't good enough. Our self-sabotage puts us at a disadvantage. Others take advantage of the opportunity we have created for them. When they do, we tend to feel trapped, discouraged and resentful of the more effective people around us. We are not really their slave. We just do not see how our feelings of inadequacy contribute to our own distress. We cannot blame ourselves because it would hurt too much. So we must blame others for our difficulties, making our problems insoluble. We are the prisoners of our own self-doubt.

11. Feelings of Dependency – When we cannot trust our competence to cope with the tasks of life, we feel compelled to depend on the resources of individuals who seem to be more adequate than we are. Our advantage in being dependent on others is that if there is a disaster, it will be their fault, not ours. Since we are exempt from responsibility, our dependency has been converted from a liability into an asset. We can not see any advantage under these circumstances to becoming independent. It isn t worth the grief. When our partner lacks self-respect, he or she depends on our dependency. We are mutually dependent. We have *co-dependency.*

12. **Allergic to Accomplishment** – When we do not have self-respect, we have no hope of accomplishing anything of significance in the world. We cannot, therefore, take the initiative in accomplishing anything useful and constructive. Even when we do accomplish a task, we are quick to pooh-pooh it. This is called *undoing.* In our despair, all we deserve is negative accomplishment. We succeed in accomplishing things that do not need to be accomplished; we make mischief. We succeed at failing. We become destructive of ourselves and others. We may fail passively through inaction or actively become destroyers with no thought to what will take the place of what we have torn down.

13. **Allergic to Success** – Many of us suffer from the conviction that we "can't win for losing." We have the Reverse Midas Touch: Everything we touch turns sour. Our behavior is consistent with these attitudes and we arrange to snatch defeat from the jaws of victory every time. We succeed at failing. It isn't much, but it's all we've got.

14. **Negative Success** – We arrange to succeed at failing because we are afraid to succeed at succeeding. We have the attitude: "If I succeed on Monday, they'll expect me to do it again on Tuesday. I'm not sure I can do it two days in a row, so I'd better not start anything I can't finish. Besides, who am I to succeed at succeeding? I don't deserve to. I am unworthy. I'd only feel guilty of perpetrating a fraud. They would find out how undeserving I am. It would be humiliating. I can solve the whole problem by sabotaging myself and arranging to succeed at failing."

15. **Lack of Confidence** – "If I've never succeeded in the past, how can I expect to succeed in the future? My skills aren't good enough, my judgment isn't good enough. I'd only make things worse, so why try?" We call this attitude, *negative confidence* – "I know I'm going to screw it up. I can count on it."

16. **Lack of Courage (Discouragement)** – This is the attitude, "I am not willing to take the risks required to live in the real world. I might fail to be good enough and the pain would be unbearable. Everyone would know how inferior and inadequate I really am. It's not worth it. What's the use of trying? I know in advance I am not going to succeed."

17. **Inappropriate Responsibility** – When we do not trust our competence to assume appropriate responsibility for the tasks of life, we may try to solve the responsibility problem by assuming more — or less — responsibility than the situation requires.

The purpose of our taking on too much is not to get the job done faster, but to prove we are not inadequate to cope after all. We become super-responsible, which is a good intention to do more than reality requires us to do. We cannot keep it up. We will burn ourselves out in the end.

At the other end, we may seek to exempt ourselves from our responsibilities by devising ingenious cover stories with which to deceive the important others in our life, as well as ourselves. For instance: "I'm not feeling well today" or "I'm just too busy." Our logic is: "The less I do, the less I'll screw up. If I don't do it, no one will ever know how inadequate I am. Then I can't fail." We never question the validity of our prophecy that we are going to fail. It is consistent with our self-contempt.

18. **Mismanaged Anger** – Many of us fail to learn how to manage our anger appropriately. We have come to believe that our anger is not a legitimate emotion: Since *we are not valid, our anger cannot be valid either.* Invalid anger cannot be expressed appropriately. We can only suppress it until we reach a point where we cannot suppress it any longer. When something in the present provokes us to the breaking point, we erupt all over the place. This inappropriate overreaction confirms our negative attitudes towards ourselves, our anger and the consequences of expressing it. We suppress it again and the cycle of stuffing exploding, repeats itself.

19. **Distrust of Our Own Judgment** – When we do not respect ourselves, we have contempt for our decision-making ability. We have contempt for our own judgment, which is the organ of decision making. We cannot trust any judgment as imperfect as our own. In trying to outsmart ourselves — "If I think I am right, I must be wrong," we make the wrong choice, thus confirming our self-contempt. Or, we make no choice at all, deferring to the superior judgment we mistakenly attribute to others. We feel trapped, but we do not usually understand our trapped feeling in terms of our

contempt for our own judgment. We cannot initiate actions. We can only react to the provocation of others, which requires no judgment at all.

Because we cannot trust our own judgment, we often find ourselves making the double error of not trusting those we should trust and trusting those we should not. We lose out both ways. We fulfill our negative expectations.

Seymour has contempt for everything that is his, including his own judgment and competence to cope with problems. He cannot trust his judgment because it is *not good enough.* He cannot trust the judgment or good faith of others since they are no better than he is. Even so, he is painfully dependent on the judgment of others and continues to ask for advice. When he gets their advice, it is still up to him to decide whether to take it or not. He cannot make that decision either because he still doesn't trust his judgment. His dilemma is insoluble. He cannot resolve it. He feels trapped because that's what he is.

20. **No Power of Choice** – When we play a role on someone else's terms, we cannot feel independent or secure. We forfeit our power of choice. All we can do is react to the other person's stimulus as they react to ours. Neither one of us is making conscious, appropriate choices in our own behalf.

We do not have free will. We can only make choices that are determined by our respective scenarios. For example, lifelong victims in a relationship with a victimizer cannot deviate from their scenario. They find themselves saying things they know from past experience will only bring down more victimization on their head, such as, "Oh yeah! I'd like to see you try!" It would be out of character to say something like, "You scare me when you talk like that." That would be telling the truth, doing the unexpected, and disengaging from the mischief.

That is what an informed, self-respecting person would say. That choice is not open to someone who is playing the role of the victim.

"We do not require perfection, we require improvement. Improvement is attainable. We are worthwhile in the meantime."

Rudolf Dreikurs

A super-responsible child cannot say, "Do it yourself." A super self-reliant child cannot say, "Can you help me with this?" A Pleaser cannot say, "It makes me angry when you do that." These choices are not open to them.

The impediment to making choices in the present is the interference of our attitudes from the past. Our attitudes predispose us to behave in certain ways. They save us the trouble of making trivial choices, such as what to do when the telephone rings. We don't deliberate, we pick it up every time, even when we know it's our mother-in-law. Our negative attitudes are useless when it comes to coping with the minute-by-minute demands of adult living.

Sometimes, however, our trusty old attitudes aren't so trusty after all. They are out of sync with our present situation. They may have been appropriate thirty years ago, but they are not appropriate any more.

Frank and Maria spent years fighting over money. Frank didn't like paying the bills and he sometimes put them off too long, running up late payment charges that could have been avoided. Maria suggested that he let her pay the bills. He couldn't bring himself to let her. "There is a higher principle here," he said. "Men control the money, not women." His father had managed his money and his father before him. He could not betray their example of masculine household management. He would feel guilty. It was less painful to screw up the checkbook himself. It was the lesser misery. This was not a rational decision. An attitude had kicked in a long time ago and he never questioned it.

Frank learned in counseling that he was the prisoner of these examples, roles and attitudes. They were not high principles at all. They were not Holy Writ. They were inappropriate carryovers from the past. They could be questioned now, examined and replaced if the reality situation required it.

Frank used his adult judgment. He chose to let go of the checkbook. That judgment wasn't perfect. It wasn't worthless, either. It was good enough. It got the job done. He felt relief, control, maturity, liberation and independence. He had the power of choice. He was not his grandfather's grandson any more. He had an identity of his own. He was not playing the role of the Man of the House, Doing His Duty. He was free to cooperate and share responsibility with Maria in an atmosphere of mutual respect.

21. **Intellectual Self-Contempt** – When we are without self-respect, we have contempt for our intelligence. We feel that if we are not perfectly smart, we are *not smart enough*. Since we do not know everything we require ourselves to know, our conviction is that we must be stupid. We may be very smart in some areas of our existence, such as our work or in remembering baseball statistics, but these mental accomplishments do not affect our underlying emotional conviction that we are not smart enough. We arrange to forget a date or to make a self-destructive remark to our boss. We have succeeded in confirming our lifelong *stupiditude*.

Some people escape from the pain of intellectual self-doubt into mindless overcompensation by playing the know-it-all role. Their watch phrase is, "I knew that!" They deceive no one.

22. **Feeling "Not Good Enough"** – When we lack self-respect, we have a vague, generalized feeling that we are *not good enough*. We do not know where we are lacking nor how to make up the supposed deficiency. We do not know how good is good enough. We only know we do not measure up to some vague standard of achievement that someone expects us to live up to. We may feel driven to prove we are good enough in one specific way or another, only to find that such irrelevant triumphs do nothing at all to relieve our unworthiness as a person.

23. **Unfavorable Comparison** – When we feel inferior to those who seem to be more self-respecting than we are, we are painfully sensitive to our inferior condition vis-a-vis our more fortunate fellows. We may resent their unfair advantage over us, and seek to pull them down to our drab level. Or we may spur ourselves to rise above them only to find that we cannot sustain our advantage. Our self-contempt catches up with us sooner or later and we crash.

24. **Confusing Cooperation with Submission** – When we feel inferior, we cannot cooperate freely with our supposed superiors. We

279

can only submit to them, rebel against them, or withdraw from them in discouragement.

When our boss seeks to secure our cooperation, we are predisposed to hear his or her request as if it were a demand that we submit to higher authority. This perceived demand makes us feel resentful, which means angry. As a result of this predisposition, we are angry most of the time. Also unemployed.

25. Denial of Unpleasant Reality – If we have contempt for ourselves, the real world cannot be perceived as friendly, It seems painful and dangerous to us. We feel inadequately prepared to cope with its demands. Debby deals with problems in the real world by denying they exist. That way, she is exempt from having to solve them and she cannot fail. She withdraws from reality and contents herself by solving problems that do not need to be solved, such as preventing others from finding out how badly she really feels about herself. She puts on a facade of cheerfulness, but it is only skin deep. When the facade cracks, everyone will be surprised. They will say, "I had no idea things were so bad for her."

26. Not Living in the Present – If we do not respect our ability to cope with the tasks of everyday life, one solution is to live in another tense, where nonexistent problems serve to distract us from uncomfortable reality. If we live in the past, we say things like, "If only I had . . ." which conveniently exempts us from having to cope with the consequences of our choices in the present. If we live in the future, we suffer from the *Someday Syndrome.* Our intention is to begin living some time in the future when certain fictitious requirements have been met. For instance, "Someday, after I get my divorce . . ." or "Someday, after I get my revenge . . ." We may spend our days trying to prevent something bad from happening in the future, as if we knew what was going to happen when.

We are not only living outside the present tense, we are also living outside the indicative mood, which has to do with things as they are. We live our lives in the subjunctive mood, which has to do with conditions contrary to fact. We live in a world of "as if," "what if," "if only" and "yes, but . . ." The reason we feel out of it is that we are.

280

We complain, "I can't feel my life." We have spent all our time arranging not to.

27. Unapproachability – If we feel badly about ourselves, we do not want others to find out how inadequate and inferior we are. We put up facades of pleasingness, shyness, intimidation or self-reliance to keep people at a safe distance. We elevate ourselves above others by attaining the heights of achievement or we fall into the pit of failure. In any case, no one will ever know our painful secret. Then, after years of putting up a defensive wall around ourselves, we wonder why we are lonely. We can't have it both ways.

28. Selfishness – If we lack self-respect, we tend to be selfish and self-centered. We *take without giving*. For one thing, we cannot give because we need it all ourselves. We have nothing to spare for anyone else. We take because we imagine that what we are grabbing for will relieve the pain of our existence. Since it never does, we need more of the same tomorrow. We are a bottomless pit of needs and wants. In addition, we cannot give of ourselves because we have contempt for anything that is ours to give. We anticipate that our worthless gift would be despised and rejected, so why bother offering it? It is much safer to take.

We are not consciously aware of our selfishness, but we are terribly conscious of the selfishness of others. We have our own self-serving definition of selfishness: "Anyone who does not give me what I want is selfish!"

29. Lack of Social Interest – If we do not respect our own worth as people, we cannot have *an appropriate regard for the well-being of our fellow humans,* which is our definition of Alfred Adler's term, *"Social Interest."* Since we do not feel equal to them, we can only feel superior or inferior.

If we feel that others are superior to us, we cannot relate to them appropriately. We can fear them and curry favor or we can try to overthrow them so that we won't feel inferior anymore, but we cannot regard them as equal members of the human race.

If we feel superior to others, we can only have contempt for them as our inferiors. Sometimes our contempt for underlings, such as our wives and children, is open and obvious. Sometimes we mask our contempt for inferiors by representing ourselves as the compassionate, but ineffectual, champions of the suffering underdogs of the world. We may even put these suffering underdogs on a pedestal, as though their suffering made them more human than those who do not suffer. We call this overcompensatory, well-intentioned role, the Champion of The Underdog Syndrome.

30. **Unlovability** – Some of us do not believe that anyone can sincerely love us. On the one hand, we predict a miserable, loveless existence for ourselves. On the other, we defeat all attempts on the part of potential partners to love us and make us happy. In our self-contempt, we can only have contempt for anyone so foolish as to love us. We cannot love such a person. We can only admire those persons who are perceptive enough to spurn us.

When we feel unlovable, we may invest much of our time and energy defending ourselves against the conviction of our own unlovability because it hurts too much. We may downplay the importance of love in our lives or escape into fantasies of super lovability. Some of us form our own religion which requires its adherents to love their master. When we do succeed in forming an attachment, we make ourselves hateful to our partner so that, when that person leaves in disgust, we can say, "I told you so. I knew you couldn't love me." We may blame the entire opposite sex for its inability or unwillingness to love us, and then become very angry at the whole gender. We may perceive individual members of that unloving gender as worthy victims of our righteous indignation. We may feel entitled to punish representatives of that gender severely for their cruelty. None of this is rational. These are all attitudes from the past that have never been outgrown.

We are not really unlovable. We are merely the prisoners of our conviction that we are. We are doomed to bring about the fulfillment of our prophecies of love and disaster forever.

Ted felt unlovable all of his life. In college, he was attractive and popular. He thought that he didn't have a problem. One night, on a date, he started to become sexually-aroused. He made an aggressive attack on Sheila, who repulsed his advances. This rejection triggered his old feeling that he was unlovable. He could not stand the pain of that confirmation. He forced himself on Sheila, not out of love or sexual tension, but to prevent the confirmation of his conviction that he is as unlovable now as he was in the playpen. He was convicted of date rape. Sheila might have loved him in time. He saw to it that she never would. He still doesn't know what got into him. We would say he had an attack of self-destructive *unlovabilitude* and *Allergic to Happiness* in a context of self-contempt.

31. Out of Touch With Reality – If we hold ourselves in contempt, we are out of touch with the reality of our fundamental worth as human beings. We cannot, therefore, be in solid contact with the rest of reality. Our perception and understanding of the real world will be distorted by the prism of our self-pain. We will be in touch with our overcompensatory needs, wants and strivings or with our fantasies about reality, and we will behave accordingly. We will operate on the basis of our mistaken attitudes towards reality, other people and ourselves.

We may even be super-intelligent, but the effective use of our intelligence will be impeded by our underlying misconceptions about our place in the world. We may suffer from the delusion that we are rational and conjure up impressive philosophical theories to explain the social, economic or political aspects of human existence. However, all such products of our intelligence will be skewed by undiscovered and unresolved doubts about our own worthiness to be happy, successful human beings. Our generalizations about suffering mankind will stem, to a greater or lesser degree, from the particulars of our own painful introduction to life on this planet. Our remedies for relieving the pain and suffering of others will have a strong connection with the relief of our own. For instance, if our parents were poor, we may feel that the problem is poverty and the solution is to give everybody money. If our parents had too much money, we may feel that human problems can be solved by taking money from those who have it and giving it to those who don't. We have mistaken sameness for equality. Our ideals may seem lofty, but they are mere overcompensations for our own self-contempt. This is the impediment that renders us unable to see reality as it is.

32. **Intolerance of Pain** – If we lack self-respect, we are more vulnerable to pain than we need to be. We perceive it as a confirmation of our worthlessness. We feel that worthless, unsuccessful people like ourselves deserve to suffer, and we see to it that we do. We mistakenly perceive pain as a victimization even where no victimization is intended. We prophesize a life of pain for ourselves and then proceed to erect pseudo-logical defenses against it. When these fictitious defenses and overcompensations fail, we blame others, which does not help, or we blame ourselves, which is worse.

We do not respond to pain in ways that are appropriate. We respond in counterproductive, nonrational ways that prevent us from getting the relief we might be able to get otherwise.

33. **Negative Compatibility** – If we lack self-respect, we often gravitate towards others like us and get married or form business partnerships. We find we have recreated relationships that we remember from our childhood, such as Victim and Victimizer, Crown Prince and Scullery Maid, Big Sister and Baby Brother, Sparring Partners, or Pleaser and Pleasee. Neither partner has enough self-respect to break the mold and put the relationship on a more appropriate basis, such as mutual respect, equality and shared responsibility.

For example, a woman who was abused by her father and brother will not be compatible with a man who is prepared to cooperate with her as an equal. She will feel uncomfortable in such a relationship and soon end it. She will not question the nature of her discomfort, nor seek to relieve it. She will persevere in her mate selection process until she meets someone at a dance who she feels comfortable with. She has no way of knowing in advance that two years into the future he will be pulling her around by her hair, just as her father did.

It is uncanny how these people find each other and then proceed to bring out the worst in each other. We do not know how they are able to penetrate the screen of "best foot forward" and link up with the destructive child behind the facade. Perhaps it is empathy that is working here, which is a little known aspect of the human condition. It is little known because it is unscientific. It cannot be reproduced under laboratory conditions, or at least it hasn't been so far.

Perhaps a woman who is compatible with victimizers like her father can sense the pattern of vibration that a charming brute radiates. Perhaps there is a constellation of vibrations that she zeros in on, like a homing pigeon. In any case, we know that the process of negative attraction is not rational or logical. We ask ourselves, "What does she see in him?" If we ask her, she will come up with some cover story like, "He is so strong, so sure of himself." It is exactly these qualities that will break her cheekbone in three years and drive her to a women's shelter in four.

It is the task of the counselor to identify these negative predispositions and change them. The change is not accomplished by a direct frontal assault on the subject's dating patterns. It is done by replacing her self-contempt from childhood with self-respect in the present. Her taste in men will change accordingly. She will not be negatively compatible any more; she will be positively compatible with men who respect themselves. Her discomfort will have disappeared.

34. Fear and Anxiety – If we lack self-respect, we live in fear. Many of our fears have a specific object such as snakes. Other fears seem to have a definable object such as failing the mid-term, failing to close a deal, or failing to get a date for the prom. These fears often exist in an aura of anxiety, which is undefined and free floating. These are not true objects, they are merely occasions for our preexisting anxiety. When we define the true determinants of our anxiety, our feeling of not knowing is replaced by knowing. We feel back in control. The anxiety is relieved. These are some of the factors that contribute to our painful anxiety:

- *Anger out of control*. When our anger is out of control, *we* are out of control. We feel like something terrible could happen to us.

- *Living in the future*. When we feel inadequate to cope in the present, we predict disaster ahead. We render ourselves out of control. We scare ourselves in advance.

- *Living on other people's terms.* When we play a role opposite someone else's role, we make our lives unpredictable. We are dependent on the other person who is just as dependent on us. We say that he or she is dependent on our dependency.

We give away our judgment and with it our ability to exercise positive control over our lives.

- *Out of control.* When we define *control* in ways that do not work, we cannot be in control of our lives. When we try harder to control in the wrong ways, we make things even worse. We are sure something terrible is going to happen and we can't prevent it. That's scary.

- *Insecurity.* When we define security in childish ways, we create problems we do not know how to solve. We feel exposed, vulnerable and threatened. We feel unable to protect ourselves. We try to protect ourselves in ways that do not work, such as with money, guns, electrified fences and Dobermans, only to find that our insecurity comes right back.

- *Fictitious guilt.* As unself-respecting people, we suffer from fictitious guilt. We have a feeling we identify as guilt from our childhood, but we have not committed an offense against the law. We may have said something displeasing to the neighbor's mother-in-law, failed to prevent something from happening, or failed to be perfectly responsible. We are afraid that our guilts will be uncovered and we will be sent to our room forever. This anticipation of exposure in the future sets up the out of control feeling we experience as anxiety.

- *Real guilt.* We really did do something terrible to our little sister. We live in fear of being found out. This painful fear is our punishment and that is what guilty people deserve. We would rather punish ourselves forever than let someone else do it. It hurts less this way. In the meantime, we dread the future. We can have no hope of happiness.

286

- *Fear of change.* As unhappy as we are, we are afraid to change. In our pessimism, we cannot imagine that the change will be for the better, only for the worse. We are afraid to break the continuity of our existence. We wouldn't know who we were any more. We prefer the lesser misery of staying the way we are to the even worse misery of risking annihilation.

- *Fear of abandonment.* We may have felt abandoned by a loved one in childhood, if only for seven seconds. We may have felt terrified that we would never see them again or that we would die of heartbreak and neglect. We are afraid it will happen again. Our priority is to prevent it. Even the thought of being abandoned makes us angry. We feel powerless to prevent an impending loss. We are angry at ourselves for being so vulnerable. All of these out of control angers turn into anxiety, which compounds our original fear of being abandoned.

- *Fear of betrayal.* Betrayal hurts. When we trust our little friend with our favorite toys and then find they are missing the next day, we become very angry. We become angry with ourselves for being so trusting and so *good for nothing*. We resolve not to trust again. That way, we will never be betrayed.

- *Fear of ridicule.* Failure is embarrassing. Since that is all we can predict for ourselves, it is only a matter of time before our inadequacy to cope will be exposed before the whole community. We will be ridiculed for our failure and for our absurd attempt to make people think we were just like them.

- *Fear of criticism.* To prove that we are not worthless, we strive for perfection. A criticism points out that we have missed our goal. Our goal now is to do even better next time so no one will criticize us. There is no middle ground between perfect and worthless. In the meantime, we are not living in the present. Striving is not living. It is a good intention we have for ourselves.

- *Fear of being wrong.* As a child, there was no middle ground between right and wrong. Wrongness was punished severely. We had no hope of being right; our prayer was to be not wrong, which is a negative ambition. Since we can never be perfectly right, we are doomed to be wrong forever. It is only a matter of time until our wrongness is exposed and we will be punished. We cannot stand the suspense. We confess our wrongdoing and sabotage relationships that do not need to be sabotaged.

- *Fear of anger.* We feel inadequately prepared to cope with our anger situation. Some of us are afraid we will lose control and kill somebody. Some are afraid that if we express anger, we will be punished, victimized, abandoned or annihilated. We are afraid of other peoples' anger. We feel surrounded by angry people or the threat of their anger. We walk on eggs to avoid provoking them.

These fears are scary enough, but there is something more. We are afraid that if any of these scary eventualities come to pass, we will ultimately be *annihilated*. We will die of shame or grief. We will cease to exist. On a still deeper level, the terror will not end with our death, which is bad enough, but for unself-respecting people, death is not just the end of them. Their death is the end of the world! That is too scary to bear.

- *Panic.* If anxiety means feeling out-of-control because something bad is going to happen in the future, then panic is the feeling, the conviction that the bad thing is happening right now and that we are going to die. We are made susceptible to this horrible malady by our lifelong underlying conviction that we are not good enough. We are worthless – worthless things deserve to be destroyed and this is it! Our prophecies of disaster are being fulfilled right now!

35. **Vulnerability to Temptation** – If we lack self-respect, we are in a lot of pain. We imagine we can relieve our pain by escaping into negative excitement. We are vulnerable to making exciting, self-destructive mischief. We are not dissuaded by the danger, even deadly danger. If we die, that is what worthless people deserve anyway. Our pain will end forever. In the meantime, we are temporarily numbing out the pain of our self-contempt by engaging in

forbidden behaviors. Our guilt in the morning after will confirm and prolong our worthlessness.

36. **Internal Conflict** – If we lack self-respect, we hold ourselves in contempt. We despise our *stupidity, weakness* and *inadequacy to cope.* We hate the roles we have learned to play: The Pleaser, the Victim, the Good-For-Nothing, etc. We wish we could escape from the pain of our self-hatred, but we do not know how. We carry it with us wherever we go. We cannot be at peace with others because we are not at peace with ourselves. The stakes are higher than we can consciously know. We must redouble our striving to prevent disasters from happening. We are at war with ourselves.

These are just some of the facets of self-contempt. The infinite number of possible combinations and permutations of these facets, in their various strengths and degrees, accounts for the endless variety in what we call the "human personality." Individuals may not be consciously aware of these facets. We are attached to the mistaken ideas we acquired about ourselves as children, such as "I'm not good enough" or "People are out to victimize me." These ideas are no longer conscious, either, but we carry a load of negative emotional freight with us. We have become predisposed to think, feel, perceive, dream and behave in certain ways as an adult. These carryovers have become underlying attitudes.

For example, Steve is a manager. When he is required to make an adult business decision, his judgment will be colored by carryover attitudes from the past that are irrelevant and inappropriate in the present. He may, as a result, decide not to discipline an employee who deserves it because, "He won't like me anymore." He may overcompensate for feelings of self-doubt by giving the employee a pass. Since overcompensation is always counterproductive, the employee, who knows he deserves to be disciplined, will respect the manager even less and behave accordingly.

Our purpose in drawing up this lengthy list of components is to show how multifaceted the problem of self-contempt really is, and how it underlies so many of the problems we have been focusing our attention on for all these years.

289

We hope that it has become apparent now that all of these facets are interrelated, which means that a problem such as insecurity, indecision or loneliness is not the issue in and of itself. It is part of a larger issue further down. We also wish to make it clear that, as we gradually solve more and more of our life problems in this new way, we are also replacing our underlying self-contempt with self-respect. Even the other facets of our self-contempt, which may not have been as apparent, will be relieved and replaced by the corresponding facets of self-respect.

THE COMPONENTS OF SELF-RESPECT

Self-respect is a complex attitude towards ourself that includes the following positive feelings and emotions, each of which corresponds to a facet of self-contempt.

1. **Relief –** People who learn how to replace their self-doubt with self-respect experience a feeling of relief from pressure, tension and stress. This feeling includes relief from the pressures of having to prove that they are not worthless, the pressure to succeed perfectly, and to avoid displeasing others; the tension that comes from having to prevent bad things from happening; from the stress that arises when our perceptions about reality are not congruent with the real world, and from the stress of having to maintain a facade of self-confidence and success to conceal from others our underlying feelings of worthlessness and inadequacy. These pressures, tensions and stresses preclude happiness. They can make us physically and mentally sick.

2. **Power and Control –** People who respect themselves feel that, although they are not perfectly in control of their situation, they are able to function well enough in the real world. They do not define control in terms of controlling others, life or their emotions — all of which would only set them up to fail and feel even more out of control. They do not define control in terms of preventing bad things from happening. Instead, they define control *as the ability to make things happen* (which includes the choice not to make things happen) and *taking life as it comes and doing the best they can with it.* Positive control is predicated on trusting in their judgment as to what the

290

reality of the situation requires them to do, and having the courage do it. Constructive power is the energy required to make positive things happen.

3. **Identity** – Self-respecting people have an identity of their own as persons in the world. They do not live in other people's eyes or on other people's terms. They know where other people end and they begin. They are able to cooperate with their fellow human beings without fearing that their selfhood will be compromised or engulfed by others. Nor do they seek to enhance their selfhood by engulfing others. They know their identity as worthwhile human beings cannot be enhanced nor diminished by external considerations. They do not play childhood roles in their adult relationships. They are flexible in their relationships with their spouses, children, bosses, friends and subordinates. They are able to play appropriate adult roles as the changing reality of the situation demands, but they know all the while who and what they really are: Worthwhile human beings in their own right.

4. **Maturity** – Self-respecting people feel they are at an appropriate stage of development for their age. They will not feel older than their years, nor will they feel childish or faintly ridiculous. They will not be vulnerable to postponing their lives until some day in the future when they are better prepared to handle it. They will be living their lives in the present and deriving appropriate gratification from it. Under extreme stress, they may find themselves reverting to child-hood roles, attitudes and behaviors, but they will have the resilience to recuperate quickly from these temporary regressions.

5. **Belonging** – Self-respecting people do not question their *belong-ingness*. Wherever they happen to be, that's where they belong. They feel themselves to be members in good standing of the human race. They have a sense of embeddedness. They belong to themselves, to their families and to their community. They are secure in their belonging. It is not conditional and no one can take this belonging away from them. Moreover, it is portable. They can take their belongingness with them wherever they go.

6. **Security** – Self-respecting individuals feel secure within themselves. They feel secure in their ability to cope with the ups and downs of life. They do not live in fear of disasters. They do not

291

prophesize disasters in the first place. They know they can tolerate more distress and pain now than they could as children. They are not afraid of pain. They can take it as it comes. They do not live in the future, which is a setup for insecurity and anxiety. They live in the present.

7. **Trust** – Self-respecting individuals can trust others because they trust themselves. They trust their own ability to discriminate between people who are worthy of their trust and those who are not. Even if their judgment isn't perfect, they can trust their competence to deal with a mistaken judgment if and when it happens. It will not shake their trust in their judgment. It will only prove that their judgment isn't perfect. It is still good enough.

8. **Equality** – Self-respecting individuals do not feel inferior to others, nor do they feel the need to overcompensate by imagining themselves to be superior. They are not consciously aware that they feel like an equal human being, but they do and they behave accordingly. They can respect themselves in the presence of the governor as well as in the presence of children.

9. **Relief from Guilt** – Self-respecting individuals are less prone to feeling guilty than individuals with self-contempt. If they make a mistake, they don't feel guilty of failing to live up to expectations. They perceive it in the context of their human imperfection and they can learn from it. If they should behave inappropriately, as imperfect people sometimes do, they don't wallow in useless, phony guilt feelings. They are able to take appropriate remedial action and to feel active remorse to an appropriate degree. They know, consciously or not, that imperfection is not a crime, and they are not guilty. They feel appropriate regret and are able to make restitution on an appropriate basis.

10. **Liberation** – Individuals who come to respect themselves feel liberated, not from the demands and expectations of others, but from their vulnerability to them. They feel liberated from carryover attitudes and misperceptions that have been interfering with their happiness and success since childhood. They are no longer victims. They can deal effectively with those who seek to victimize them. They are no longer rebels, mindlessly reacting when they don't get their way. They can solve problems constructively and choose to

make other arrangements. They feel liberated from their childhood roles, fears and doubts. They have the feeling that they have liberated themselves, which is the only way it can be done. They cannot begin to liberate anyone until they have liberated themselves. Once they have done so, they will be able to set an example of liberation for other people to follow if they choose.

11. **Independence** – Having liberated themselves, self-respecting individuals have the feeling that they are independent entities in their own right. They are not dependent on others to validate their existence as persons in the world. They can, and do, validate their own worth in spite of their faults and imperfections. They are free to enter and maintain interdependent relationships with other independent human beings as equals.

12. **Accomplishment** – When self-respecting individuals complete a task, they experience a feeling of accomplishment. They do not undo or minimize their achievement out of false modesty. They don't blow it out of proportion, either. They can accept appropriate commendation for it. They know what they did and they know it was good enough.

13. **Success** – Self-respecting individuals are free to experience themselves as having succeeded. They have earned the right to feel successful. They deserve it. Since their effectiveness in the world is no longer hampered by self-doubt, they are more likely to succeed at solving problems than they were before they acquired their self-respect. They are not driven to succeed. They are free to succeed.

14. **Courage To Succeed** – Self-respecting people are not afraid that their success in the present will lead to higher expectations which they will fail to achieve. They take success, like failure, as it comes. They feel they deserve to succeed, no more and no less than anyone else. They do not fear that their happiness will end in disaster. They do not abort their happiness to get it over with. They are willing to take appropriate risks. They can tolerate a successful outcome.

15. **Confidence** – Having succeeded once, people have earned the right to conclude that they can do it again. They are confident that their worth as persons is not threatened by the ups and downs of life. They feel adequately prepared to take them as they come.

16. **Courage** – Self-respecting people are willing to take appropriate risks. They can draw confidence from their successes. They become willing to take the greater risks that life requires them to take. They can use their adult judgment to discriminate between those risks that need to be taken and those that do not. They are no longer discouraged. In having the courage to make their success happen, they have encouraged themselves. They do not wait for the courage to come. They go ahead and do it anyway. The courage comes afterward.

17. **Appropriate Responsibility** – Self-respecting people are able to assume as much responsibility as the situation demands, not too much and not too little. They are able to assess the situation objectively and to respond appropriately to it. They know there are no rights without responsibility, and they are willing to pay that price.

18. **Appropriate Anger** – Self-respecting people are enabled to respond appropriately to anger-provoking situations. They do not get angrier than they need to be, nor do they deny or suppress their anger. They feel free to express their legitimate anger in mature, responsible ways. They have the responsibility and the right to do so.

19. **Trust In Their Own Judgment** – Self-respecting people learned in childhood or through counseling that their judgment can be trusted. It isn't perfect, but it doesn't have to be. It is good enough. They do not try to prevent mistakes by refusing to decide. They trust their competence to take the appropriate corrective action if their judgment turns out to be mistaken. They are open to learning from experience.

20. **Power of Choice** – Because self-respecting individuals respect their judgment, they are free to make choices. They know they can live with the consequences of their decisions. If they are mistaken, they know they can learn from their mistakes and correct them. They appreciate their freedom to make choices and they are prepared to assume the responsibilities that go with that freedom.

21. **Intellectual Self-Respect** – This can be expressed as, "As smart as I am right now, that is smart enough. If I am smarter still tomorrow, that is all right too. In this meantime, I am smart enough."

294

22. Self-acceptance – Self-respecting people accept themselves as they are right now. They do not qualify their self-acceptance in terms of such considerations as appearance, popularity, success, intelligence, sexual prowess or athletic achievement. They feel *good enough* They do not require themselves to feel any better than that.

23. Counting Their Blessings – Self-respecting individuals recognize their blessings and appreciate them appropriately. They are content. It is enough. If more comes tomorrow, that will be enough too.

24. Securing Cooperation – People who respect themselves are free to solve problems by securing the cooperation of their fellow human beings. They do not submit nor do they require others to submit to them. Because they respect themselves, other people are more likely to respect them and to cooperate with them in an atmosphere of mutual respect.

25. Acceptance of Unpleasant Reality – People who have achieved self-respect are not as vulnerable as they used to be to taking a mishap as a personal affront. They are not devastated when they do not get their own way. It is not the end of the world. It is only a disaster if they don't learn from it. They do not resign themselves to life. They accept it as it comes and do the best they can with it, even under difficult circumstances.

26. Living in the Present – People who have self-respect are able to experience themselves as functioning effectively in the real world right now. They do not wallow in the past, nor do they try to prevent the future. They are prepared to take life as it comes and do the best they can with it. They can learn from the past and make effective preparations for the future, but they do it in the present.

27. Approachability – Because they accept themselves as worthwhile, self-respecting people, they are prepared to accept others as being worthwhile also. Other people sense their openness, trust and appropriate regard for them as equals. Other self-respecting people find these qualities attractive and seek them out.

28. Unselfish – People who have an appropriate regard for themselves as worthwhile human beings in spite of their faults and imperfections are free to give of themselves to their fellow human beings. They are not afraid that their gift of self will be rejected as worthless. They are free to receive from others as well. Their ability to accept the offerings of others is not impeded by feelings of unworthiness or guilt. They know that the more they give, the happier they will be, but that's not why they do it. They do it because it is appropriate. They can even give to themselves. They can do what pleases them without overdoing it.

29. **Social Interest –** Self-respecting people are free to have an appropriate regard for the welfare of their fellow human beings. They are not driven by self-serving, overcompensatory good intentions, nor are they wallowing in miserly self-interest. They understand that the better off the community is, the better off they and their children will be. They can serve the community in a spirit of enlightened self-interest. They do not operate out of mindless idealism, nor do they sink into cynicism when society does not measure up to their expectations or when society does not express sufficient gratitude for their exertions in its behalf. They do what they feel they have to do. They do not care too much or too little. They care just enough to do the things that need to be done.

30. **Lovability –** People who have self-respect feel they can be loved. They do not compare themselves unfavorably to movie stars or athletes who seem to be more lovable than they are. Nor do they compare themselves favorably to persons who have apparent difficulty in finding a mate. They do not define their worth as a person in terms of being loved by a particular person. They are, therefore, less vulnerable to being personally devastated by the loss of that love. They are able to relieve their distress somewhat by reminding themselves they are worthwhile human beings in spite of such losses. They are confident that, having found this love, they are quite capable of finding the next one.

31. **In Touch with Reality –** People who have a realistic perception of themselves as persons of worth in the world are in a much better position to perceive the world around them objectively and appropriately than those whose perception of the world is clouded by self-doubt and despair. They are also more likely to respond to emotional situations with the appropriate reaction. They are more likely to have success in solving their life problems and in relating to their fellow

human beings than those whose perception is impaired by feelings of worthlessness. Because they trust their competence to cope with reality, they have fewer crises in their lives.

32. **Tolerance of Pain** – Self-respecting people do not make the pain of their existence worse than it needs to be. They don't make the mistake of taking their pain as a punishment for guilt or as a reflection on their worth as persons. They do not take their pain as personal victimization. They do not spend their life trying to prevent pain and they do not blame themselves for failing when they cannot do so. They can learn useful lessons about themselves, others and about life from the unhappy, disappointing events that befall them just as such events befall everyone else.

33. **Positive Compatibility** – Self-respecting people are compatible with self-respecting life partners. They will not be compatible with mischief makers, excitement-seekers or negative role players. They will set an example of mutual respect and cooperative problem solving. They will deserve to be happy and will enjoy making each other happy. They will trust each other positively, not negatively. They will belong to themselves and each other.

34. **Relief From Fear and Anxiety** – Self-respecting people do not terrify themselves with predictions of failure and disaster in the future. They live in the present. They do not live on the unpredictable terms of other people. They have their own valid terms. They do not set themselves up for scary failure by requiring perfection of themselves. They feel adequately prepared to take life as it comes. They express their anger appropriately in the present so it does not go out of control and give rise to feelings of anxiety and paranoia.

35. **Less Vulnerable to Temptation** – Self-respecting people do not need exciting mischief to relieve the pain of their existence. They strengthen their self-worth by making appropriate, responsible choices. They can pass up opportunities to engage in self-destructive mischief, not because they are morally superior but because it is inconsistent with the way they feel about themselves. They can resist temptation, not because they are terrified of the consequences, but because self-indulgent, destructive behavior is inconsistent with their self-respect. They deserve to be happy in constructive, productive ways. They even deserve to enjoy their happiness. They can also

resist the temptation to stand in moral judgment upon their more vulnerable fellows. They are not moral because of promised rewards here or in the life to come. They are moral because the situation demands it and it is appropriate. They cannot do otherwise. Immorality is inconsistent with their self-respect.

36. **Serenity** – Self-respecting individuals are not at war with themselves. They do not hate their human shortcomings or themselves for having them. They do not compare themselves unfavorably to people who are luckier or better off than they are. They experience peace of mind, peace of soul and serenity. They do not live in fear that their inadequacies will be revealed, and they do not strive to prove their worth through endless overcompensation. They are not afraid of losing control. They are at peace with themselves and are free to be at peace with their neighbors.

Just as with self-contempt, there are many more facets of self-respect, but these examples will serve to demonstrate the complexity of this very basic human condition. If our basic attitudes and feelings about ourselves are appropriately positive and realistic, then our thoughts, expectations and behaviors will be positive and effective. The rewards for our effectiveness in the world will be appropriately gratifying and will provide us with a reasonable basis for expecting continued success in the future. We will be free to cooperate appropriately with other self-respecting human beings in the accomplishment of our life tasks: including the tasks of love, work and friendship. This also includes the task of building a better saner world for our children and our children's children.

Appendix C

SUMMING UP

You have come a long way since you first sat down to read this book, and we hope you have learned some things about anger and self-respect that you did not know before. We further hope:

- That you have had a chance to do a Homework in the real world and that, as a consequence, your anger illiteracy is being replaced by anger literacy.

- That angerphobia has been replaced by the courage to take appropriate risks.

- That you now have choices that you did not have before.

- That you can now solve problems that *nice* people weren't even supposed to have.

Finally, we hope you can apply these techniques in your own life as you weather the ups and downs at home, at work, and at play. Your success with these new choices will serve as a model for other people to follow, should they choose to. By your example, you will be spreading the word that anger is a legitimate part of the human condition and that it can be managed if you know how.

299

This book wasn't just about anger though, was it? It is a handbook of suggestions that counselors, teachers and other helpers can use to understand their charges' anger problems in a new light. Anger is not a mysterious instinct or an irresistible natural force. *It is an emotional response to a grievance.* Human beings can learn to perceive their grievances in less painful ways, thereby relieving the consequent emotional pain. The reduced pain is more manageable. It helps even more when we have tools to manage it with. The emotional pain goes away sooner when you know what is going on.

These anger management techniques are also useful to nonprofessionals, such as parents, siblings, neighbors, co-workers and everyone else who deals with imperfect human beings on a daily basis.

We understand our fellow human beings as people who are trying to relieve their painful feelings of inferiority and inadequacy through overcompensatory striving for superiority. If not positive superiority, then negative superiority will do. This understanding of human nature is based on the psychology of Alfred Adler and, his student, Rudolf Dreikurs. We have included some of their books as references for additional reading. We find this school of psychology to be very practical and immediate. Once we identify negative behavior as overcompensatory mischief, we are enabled to cope with it more successfully. We can stop taking the misbehavior personally and begin to disengage from it. The results are often gratifying to us and to the individual who was misbehaving. Negative behaviors can now be replaced with more constructive ones — to the benefit of all.

We encourage you to use this book as a resource for yourself and to share it with others. When you see people struggling with an anger situation you have read about, you can choose to show them the page and let them learn for themselves about the new choices they have available if they wish to use them. They will be relieved, and so will you. That is not just a good intention. It is a real intention.

This book is not a substitute for competent counseling. When we are too close to our problems and cannot see ourselves as others see

300

us, we may have to pay someone to give us the feedback about our attitudes and behaviors that we cannot give ourselves.

Otherwise, there are the emotional cuts and bruises of everyday life that do not require the services of a professionally trained practitioner. We can learn to take the sting out of an anger attack by disengaging from it emotionally and choosing to tell the truth: *"I'm sorry you're so angry."* How many hours of our lives are wasted every year in painful, useless skirmishes over who has the right to be angry at whom? How many hours are wasted trying to prevent waste!

Trust is an emotion, too, and it sometimes needs first aid. For instance, if we do not know that we are abusing a loved one's trust, we are liable to lose it forever. The emotional cost of these silent, invisible losses is beyond calculation. We can learn to prevent these avoidable losses and their consequent griefs by doing our Homeworks as life gives us the opportunity to do so. If life is a journey, we want you to enjoy the ride. It costs no more.

Appendix D

REFERENCES

Adler, A. (1968). *The Practice and Theory of Individual Psychology.* New York: Littlefield, Adams & Co.

Adler, A. (1964). *Social Interest: A Challenge to Mankind.* New York: Capricorn Books.

Angier, Natalie (1990). "Chronic Anger May Lead to Early Death." Chicago Tribune, December 20.

Dinkmeyer, D. & McKay, G. (1973). *Raising A Responsible Child.* New York: Simon & Schuster.

Dreikurs, R. Grunwald, B. & Pepper, F. (1971). *Maintaining Sanity in the Classroom.* New York: Harper & Row.

Dreikurs, R. & Grey, L. (1968). *Logical Consequences: A New Approach to Discipline.* New York: Hawthorn Books.

Dreikurs, R. & Soltz, V. (1964), *Children: The Challenge.* New York: Hawthorn Books.

Gilbert, Jerrold I. (1986). *Logical Consequences: A New Classification.* Individual Psychology. 42:2:243-254.

Kübler-Ross, E. (1969). *On Death and Dying.* New York: MacMillan Publishing Co.

Montagu, Ashley (1973). *Man and Aggression.* London: Oxford University Press.

Mosak, Harold H. (1977). *On Purpose.* Chicago: Alfred Adler Institute of Chicago.

Peele, Stanton (1976). *Love and Addiction.* New York: New American Library.

Peele, Stanton (1989). *The Diseasing of America.* New York: New American Library.

Powers, R. & Griffith, J. (1987). *Understanding Life-Style: The Pyscho-Clarity Process.* Chicago: The American Institute of Adlerian Studies, Ltd.

Siegel, Bernie S. (1986). *Love, Medicine and Miracles.* New York: Harper and Row.

Stein, H. (1991). "Adler & Socrates: Similarities and Difference." *Journal of Individual Psychology.* 47:2:241-246.

Tavris, Carol, (1989). *Anger, The Misunderstood Emotion.* New York: Simon and Schuster..

INDEX

Index

309

Selected Books from the Anger Institute

The following titles are a sampling of the publications available from the Anger Institute. We provide these books as one way of helping you discover new ways of managing your anger and the anger of others.

Managing Anger

by Mitch Messer **$18.95**

How do you manage an emotion that civilized people aren't supposed to have? We are busy suppressing and denying that we are angry on a daily basis. Sometimes, we even fail to identify our emotion for what it is even though that would be the first step toward managing it on a rational basis. Nice people get angry every twelve minutes — on a slow day. They just don't know how to manage it. So they *mis*manage it to the detriment of their marriages, their friendships and their relationships at school or work. You can learn to express your legitimate anger in the "middle ground" between too much and too little. *Managing Anger* demonstrates techniques for managing anger using real-life situations to show you how to make your life better for everyone concerned. *Order book #100*

Selected Books from the Anger Institute

Professional Series

The books and papers in this series are intended primarily to help therapists and professional counselors teach their clients new ways to resolve anger issues and improve their relationships. The tips and techniques are immediately useful, the distillation of more than three decades of Mr. Messer's therapeutic work with thousands of clients. (They may also be valuable as personal self-help guides.)

The Socratic Questions

by Mitch Messer $14.95

On what day did you solve the mystery of who you were? Graduation Day? Your Wedding Day? Maybe you haven't solved it at all. *Socratic Questions* helps you answer the question of how to get there from here while you're still young enough to enjoy it. Some of us have trouble asking for help in solving problems we can't even identify. What has to happen first? You have to know what those questions are. What if your parents and teachers didn't know what those questions were because no one ever told them! Then you will dwell in the darkness of not knowing forever. *Socratic Questions* helps you to ask the right questions as a first step toward getting the right answers. . . .*Order book # 101*

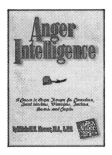

Anger Intelligence

by Mitch Messer $18.95

The human race has acquired knowledge about the depths of the sea and the birth of stars, but we don't know very much about the unexplored emotions in our heart. We have attitudes towards our emotions that predispose us to put external, tangible things first and our humanity last. This silent predisposition accounts for our anger illiteracy. *Anger Intelligence* fills the void where your anger competence should be. Anger is not wrong, it is not a weakness in our character, it is an emotional response to a grievance. If we are uninformed about anger, we are liable to mismanage it and do harm to ourselves and others. Anger Intelligence shows you how to peel away the self-imposed censorship of your legitimate emotions. You will learn how to relieve the pain they cause you every day. This education can make your relationships stronger. Not knowing how to solve anger problems drives people further away from the ones they love the most. Knowing is much better.
.... *Order book # 102*

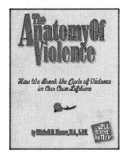

Anatomy of Violence

by Mitch Messer $14.95

We behave as if violence could be prevented if we could just find out what's causing it and tell them to stop. Violence has purposes. There are attitudes kicking in below conscious awareness, there are contexts in which out-of-control anger flourishes. There are counterproductive good intentions on our part that make the behavior worse instead of better. *The Anatomy of Violence* breaks the problem of violence down into its components. When each component is put in a realistic perspective, the problem of violence becomes more manageable and not until. .... *Order book # 103*

Selected Books from the Anger Institute

Personal Series

The books and papers in this series are intended to help individuals identify and manage anger in their own lives. They focus on relationships between husbands and wives, parents and children, extended family, friends and business colleagues and, perhaps most importantly, your personal relationship with yourself. (Many of these publications provide additional insights valuable to professional counselors.)

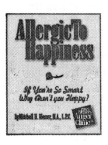

Allergic To Happiness

by Mitch Messer $18.95

Do you find yourself sabotaging your own happiness? Do you feel you don't deserve to be happy? Can you allow yourself to be happier than your unhappy parents? *Allergic to Happiness* shows you how to identify and outgrow your old impediments to happiness. You will learn why you deserve to be happy after all. You will learn how other people identified the bumps in the road to happiness. You will see what they did that was different. You can do it, too! The answer to the question, "Do you deserve to be happy?" is: Yes! You always did. You just didn't know it. It's time you found out. . .
. . . .*Order book # 200*

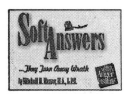

Soft Answers

by Mitch Messer $10.95

When we are provoked to anger, our adult judgment flies out the window. Our old attitudes take over and do our thinking for us. We often regret our thoughtless comeback, but it's too late. Words, and the hurt they cause, cannot be mended by issuing a retraction. Sometimes our response adds fuel to the fire and the battle is on, to our mutual regret. We didn't want it to happen but it happened anyway. *Soft Answers* provides the tools to break the cycle of tit for tat we learned as children. Your relationships will come out stronger than they were before. . . . .*Order book # 201*

The Suicide Dialogs

by Mitch Messer $24.95

When parents and teachers hear kids wishing they were dead, they don't know what to say or do. They didn't go to school for it. *The Suicide Dialogues* is a compilation of scenarios that show how these painful occasions can become an opportunity to peel down the layers of defense and uncover the painful truths deep within. The young person hears himself or herself being encouraged to talk as an equal member of the human race. They hear their hopes and fears being validated and taken as a serious area for exploration on an informal basis. These responses get to the heart of the problem and, at the same time, they bind up the wounds. *The Suicide Dialogues* reveals that the surface issues are not the real issues at all, which usually go undiagnosed and untreated. These issues can be brought to the surface by asking the right questions. This book shows you how. It is a book you and your child can read together in an atmosphere of mutual respect. *Order book # 202*

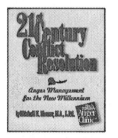

21st Century Conflict Resolution

by Mitch Messer $18.95

Although a new millennium is beginning, our problems with anger and conflict are ageless. People have always fought. It's human nature, but down through history we have learned precious little about the underlying causes of conflict. Now we are starting to understand. *21st Century Conflict Resolution* teaches more effective choices for managing and resolving conflicts in everyday life. . . . . *Order book # 203*

Selected Books from the Anger Institute

Yours, Mine, Ours

by Mitch Messer $14.95

How much did you know about your spouse before your marriage? What roles are you playing in this relationship? Where did you learn this role? Are the roles you play positive and constructive or negative and destructive? Is it too late to find out? Can you spare yourselves years of painful, preventable "misunderstandings" and heartbreak?

Yours, Mine, Ours could be called: "Getting to Really Know You." It will show you the components of mutual respect. It will show you the difference between dependency and interdependence as equals. Find out what happens when you remove the impediments to the joy you deserve to have. ....*Order book # 204*

To order these or any other
publications from the
Anger Institute
call 312-263-0035 or 800-334-2647
or use the order form
in the back of this book.

Volume and school discounts available.

Check out our websites:

www.angerinstitute.org
www.angerclinic.com

Order Form

Make checks payable to: **The Anger Institute**

Book #	Book Title	Price	Quantity	Total
		Subtotal		
	Sales Tax	Illinois residents please multiply subtotal by .085		
	Shipping and Handling	Add $3.50 per book. (For 5 or more books call for special rate.)		
		TOTAL		

Payment Information

Check enclosed ☐   Visa ☐   Mastercard ☐

Credit card # ☐☐☐☐ - ☐☐☐☐ - ☐☐☐☐ - ☐☐☐☐   Exp date ☐/☐

Name _____ Signature _____

Address _____

City _____ State_____ Zip_____

Please do not add me to the mailing list ☐

Order Form

Shipping Information

Fill in this shipping label only if you want your books shipped to an address other than your billing address.

Name _____

Address _____

City _____ State _____ Zip _____

Complete the order

Tear this sheet out of your book and mail it today to the following address:

**The Anger Institute
111 Wabash
Suite 1702
Chicago, IL 60602**

If you are paying by credit card, you may fax it instead to:

**The Anger Institute
847-674-4577 fax**

Thank you for your order.

If you have questions regarding your order, please call **312-263-0035**.

If for any reason you are unhappy with your purchase, please return the books in saleable condition to the address above for a refund. Sorry, shipping charges are not refundable.